Launching a Successful eBay® Store

Ron Mansfield

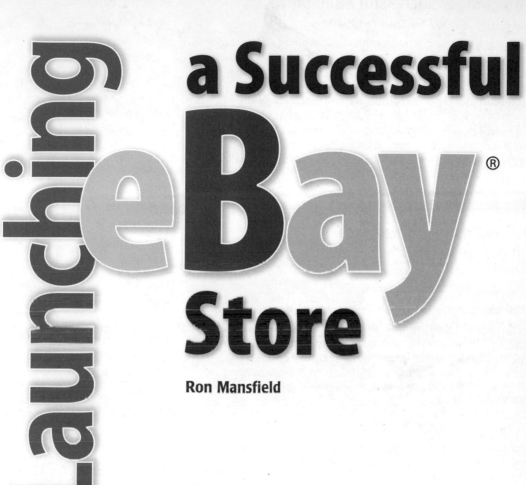

800 East 96th Street,
Indianapolis, Indiana 46240 USA

Launching a Successful eBay Store

International Standard Book Number: 0-7897-3575-X

Library of Congress Catalog Card Number: 2006922246

Printed in the United States of America

First Printing: August 2006

09   08   07   06   4   3   2   1

Trademarks

Warning and Disclaimer

Bulk Sales

Que Publishing offers excellent discounts on this book when ordered in quantity for bulk purchases or special sales. For more information, please contact

U.S. Corporate and Government Sales
1-800-382-3419
corpsales@pearsontechgroup.com

For sales outside of the U.S., please contact

International Sales
international@pearsoned.com

Associate Publisher
Greg Wiegand

Acquisitions Editor
Stephanie McComb

Development Editor
Rick Kughen

Managing Editor
Patrick Kanouse

Project Editor
Mandie Frank

Copy Editor
Bart Reed

Indexer
Julie Bess

Proofreader
Paula Lowell

Technical Editor
Michele Brantner

Publishing Coordinator
Cindy Teeters

Book Designer
Anne Jones

Page Layout
Nonie Ratcliff

Contents at a Glance

Table of Contents

About the Author

Ron Mansfield is an eBay consultant, instructor, and freelance writer. Besides helping people learn how to start and run their own successful selling businesses, Ron operates childhoodradio, an active eBay store offering unique items of interest to enthusiasts who collect, restore, buy, and sell electronics from the fifties and sixties. He has been selling on eBay since 1999, and runs an active online community for enthusiasts of mid-century electronics (www.ChildhoodRadios.com). His best-selling, award-winning books have been published by Que and others in 18 countries, in more than a dozen languages.

Dedication

To An, the love of my life.

Thanks.

Acknowledgments

Book teams are odd communities. Except for the occasional meeting at a seminar or conference, many of us never see each other. Authors often work at home, as do technical editors and all manner of other participants. We exchange emails and the occasional phone call, but for the most part we wouldn't recognize each other in line at the supermarket. And so, whenever I write an acknowledgement page I know that I have forgotten someone who has poured his or her heart into the pages you hold in your hands. If that's you, I apologize, and want you to know I appreciate all your hard work.

Thanks again to my agent, Carole McClendon, and the rest of the folks at Waterside. Splendid as usual.

A lot of people at eBay helped on this one: Walt Duflock, Chris Tsakalakis, Elizabeth Ferguson, Darlene Clementz, and countless tech support gurus. See you all at eBay Live! I hope.

The Que publishing team is not only amazing and hard working, these folks are patient, too. Thank you Greg Wiegand, Stephanie McComb, Mandie Frank, Patrick Kanouse, Rick Kughen, Sharry Gregory, Bart Reed, and my hard working technical editor, Michele Brantner.

Thanks as well to the many eBay store owners whose storefronts have been included in this book. Continued success to you, one and all.

We Want to Hear from You!

As the reader of this book, *you* are our most important critic and commentator. We value your opinion and want to know what we're doing right, what we could do better, what areas you'd like to see us publish in, and any other words of wisdom you're willing to pass our way.

As an associate publisher for Que Publishing, I welcome your comments. You can email or write me directly to let me know what you did or didn't like about this book—as well as what we can do to make our books better.

Please note that I cannot help you with technical problems related to the topic of this book. We do have a User Services group, however, where I will forward specific technical questions related to the book.

When you write, please be sure to include this book's title and author as well as your name, email address, and phone number. I will carefully review your comments and share them with the author and editors who worked on the book.

Email: feedback@quepublishing.com

Mail: Greg Wiegand
         Associate Publisher
         Que Publishing
         800 East 96th Street
         Indianapolis, IN 46240 USA

Reader Services

Visit our website and register this book at www.quepublishing.com/register for convenient access to any updates, downloads, or errata that might be available for this book.

Introduction

When the first eBay store launched around 2000, those of us selling then were pretty unimpressed. In fact, most of us probably never even saw that first store.

eBay wanted to help sellers categorize and show-case fixed-priced items, but setting up a store seemed like a lot of extra work for a dubious return. And we were, after all, mostly auctioneers at heart.

Well, this has changed of course. That first store has grown into thousands and thousands of eBay store-fronts, offering a bewildering array of items from garage sellers and world-class retailers alike. Stores still help organize fixed-priced items, enabling buy-ers to more easily find them, but now, thanks to hundreds of new features added by eBay, stores do much, much more.

As you will see in this book, an eBay store can greatly enhance your selling presence on eBay. A store can also draw traffic from elsewhere on the Internet to your items, be they fixed price or on auction.

Store selling, when done properly, can be less costly than auction-only selling. The tools provided with an eBay store can help you get a handle on your profitability, let you see where traffic comes from, help you track and understand how buyers react to your listings, and even help you build a loyal following.

Who Should Buy This Book?

If you are serious about selling on eBay, you need an eBay store. Stores are now remarkably easy to start and run, and they can grow in sophistication right along with you. So, beginners, use this book to get started. Those of you with a store up and running, use the tips and suggestions you'll find here to take your store to the next level.

Part I: Store Basics

Part I of this book gives you the basics. You'll learn what makes store selling different from traditional auction selling, and you'll see examples of both simple and complex store designs. You will learn how to set up a store with the features you need. We'll also explore the selling formats used in stores.

Inventory is the key to any selling operation. You'll find ways to locate items to sell in your store. Can you make money buying items on eBay and reselling them in your store? Perhaps. Are there wholesale lot and liquidation resources worth exploring? The answer for many of you is, yes. Does it make more sense to manufacture your own items for sale in your store, or add value to everyday items for a profit? Explore these concepts and come to the conclusions that are right for you in Part I.

Brand building, the art of making your company recognizable in this cluttered world, is an important aspect of retailing. You will learn how to build branding into your store design. What should you name your store? What will the logo look like? Where can you get a logo if you aren't artistically inclined? What colors should you use? How do you develop a "look and feel" for your store that's inviting and in keeping with the merchandise you sell?

You will also learn about the importance of picking and naming store categories—the departments and aisles of your online store. And you'll learn how to create a wide variety of custom store pages—the key to standing out from the crowd.

Part II: Managing Your Store

Next we'll explore the powerful store-based management tools you can use for selling and wrangling not only fixed-price store items, but items using active and closed auctions as well. eBay's recently added Selling Assistant Pro features can be so tightly integrated with eBay stores that I can't imagine running an eBay business without them.

Part II will show you how to set up listing templates, manage inventory counts, track inventory costs, serve photos, monitor bidders and payments, integrate your selling results with QuickBooks for accounting purposes, and even automate and track daily shipping tasks.

Part III: Promoting Your Store

You can have the best retail store in town, but if nobody walks through the door, you will fail. It's the same for online sellers. We need eBay shoppers. We need them seeing and purchasing our eBay Items with regularity.

Effective promotion can dramatically increase visits and sales. In Part III, you will see how to cross-promote your store and traditional auction items, both on and off of eBay. Froogle, eBay Express, Shopping.com, and other comparison sites can draw customers to your eBay items. You'll learn how to make it happen in this part of the book.

Opt-in email marketing is discussed. You'll learn about eBay's Store Directory and how to get above-average visibility in it. Blogs, community building, and techniques that push buyers from other sites to your eBay store can all boost your sales.

Really Simple Syndication (RSS) is starting to really take off. It's a technology you can use to be sure your customers get up-to-date information about what you have to offer. Did you know you can create RSS feeds containing information about your eBay items? Find out how to and why you would want to in this book.

Were you aware that when someone purchases your eBay store items as a result of following links to them from non-eBay sites, you, as the seller, can get a significant eBay fee discount? The concept is called *Store Referral Credits*, and the simple-but-important steps you must take to get these discounts are discussed in Part III.

Part IV: Reports

For many of you, I've saved the best for last. eBay store operators have a mind-boggling amount of management information at their fingertips, right down to who came to their stores, where they came from, what they looked at, what they bid on, what they bought, what else they looked at during their visit, how wide their computers display screens were, and so on. You'll learn which days of the week work best for you, which ending times are best, which categories draw the most shoppers, and so much more.

Once you have discovered eBay's intoxicating research tools, the hardest part will be pulling yourself away from them and getting back to listing and shipping. Reports can really help you work *on* your business as well as *in* your business, and they are reason enough for many sellers to open a store.

Come on. Let's take a look!

Part I

Store Basics

Why You Need an eBay Store

Although there are PowerSellers who do not have eBay stores, others have multiple stores, both plain and fancy. There are at least 10 good reasons for any eBay seller (whether you are an existing PowerSeller or are fairly new to eBay selling) to consider opening an eBay store. Let's take a moment in this chapter to get an overview of the "whys" and then dig into the "how-to's" throughout the rest of the book. Stores can help you do the following:

- Control and monitor your inventory
- Showcase your merchandise
- Get your own private search engine
- Cross-promote your items on eBay
- Reduce eBay Selling Fees
- Become visible to search engines
- Learn from store reports
- Save time listing and relisting
- Get marketing help from eBay
- Improve your image

These reasons are fully explored in this chapter. And don't worry if all of this seems like too much to grasp all at once. I'll explain every last little detail in the coming chapters. Just think of this chapter as a preview of all the great things you can do with your own eBay store.

Control and Monitor Your Inventory

If you use Selling Manager Pro in your eBay store, you will be able to keep an eye on your inventory items, see which things are selling best, and know when to reorder. Take a look at Figure 1.1.

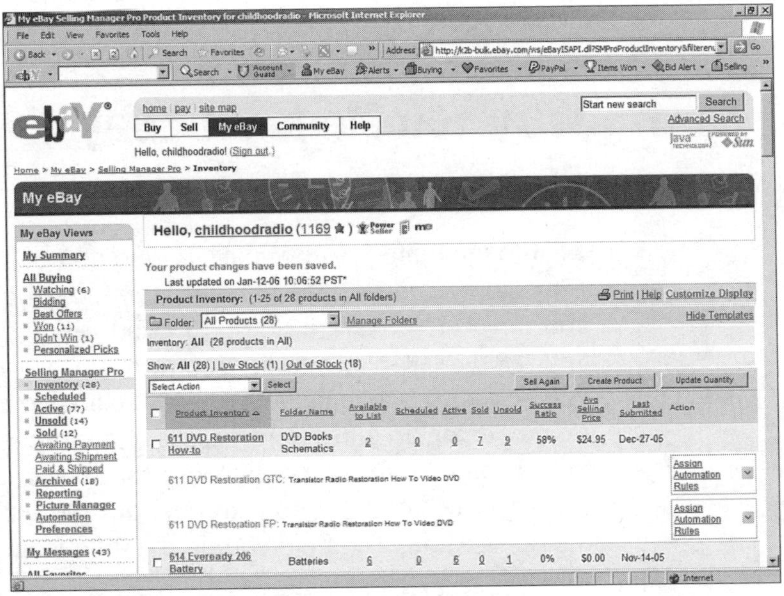

FIGURE 1.1

Monitor and control your store inventory with Selling Manager Pro.

Your "My eBay" page will include a series of new Selling Manager Pro choices on the left side of the screen, including a way to see and manage inventory.

In this figure, you can see two of the products I sell in my store: a DVD and a battery. You can tell how many of each are available to list, how many are active on eBay, how many sold and how many did not, success ratios, and more. You'll learn the details in Part II, "Managing Your Store," but for now the take-away is that a store, in combination with Selling Manager Pro, can help you manage your inventory.

By the way, if you are wondering why there are two lines for the DVD in Figure 1.1, it has to do with creating templates for different selling formats; this is covered in Chapter 3, "Types of Store Selling Formats."

Showcase Your Merchandise

Perhaps the coolest thing about an eBay store is the way it lets you organize and present items you have for sale. Figure 1.2 shows the "landing page" for a store that sells baby items.

FIGURE 1.2

Stores help you showcase your merchandise.

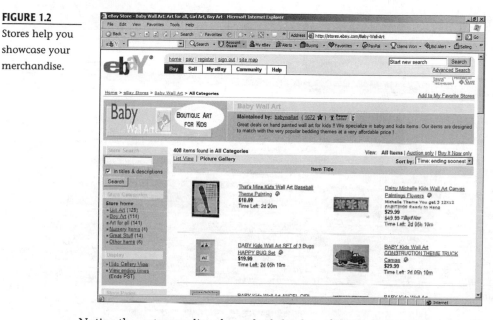

Notice the category list along the left edge of the store landing page. The categories this seller chose (Girl Art, Boy Art, and so on) help visitors zero-in on products they are interested in purchasing.

The store example in Figure 1.2 presents all of the store's items in Gallery view to the right of the category list, with the items ending soonest shown first. Store sellers have great control over what's displayed in the main area of the screen, as you will see throughout the book. In the Figure 1.2 example, a shopper interested in art for a girl's room could click the Girl Art link at the left side of the screen and view just items the seller thinks girls will like. Figure 1.3 shows that resulting view.

Gone are the baseball bat and the cement truck. In their place are bugs and angels and flowers.

There are other ways to use categories. For example, some sellers use categories to display specific sizes and colors. Or, as you can see in Figure 1.4, you can have shoppers select desired brands. This seller has organized cell phones by maker and carrier.

FIGURE 1.3
Categories help shoppers narrow down their choices.

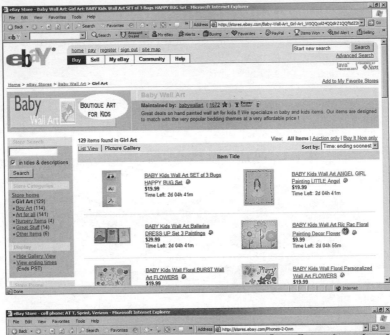

FIGURE 1.4
Store categories can be used to filter size, color brand, and more.

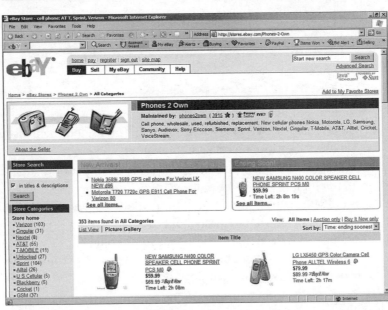

Categories cut the clutter. You can have up to 300 categories and subcategories, and use them to organize your merchandise in ways that make it easy for buyers to browse as well as to quickly find what they want.

But what if you sell such a diverse product mix that 300 categories can't cut the clutter? By adding custom landing pages with their own links and search filters, you can create a full-blown searchable catalog with level after level of subcategories (see Figure 1.5).

FIGURE 1.5

Custom landing pages help you create large, searchable "catalogs."

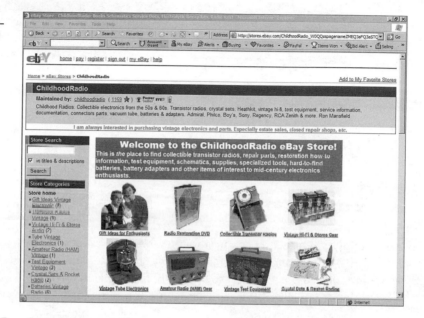

For example, I use 20 categories in my store and have created a custom landing page with "icons" representing those 20 categories. Clicking the links or photos takes visitors to the listings in their specific categories.

Several categories will eventually have hundreds of different items each, with enough diversity to need further subdividing. For instance, my Parts and Books categories will get their own directory pages created using search and custom page techniques described in Chapter 8, "Custom Store Pages." So, as I add repair manuals, schematics, books on theory, and hundreds of other items to my store's Books category, I can subcategorize them using the tricks you'll learn in Chapter 8.

Get Your Own Private Search Engine

Speaking of searching, did you know that stores have their own private search engines? Suppose you are a collector of vintage Sony radios. Type "Sony" in my store search field, and you will see all my Sony-related products, as shown in Figure 1.6.

FIGURE 1.6

Stores have their
own built-in
search engines.

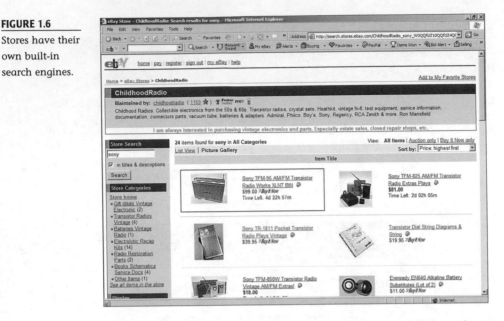

Today, when I searched my store there were 24 listings relevant to Sony enthusiasts. These were from a variety of my store categories (Transistor Radios,
Batteries, Recap Kits, and so on). Only my items, not items from other sellers,
show up when a visitor searches within my store. Is that cool or what?

Cross-promote Your Items on eBay

Stores also help you cross-promote items on eBay. When you scroll to the bottom of any of my listings, regardless of format (auctions, Buy It Now, Good
'Til Cancelled, and so on), you will see pictures of other items of mine, and a
link to my store, as shown in Figure 1.7. You can do this, too.

There are lots of other ways stores help promote your eBay items. For example, you can place a variety of boxes on your store pages to highlight new
merchandise, items ending soon, and so on. Figure 1.8 shows two examples.

You have lots of control over what's displayed in these promotional boxes and
where they appear on your store pages. You'll learn more about this feature in
Chapter 8.

FIGURE 1.7
Stores help you
cross-promote.

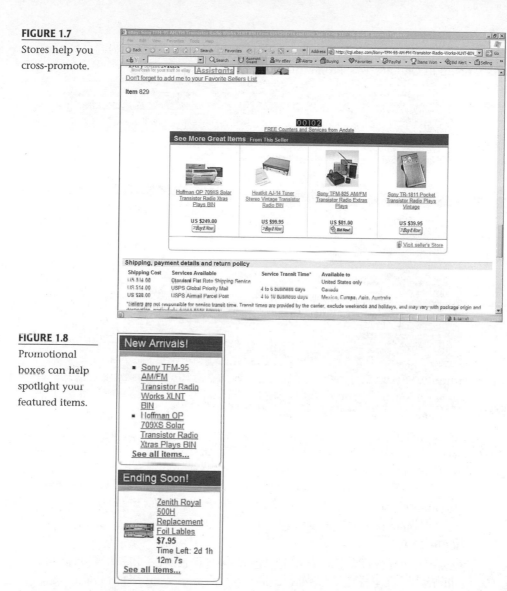

FIGURE 1.8
Promotional
boxes can help
spotlight your
featured items.

Reduce eBay Selling Fees

One of the most intriguing aspects of running a store is the opportunity to get an eBay fee reduction when people come to your store to purchase items as a result of clicking an "off-eBay" link. For example, when visitors to my hobbyist website ChildhoodRadios.com click the Store button at that website, shown in Figure 1.9, they are taken to my eBay store, and my eBay selling fees are reduced when they purchase store items during their visit. This is discussed in detail in Chapter 16, "Promoting Your Store Outside of eBay."

FIGURE 1.9

Store sales referred from "off of eBay links" can qualify for discounted selling fees.

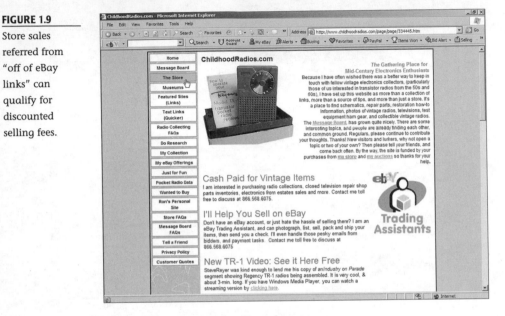

Become Visible to Search Engines

Auctions don't last very long, and therefore do not get indexed by Google and other search engines or have such low ranks that they are rarely seen by searchers. But eBay store items do get indexed. Wouldn't it be cool to get the top line of a Google search for only the cost of an eBay store? Well you can! Checkout Figure 1.10. If you Google "recap kits," you get my eBay store.

The Froogle hits are even sweeter. Check out the whole first page of Froogle in Figure 1.11.

Now, let's not kid ourselves. Recap kits are pretty obscure items, and if you are selling iPod accessories or cell phones, you are not going to land on the top of search pages by simply opening a store. But as you can see, stores can make your items plainly visible to the whole world.

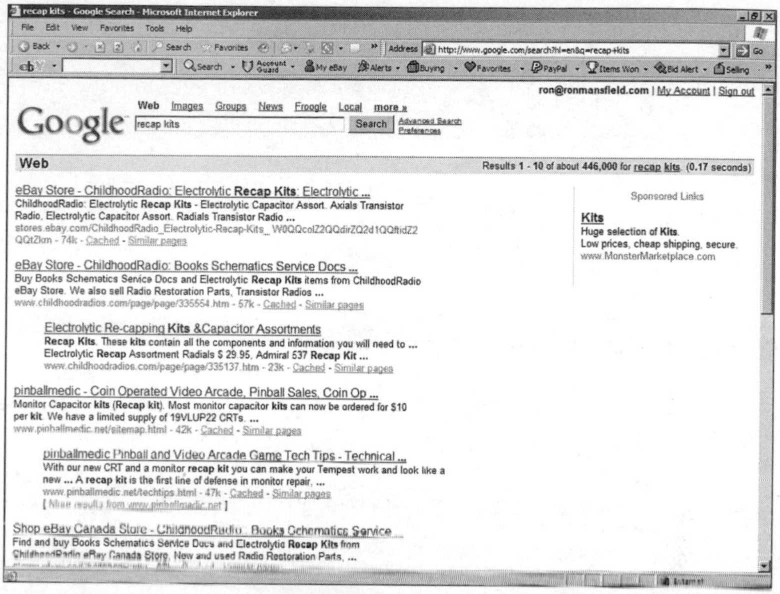

FIGURE 1.10

Store items get indexed by Google, Froogle, and others.

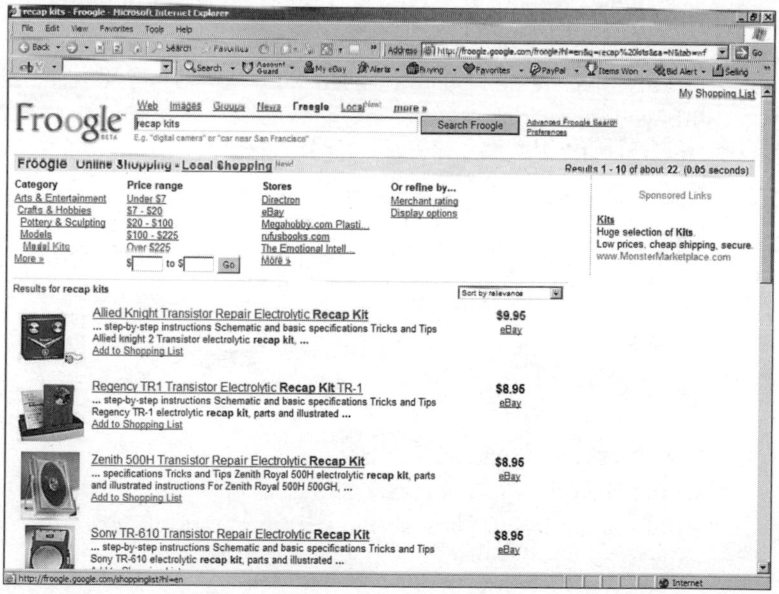

FIGURE 1.11

Froogle does a really nice job of showcasing eBay store items.

Learn from Store Reports

Then there are the store reports. Wow! Where to begin? Figure 1.12 will give you just a taste, and we'll explore reports in detail in Part IV, named, oddly enough, "Reports."

FIGURE 1.12

Store reports will change the way you look at your eBay items forever.

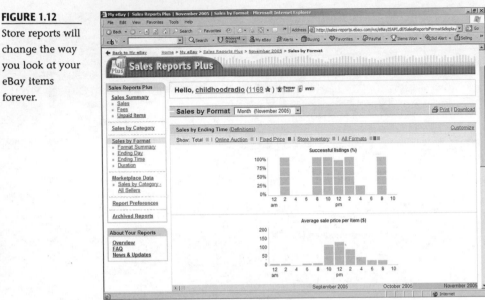

Look how easy it is to see the best times of day for my high-ticket items to end.

But my favorite new pastime is learning how buyers cruise my site. What things do they look at and ignore? What makes them tick? Check out Figure 1.13.

FIGURE 1.13

Traffic reports can tell you a lot about shoppers' behavior.

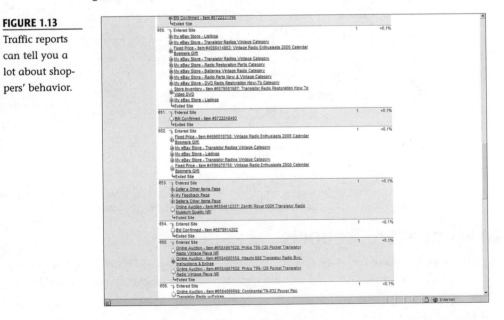

In Figure 1.13, visitor 650 came into the store, looked at several of my store categories, and then left. Shopper 651 came knowing exactly what to buy and bought it. Shopper 652 was drawn to the store from a fixed-priced auction (the calendar), looked at the radios I had listed, and left. After looking at these reports for a while, you can see which categories are getting traffic, what drives traffic to your store, and much more.

Save Time Listing and Relisting

Once you have created listing templates in Selling Manager Pro, you can restock your store and relist items with a few mouse clicks, as shown in Figure 1.14.

FIGURE 1.14
Store listing templates save time.

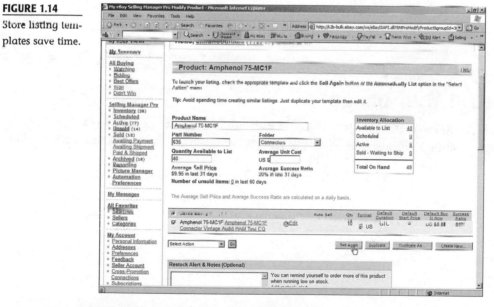

Get Marketing Help from eBay

As you read this book, you will uncover many additional ways that eBay can help promote your store, and thus your auctions. For example, you can create and maintain an opt-in email newsletter campaign, as shown in Figure 1.15.

FIGURE 1.15

Store owners can create eBay opt-in email campaigns.

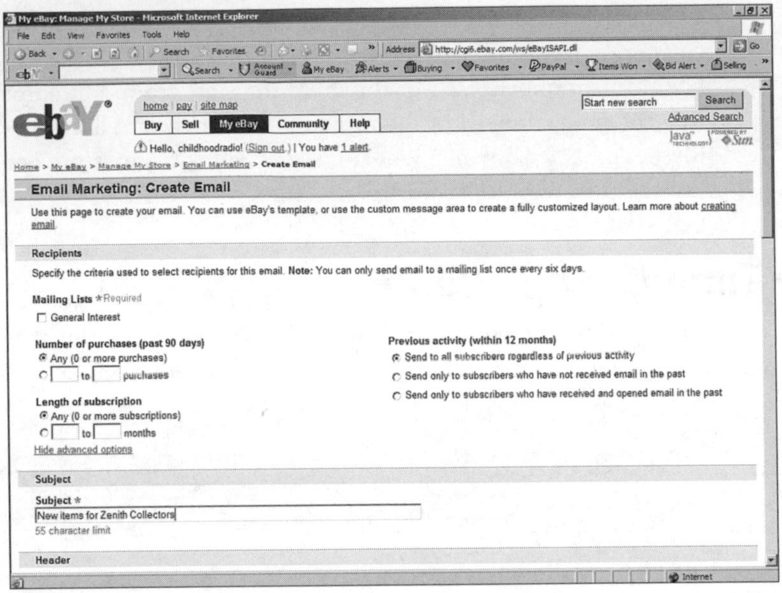

Improve Your Image

Finally, you can use your store to enhance your image as a seller. Stores can make your listings, and thus your entire business effort, look more substantial than other sellers without stores. The next chapter shows some examples of just how far you can take an eBay store to help you decide what to do next.

Examples of Stores, Plain and Fancy

Stores are like gardens. Some are plain, others fancy. You can start small and enhance them over time. Regardless of how fancy you make your store, it's important that you tend to it constantly. A little preplanning before you launch your store is a good idea as well.

Whether you are thinking about your first store or getting ready to improve an existing one, it's a great idea to look at what other people have done with their stores. The easiest way to do that is to visit the eBay Stores page and do a little window shopping. The URL is http://stores.ebay.com, or you can reach the Stores page by clicking the Stores link near the upper-right corner of the main eBay page. Either way, you will be presented with something similar to Figure 2.1.

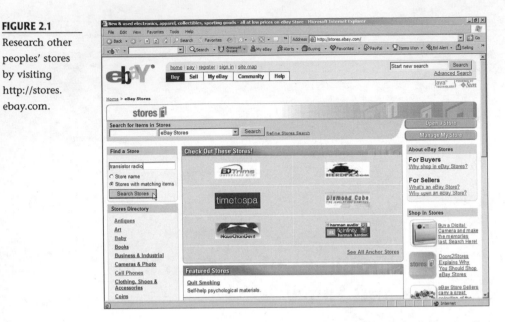

Those store logos you see popping out in the middle of the page are featured stores, something we'll talk about later in this chapter. Featured stores are obviously worth a visit, but don't spend all your time in them. Instead, click the links at the left of the screen that pertain to the categories of items you intend to sell. If you sell coins, click the Coins link, handmade quilts, click Crafts, and so on.

But don't stop there. Notice back in Figure 2.1 I've entered a search term and clicked the "Stores with matching items" button. You can use this search tool to find stores that sell products similar to yours.

As you can see in Figure 2.2, the search for stores selling transistor radio–related items turned up 354 stores. I'm not alone after all. The obvious next step is to look at some of the competitors' stores.

You will notice an amazing difference in the look, feel, and sophistication of the stores you encounter, even within the same category. And although your initial reaction might be to dismiss the plain-looking stores, thinking they are less-worthy competitors than the fancy stores, that's not necessarily the case. Let's look at some examples.

A No-frills Store

Figure 2.3 shows about as basic a storefront as you can build. There's an unembellished header, store categories on the left, and a list of available products ordered by price in the center. The owner is a PowerSeller, which tells you the store is probably working just fine. Although I am not a map collector, to me the categories look like they would be helpful to a map shopper. It's no-frills selling, probably very easy to maintain and a worthy store.

Some things worth noting about the store in Figure 2.3 include the fact that the list of items is presented by price (as opposed to year, or continent, or something else probably of more interest to collectors). Also, notice that this seller has not chosen to "brand" the store with a logo or tell us anything about him or herself with an "About the Seller" page. This eBay seller's ID doesn't really scream "Get your maps here!" either, but the store's name accomplishes that.

note This seller actually uses photos in auctions, but is not checking the appropriate Listing Contains Photos box when creating listings. If you don't use Gallery photos and you host your own photos, remember to check the Listing Contains Photos box so that at least the little camera icon will show up in searches, indicating that your listings have photos.

A quick way to embellish this store would be to include Gallery photos, or at least indicate that photos are available in the listings (which is the case with this seller). Look at Figure 2.4.

FIGURE 2.3

An example of a "no-frills" store.

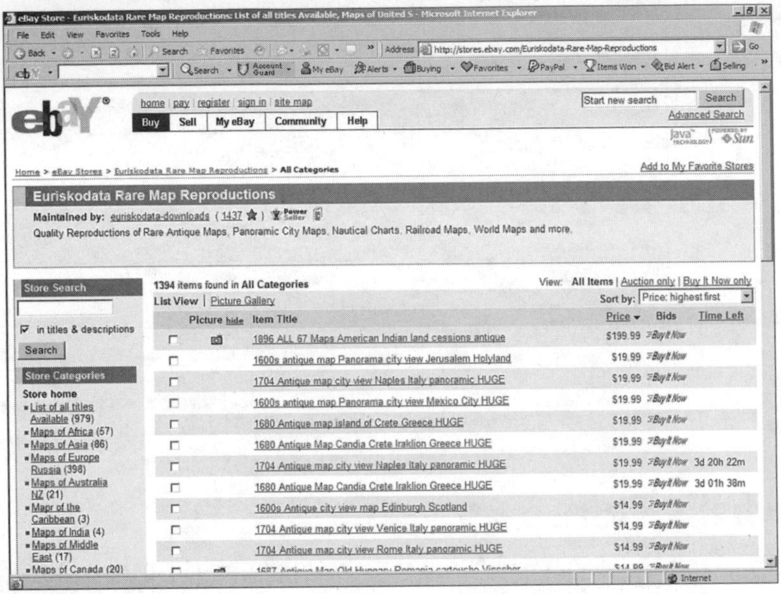

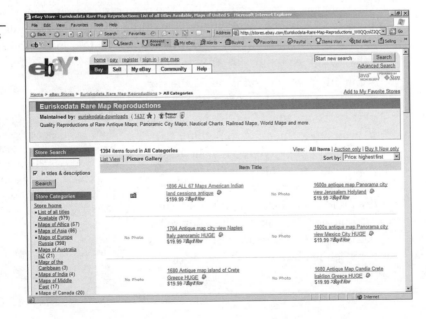

FIGURE 2.4

This store needs to work on its photos.

As you will see in the next store example, the addition of Gallery photos can really "draw shoppers in." These photos cost money, of course, and this does add up. Because Euriskodata has 979 titles, and because Gallery photos cost $0.35 each, it would cost more than $300 to add Gallery photos to this store. But if the seller uses the right listing strategy (Good 'Til Sold, multiple items per listing, and so on), Gallery photos would almost surely pay for themselves. To see what I mean, let's look at the next example, a competing map store.

Easy, Popular Store Features

Figure 2.5 shows a competing reproduction map site. It uses Gallery photos. "Wow," I thought when I landed on this one, "Cool old maps! I wonder if they have one for my town?" I had been drawn into the store even though I am not a map collector.

The custom store logo is a nice, touch. The seller ID (maps-of-the-past) is unambiguous. The store has a great index that breaks the items down into logical, manageable chunks. Also, the seller has added both an About the Seller page and a Store Policy page, with links to them at the left edge of the store screens.

Obviously, if feedback is any indicator, this seller moves a lot of maps. As you will see momentarily, I think there might be some ways to squeeze more out of the landing page (the first page visitors see), but this is a first-class store already.

The header text in Figure 2.5 is nice, too. Lots of good search terms in there (USGS, Topo, and so on). Also, there's a good explanation of the store's focus.

This was all accomplished with very little extra work, and just a little extra expense. Gallery photos are easy to add if you've already taken good product shots, and although they are not free, they quickly turn your storefront into a compelling catalog cover.

But wait, as they say in those midnight infomercials, still more can be done.

> **note** If you sell really inexpensive "one-of-a-kind" items and therefore Gallery photos cost too much, consider creating a landing page with some compelling "category" photos that link to your unembellished listings. You'll see an example in this chapter and learn how to do it yourself in Chapter 8, "Custom Store Pages."

FIGURE 2.5

Gallery photos and the logo really draw you into this one.

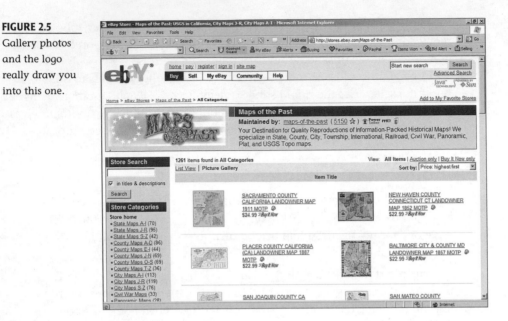

Advanced Store Features

If you have the time, money, and skills, you can turn an eBay store into a fancy, bell-and-whistle-laden presence rivaling a multinational retailer's site. In fact, some multinational retailers have eBay stores.

That said, some of the biggest retailers on eBay have relatively simple eBay stores. Stick with me. It will all make sense by the end of this chapter.

Design and Window Options

When designing your store, you can add preconfigured eBay store features and still have quite a bit of control over where you plop things, the colors, the "themes" used to decorate your store, and so on. Look at Dave and Adam's Card World (maintained by greatboxes) in Figure 2.6.

Dave and Adam have added "Ending Soon!" and "New Arrivals!" boxes at the top of their store landing page. These are standard eBay features, and you can tell eBay whether you want to use them and, if so, where to plunk them. Dave and Adam apparently want to create a sense of urgency (always a good sales tactic) by putting the "Ending Soon!" box right where we tend to look first.

To the right is the "New Arrivals!" box, which will appeal to regular visitors who don't want to slog through nearly 16,000 items in this store (yes, you read that right) to find the new stuff.

FIGURE 2.6

It's easy to change the appearance of your store using built-in store-creation features.

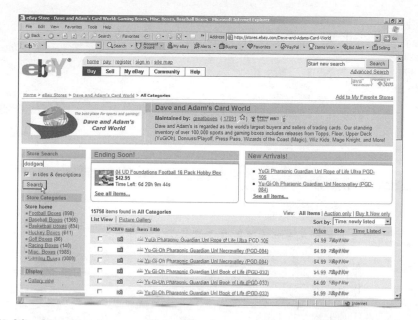

Unlike the other stores we have visited so far, this one displays the most recently listed items first, a good strategy for a seller with many new items every day.

Figure 2.7 shows a completely different approach to using the topmost, highly visible portion of the store landing page. The Oxford Diamond Co. store (maintained by oxforddiamondco) uses HTML to put links to clearance items, provides links to its other eBay site that sells closeouts, and offers a phone number.

This is a lot like hanging paper signs in the windows of a real brick-and-mortar stores. Closeout! Sale! It's harder for shoppers to peek in at the merchandise inside, but it draws their attention to important news or options. This can be a very effective way to present different elements of your business.

Africa Direct (maintained by eliza500) is a lovely, clean-looking store with a beautiful logo and matching color combination (see Figure 2.8). A single "Ending Soon!" box along the top further adds to the uncluttered look. Items presented in Gallery view allow shoppers to immediately see the lovely objects for sale when they enter the store. Notice the links along the top to the About the Seller and Store Policies pages.

FIGURE 2.7
FIGURE 2.7

The top of this landing page directs you using HTML links.

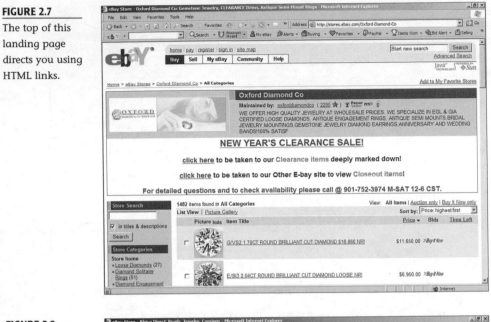

FIGURE 2.8

Here's a simple, clean storefront that opens in Gallery view.

Sellers Elizabeth Bennett and Sara Luther carry this clean look to their About the Seller page, and have used HTML to insert a personal photo, which I think is always a nice touch on eBay (see Figure 2.9).

FIGURE 2.9

You can use
HTML and other
tricks in custom
store pages.

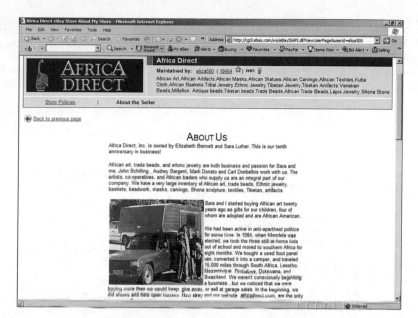

Turning Landing Pages into Catalog Covers

So far we've looked at stores where the main portion of the screen was filled
with listings fed directly from eBay in the way we are accustomed to seeing
them when we do our own searches as buyers.

The sellers in the examples so far in this chapter have decided for us whether
we will see their items in List view or Gallery view, and how they are sorted,
but basically these are vanilla eBay search results.

Custom Store pages can take this to the next level. Consider Figure 2.10,
SuperCrafty Craft Supplies, maintained by eBay seller, supercrafty!.

It almost looks like SuperCrafty has hijacked eBay. Where are the familiar listings, little Gallery images, and so on? They have been hidden by a custom-
built, HTML-driven landing page that opens instead of search results when
you reach this seller's store.

Those little boxes are clickable, and when you click them you go to more custom pages before you actually see the listings. "Why?" you wonder. It's a great
way to overcome the 20-category limitation. Check out Figure 2.11.

Yikes! SuperCrafty sells a lot of different stuff, and it needs to be organized
(and therefore purchased) by brand, style, and size. Without a ton of store categories, this could require shoppers to do a lot of needless browsing or clever
searching.

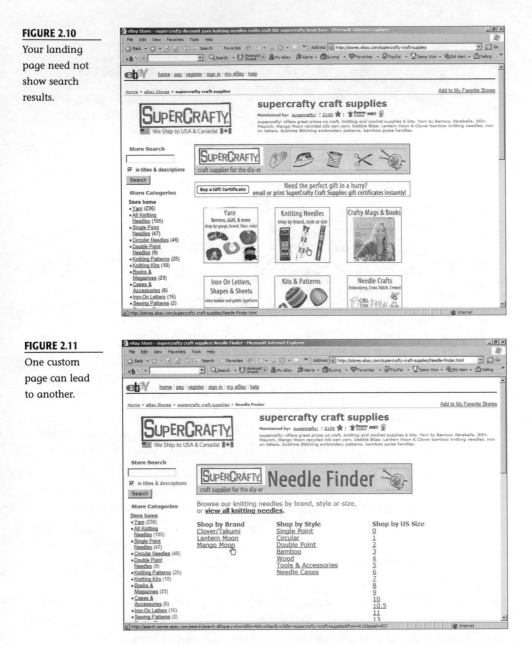

FIGURE 2.10
Your landing
page need not
show search
results.

FIGURE 2.11
One custom
page can lead
to another.

This seller has done the searching for the shoppers, and made it easy for visitors to hone in on their objects of desire. Those links you see (Mango Moon, for example) run eBay searches within the store and, if done properly, present only the items of interest. This is accomplished without shoppers needing to know a whit about eBay search techniques. You'll learn more about this technique in Chapter 8.

The by-now famous sellers at Period Paper have taken this trick yet another level higher. As you can see from Figure 2.12, hovering over an image in the store's landing page enlarges the image and dims the rest. Clicking takes you to the next level of custom pages to help further narrow your search, as shown in Figure 2.13.

Beautiful pages such as these are not the result of rocket science, but they do require the time and attention of folks with both graphic design and web design skills. The results can be stunning.

However, once introduced, this level of artistic flair needs to be maintained, and at a minimum, you need to think carefully about whether such a fancy design will make it difficult or expensive for you to add new categories or otherwise redesign your store down the road.

Remember, too, that if your store uses features that are too overwhelming, such as Flash animation and so forth, some shoppers with marginal computing skills, old or very basic computers might have trouble seeing your listings.

FIGURE 2.12

Popping images and other tricks can add eye appeal.

FIGURE 2.13

FIGURE 2.13

Remember, one custom page can, and often does, lead shoppers to another.

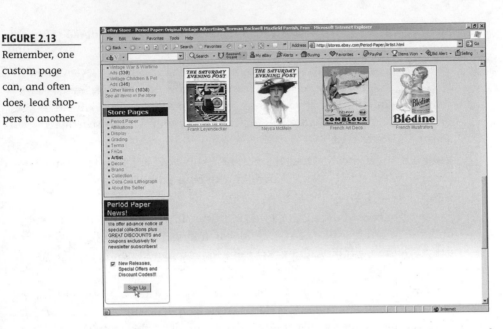

Which brings us full circle. Earlier I mentioned that many international retailers with major websites also have eBay stores. The Sharper Image is one of those eBay sellers. If you have ever read a Sharper Image catalog or visited its website or retail stores, you know that the company is very image conscious and spends a lot of time, money, and energy on the look and feel of its marketing materials and stores. Now check out its *eBay* store in Figure 2.14.

FIGURE 2.14

Sometimes simple is all it takes.

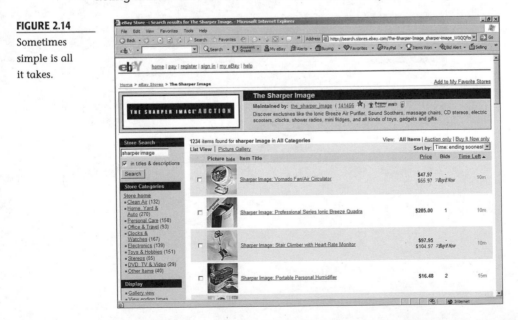

The Sharper Image uses its eBay store to liquidate obsolete inventory and sell refurbished (returned) items. This is ideally a low-budget, high-volume selling activity that should not compete too much with its "real" business.

The Sharper Image uses the basic tools you read about early in this chapter—categories, Gallery images, a custom logo in the header, and so on. But there is an absence of flash in every sense of the term. Load 'em up and move 'em out. Ya want fancy? Shop our retail operations.

A simple site like this can be almost automatically fed new products, as you will learn in Chapter 10, "Creating Listings and Templates."

Store Listing and Final Value Fees

For the time being at least, store inventory creation is a bargain. And, as I have already mentioned, if you bring shoppers from outside of eBay to your store, final value fees can be dirt cheap. Have a look at Table 2.1 and Table 2.2.

Table 2.1 Insertion Fees

Duration	Insertion Fee	Surcharge	Total
30 days	$0.02	N/A	$0.02
60 days	$0.02	$0.02	$0.04
90 days	$0.02	$0.04	$0.06
120 days	$0.02	$0.06	$0.08
Good 'Til Cancelled	$0.02 / 30 days	N/A	$0.02 / 30 days

The insertion fee covers any quantity of items with a single listing, whether you list 1 or 1,000 of the same item. The insertion fees vary based on the duration of your listing, not on quantity. Good 'Til Cancelled listings will be charged the relevant fees every 30 days.

Table 2.2   Final Value Fees

Closing Price in U.S. Dollars	Final Value Fee in U.S. Dollars
Item not sold	No fee
$0.01–$25.00	8% of the closing price
$25.01–$1,000.00	8% of the initial $25.00 ($2.00), plus 5% of the remaining closing value balance ($25.01 to $1,000.00)
More than $1,000.01	8% of the initial $25.00 ($2.00), plus 5% of the initial $25.01–$1,000.00 ($48.75) plus 3.00% of the remaining closing value balance ($1,000.01 to closing value)

To explore these options in more detail, visit http://pages.ebay.com/ storefronts/subscriptions.html.

Saving Final Value Fees with Your Store

Store sellers can earn a store referral credit and save 75% off final value fees of store inventory listings when they drive traffic to their store. Now reread that sentence!

Remember, if a buyer comes to your store from outside of eBay and then buys something from your store, you save 75% off of the eBay final value fees. This should be reason enough to consider setting up a private website (like mine, ChildhoodRadios.com) and use it to "push" buyers to your eBay store. You will learn more about this in Chapter 16, "Promoting Your Store Outside of eBay."

But now, let's look at the selling formats available to store operators in Chapter 3, "Types of Store Selling Formats."

3

Types of Store Selling Formats

If you have been selling for a while, chances are you already know quite a bit about the auction formats and options available to you on eBay. You probably have your favorites. But stores throw some new wrinkles into the equation, offer additional opportunities, and might make you rethink your selling strategies. If you're a new seller, then read this chapter carefully.

The Importance of Mixing Selling Formats

While reading the rest of this chapter, keep the following point in mind: When you run an eBay store, it's a good idea to use many, if not all of the available selling formats. You should always have some auctions running, and you should have auction items beginning and ending on every day of the week, if possible.

You should consider having some fixed-price items running for 3, 5, 7, and 10 days as well. In addition, you should obviously maintain an active inventory of "store" items, including some Good 'Til Cancelled listings.

You want to combine these formats and options because they feed off each other. For example, people will visit one of your auctions, and if you have done your cross-promotion work correctly, they will subsequently visit your store to purchase (or at least look at) your store items. Figure 3.1 shows some examples of this from my traffic report.

FIGURE 3.1

Auction items and store items feed traffic to each other.

37. Online Auction - Item #6584566698: Continental TR-632 Power Pac Transistor Radio w/Extras		
Previous Page	Instances	%
37a. Entered Site	106	48.8%
37b. My eBay Store - Listings	23	10.6%
37c. Online Auction - Item #6584580558: Hitachi 666 Transistor Radio Box, Instructions & Extras	20	9.2%
37d. Online Auction - Item #6584612337: Zenith Royal 500H Transistor Radio Museum Quality NR	12	5.5%
37e. Online Auction - Item #6584561563: Global GR-711 Leather Case & Box, Transistor Radio NR	11	5.1%
Show all for Online Auction - Item #6584566698: Continental TR-632 Power Pac Transistor Radio w/Extras		

38. My eBay Store - Batteries Vintage Radio Category		
Previous Page	Instances	%
38a. My eBay Store - Listings	39	17.6%
38b. My eBay Store - Store Directory	24	10.9%
38c. Online Auction - Item #6584916593: Magnavox 2-AM-60 Pocket Transistor Radio Vintage Plays	17	7.7%
38d. My eBay Store - Transistor Radios Vintage Category	14	6.3%
38e. Store Inventory - Item #6579315006: Eveready 206 Radio Battery New for Vintage Radios 9v	9	4.1%
Show all for My eBay Store - Batteries Vintage Radio Category		

This report shows how shoppers arrived at my store to view particular items. In the instance numbered 37, you can see that 48.8% of the people who looked at the Continental radio found it directly by searching for it or browsing. But 10.6% of the visitors came to the auction listing from a link in my store, and many of the others came from cross-promotions in other radio auction listings. So links embedded in a store and cross-promoted auctions gather extra eyeballs for each other.

Can *auctions* drive traffic to *stores* as well? Of course they can. Look at item 38 in Figure 3.1. Here, 7.7% of the people who looked at a battery I sell in my store got to that store listing after viewing an auction for a radio that uses the battery. This is because when I sell radios that use this hard-to-find battery, I mention in the radio auction listing that I carry this particular battery in my store. Also, I add the store batteries as one of the cross-promoted items at the bottom of the radio listing. Figure 3.2 shows an example of a cross-promotion box designed for radio collectors who might be looking for oddball batteries. I run store cross-promotion boxes like these in all of my auctions, and they work.

FIGURE 3.2

Cross-promotion boxes in auctions will drive traffic to your store.

Auction Items

Auctions are still the bread and butter of eBay. You offer one or multiple items and set a starting price for the auction, which can last 3, 5, 7, or 10 days.

Buyers visit the listing and bid on the item(s). At auction's end, the high bidder or bidders buy the item(s) from you at the ending price. Insertion and final value fees for online auctions vary with the starting price and ending price of the item. Auctions have high visibility on eBay (they always show up in eBay searches).

Fixed-price Items

The fixed-priced items feature is great. Don't confuse this with the Buy It Now feature you can add to auctions. When you list an item using the fixed-price format, buyers can purchase your item or items without waiting, and you get the price you want. There is no bidding and no auction. You're just offering one or more items for sale at a specific price for a finite period of time, (3, 5, 7, or 10 days). And, unlike auction-based Buy It Now auctions, the opportunity to buy instantly doesn't disappear simply because someone bids.

If you qualify (see the following note), you can sell multiple identical items in one listing. Buyers will see fixed-price offerings in category browse pages and search results, highlighted with the Buy It Now icon shown in Figure 3.3.

FIGURE 3.3

Fixed-price listings encourage impatient shoppers.

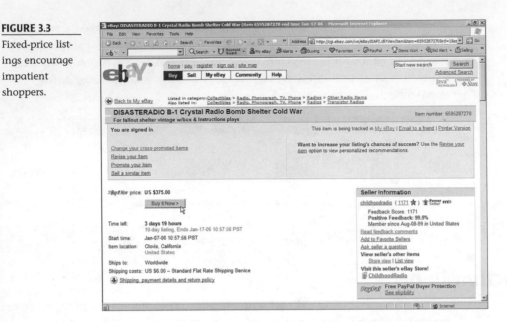

People are always in a hurry these days. I recently created a fixed-price listing for a nice radio. I set the price at $250, about $100 more than a similar one had sold for two weeks earlier.

As soon as the listing went up, I actually got a question from a radio-savvy eBayer along the lines of "What, are you crazy? $250?" Two days after the listing launched, the radio sold at the full asking price. Somebody wanted it *now*.

note You must have a feedback rating of 10 or more (or be ID-verified) to list your item in a fixed-price listing with a quantity of one. To create a fixed-price listing with a quantity of two or more, you must have a feedback rating of 30 or more and be a registered user for at least 14 days (or be ID-verified).

You can also choose to accept best offers from buyers (for example, "Buy It Now $250.00 or Best Offer"), but I am not a big fan of this. It's almost like admitting you've set the price too high.

Store Inventory Format

Here's where it gets interesting. As a store seller, you have access to an additional listing format—the "Store Inventory" format.

Store Inventory listings have a longer duration. Obviously you must have an eBay store to use this format. Items are listed at a set price (no bidding). You can create a listing for as little as $0.02 for each 30-day period, regardless of quantity! But as you read in the previous chapter, higher final value fees apply when you sell store items. You can mitigate this, of course, by driving folks from outside of eBay to your store and gaining the resulting fee reductions. The Gallery picture feature costs just $0.01, and the Item Subtitle feature costs only $0.02 when you choose the Store Inventory format.

Store duration options are 30 days, 60 days, 120 days, or Good 'Til Cancelled, which means that store inventory listings can have an unlimited duration thanks to the Good 'Til Cancelled option, described in a moment.

Store Inventory listings appear together with other listing formats in the following places:

- Your eBay store
- When shoppers click your "Seller's Other Items" link
- In eBay stores search results
- At the bottom of eBay search pages

Good 'Til Cancelled

This is another unique store feature. You choose whether you want a listing to end after 30 days or automatically renew every 30, 60, 90, or 120 days, until the item or items sell, or you end the listing.

The insertion fee covers any quantity of items with a single listing, whether you list 1 or 1,000 of the same item. Figure 3.4 shows where in the store item listing process you make the choice. You'll get more specifics in Chapter 10, "Creating Listings and Templates."

> **note** Remember, Good 'Til Cancelled (GTC) means just that. Unless you cancel the listing or sell completely out of product, you will be charged every 30 days for each GTC listing you create.

FIGURE 3.4

Creating a Good
'Til Cancelled
listing.

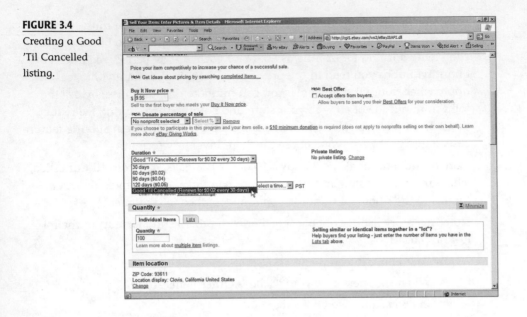

4

Sources of Items to Sell

"The best products," my grandfather used to say, "cost a nickel, sell for a dollar, and form a habit." For example, you might sell bundles of yarn and knitting instructions for a variety of projects—caps, mittens and so on. If you purchase the yarn wholesale and print your own instructions, you should be able to mark up these products quite a bit. If people love the mittens, they might come back for the hat kit. It is certainly still possible to find or create products like these for your eBay store, but many more sellers will compete with you for them now than even a few years ago.

Sometimes the best place to look for bargains is where things don't belong. Let's start with the obvious sources, and then we'll get clever.

Traditional eBay Auctions

It is still sometimes possible to buy things on eBay and resell them on eBay for a profit. I do it almost every day. It just takes more work, and a lot more digging than before, but there are some tricks you can use. It can be a little like playing "Where's Waldo?"

Sometimes the good stuff hides right there in plain sight. Check out Figure 4.1 as an example. I was browsing with the search term "vintage" I believe, and right there in the middle of a pile of stuff the seller actually described as "some old '50s junk" was the radio you see in Figure 4.1.

FIGURE 4.1

Some "old '50s" junk (a hundred dollar's worth for $0.99).

The auction started at $0.99, and because even the seller thought it was all junk, and because the word *radio* appeared nowhere in the listing, I ended up being the only bidder and won at the starting bid amount. I asked the seller to toss out all the junk *but* the radio, which she did. Keep your eyes open. Such opportunities still happen. I later resold the radio for more than $100.00.

Buy It Now, Especially in Lots

Sometimes, as you saw in the previous example, sellers don't know what things are worth. One way to profit from this is to do searches each day using keywords that find the things you hope to resell. I use the term "vintage electronics" among others, for example. Perform your searches every day, and perhaps have eBay email you reminders for high-priority items (using the

Saved Search feature) so that you will be notified when items matching your search criteria get listed.

To save a search, click the Add to Favorite Searches link that appears near to the right of the "Items found" count on search pages. To get email alerts, click the "email me daily" option on the resuting confirmation screen.

note Email search reminders often work best when using specific search phrases for rare items such as "Sony TR-650." If, on the other hand, you ask for a reminder when items are launched containing the vague phrase "vintage radio," you'll be bombarded daily.

When running your daily searches, sort them by "Newly Listed" and then (this is the important part) click the Buy It Now tab, as shown in Figure 4.2.

FIGURE 4.2

Search everyday for newly listed Buy It Now bargains.

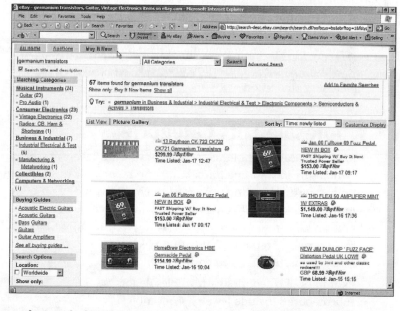

Scour the newly listed Buy It Now screens for underpriced, newly listed treasures. Then pounce. Don't forget to carefully read the descriptions to make sure you aren't buying a reproduction or badly damaged item, or are going to pay a fortune in shipping and handling. Oh, and be sure to view the listings without Gallery photos. Sometimes sellers' auction titles can disguise great finds, too.

After you have seen the day's Buy It Now opportunities, revisit the same search for auctions you might want to snipe by clicking the Auctions tab.

Selling things in lots can be tricky, and sometimes (actually, many times) things sell in lots for considerably less than they do when sold in separate auctions. This is a potential source of store inventory items for you.

For example, I recently bought a lot of duplicate vintage test gear from a trade school auction on eBay. Had the school sold the items individually, over time, as I will in my store, they could have made 10 times as much as they did. Very few buyers want 10 of the same thing unless they are interested in reselling them. Here, too, don't forget to factor in shipping, condition, completeness, and so on.

> **note** *Sniping* is the art of pouncing on an auction at the last second with the highest bid, thus beating other bidders to the punch. Often, sniping is the only way to win a hotly contested auction. Sniping can be done by hand (meaning you watch the clock and place your bid at the last second) or with specialized software, or online services such as Bidrobot.com

eBay's Wholesale Lots Categories

Many of eBay's popular categories have third-level subcategories called "wholesale lots." Sometimes, but by no means always, you can buy these multiple items in a lot and then resell them individually on eBay for a profit. This usually works best if you add some value, such as better packaging, instructions, accessories, and so on. For example, you might buy a wholesale lot of bulk yarn and repackage it with project instructions, as discussed earlier.

Examples of categories with wholesale lots subcategories include Jewelry, Collectibles, and Home & Garden. Figure 4.3 gives you an idea of some of the things sold in the Collectibles subcategory.

> **note** Some sellers list their own lots in categories without wholesale lot subcategories. Search for the word "lot" in titles.

FIGURE 4.3

A sampling of lot sales.

eBay's New Reseller Marketplace

In early 2005, eBay launched a new service for PowerSellers only called the Reseller Marketplace. You need to log into the PowerSeller neighborhood (a land you will be invited to explore after you sell at least $1,000 per month for 3 months) to even see it. Figure 4.4 shows the Marketplace.

FIGURE 4.4

The New PowerSellers' Reseller Marketplace.

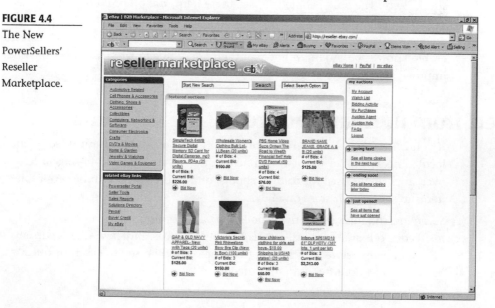

The Reseller Marketplace basically is an "off eBay" auction site, supposedly stocked by manufacturers wanting to give PowerSellers a direct shot at close-outs and such. Figure 4.5 shows a typical lot listing screen.

The jury is still out as to whether the Marketplace will provide a reliable source of merchandise to resell profitably. Remember, you are swimming with sharks here. The only people who see these items are other PowerSellers intending to do the same thing you are, which is buy low and sell high. My advice would be to try this once or twice in a category where you have considerable knowledge. Again, if you can then add value to what you buy, the odds improve considerably.

Direct from the Manufacturer

If you can make an exclusive arrangement with a manufacturer (ideally one located near you) for its distressed merchandise—returns, end-of-season left-over stock, items used for catalog shoots, and so on—these can be profitable items to sell in your store on eBay.

Some merchandise categories "spoil" quickly. Nothing loses value as fast as last-year's cell phone or last-week's basketball shoes. Buy low. Check current prices on eBay before committing to a price and then sell the stuff as quickly as you can without flooding the category.

Small, valuable items are the best targets of course. Jewelry, personal electronics, even high-end clothing should work.

How you find this stuff will vary greatly from category to category and town to town. Start at the reception desk. Ask to speak with the person who deals with returned merchandise. Meet the person, if possible, or talk on the phone. Emails will likely go unanswered. You want face time ideally, or phone time if that's the best you can do. Find out what currently happens to returned stuff and last year's models at the end of the model year. Ask if it is possible to purchase it in lot quantities.

Another option might be to offer to become their "Trading Assistant" and sell their obsolete and returned items for them on eBay in exchange for a commission.

tip To delve into these methods and strategies in more detail, check out my other book *eBay to the Max*, also published by Que.

Local Retail Stores

As with buying direct from the manufacturer, you can explore similar arrangements with local retailers, particularly independently owned stores or small local chains. If you have a local chain of car stereo installers or bike stores, for example, visit a store and seek out the manager. Ask how he disposes of trade-ins, if he takes them, and returns. Find out if this is done locally or if the stuff gets sent elsewhere. Follow the trail. Take notes. Be persistent. Tell the manager you are interested in buying wholesale lots of trade-in items and any distressed merchandise he might have. Try to convince him that this might be cheaper for the store than having a traditional sale or moving the stuff themselves.

Some shop owners won't want to deal with trade-ins at all but might be willing to hand out coupons you develop for them so that customers will bring *you* their used items so that you might sell these items for them on eBay. Again, this is explored in depth in *eBay to the Max*.

Wholesale Lots Warehouses

You have driven by them. You see them advertised on television at midnight. They are wholesalers of "deeply discounted" merchandise offering stuff you can supposedly buy and resell profitably on eBay.

It is very difficult to make money using these as your sources. First, if you see the ads, so do thousands of other eBay sellers. Next, because these are middlemen (middlepersons?), the stuff comes to you marked up once already. Check on eBay. Chances are the same stuff is selling for about the wholesale warehouse asking price, maybe even less.

There's also a good chance the house you are buying from is also competing with you on eBay. Finally, be leery of anything with a shelf life—batteries, fire extinguishers, all manner of spoiled things find their way into these warehouses.

Online Wholesale Lot Sellers

Some websites are dedicated to lot selling, and these are worth a visit, particularly if you are interested in adding some value to the items you purchase for resale. A site that's getting a lot of good press recently is Via Trading (www.viatrading.com). The home page is shown in Figure 4.6.

Be sure to read the FAQs while you are there. These do a nice job of explaining the pros and cons of purchasing distressed merchandise and "returns." In summary, much of what comes on your wholesale pallets will be incomplete or damaged in some way. You need to budget for this. Some categories of merchandise tend to arrive in better shape than others. Clothing items, for example, tend to have a higher "resalable" rate than electronic items. You should plan on cannibalizing at least part of your lot (scavenge parts, photocopy manuals, and so on) to make the rest saleable.

FIGURE 4.6

Via Trading is a popular lot seller used by quite a few eBay store owners.

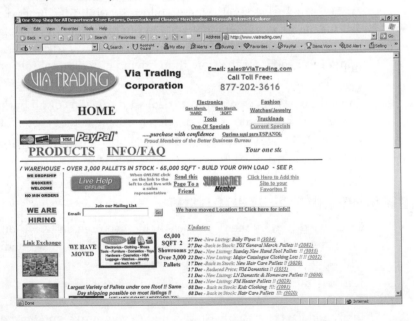

Local Auctions

You can also go to local auctions and estate sales, but this is time consuming, and you need to know what you are looking at, know how much it is really worth (on eBay), and then you must win, pay for, and get the items back to your place without damaging them.

People do this every week. Just don't assume you are going to steal much. You will likely be bidding against other PowerSellers in the audience, of course, but you will also run into people who don't need to make a profit reselling things. They want these items because they want to own them. This can drive prices up past wholesale in a hurry.

I recently saw an upcoming auction advertised over 100 miles away. There was some vintage, high-end stereo gear I was interested in, but I wanted to know more about its condition before spending the time driving both ways and standing in the sun.

The auctioneer described the items to me over the phone, without being terribly reassuring. He asked if I would like to make a proxy offer on the phone, or perhaps come to the auction. I offered a reasonable amount for untested items in questionable physical condition.

The auctioneer laughed. "Don't even bother," he said. "I collect this stuff, too. There's no way I'd let it go for that little. I'd buy it myself first!"

Hmmm. Note to self: Get a job in an auction house.

Still, it is worthwhile to get on auctioneers' mailing lists. Go once in a while. Do your homework. Be prepared. Be brave. Take a shot. It will be fun, if nothing else.

Many auction houses will send email notifications and electronic catalogs if you request them. Use Google to find local auctioneers, or visit a local antique consignment store, pick up one of those free directories you find in the front of the store, and flip to the Auctions section. There should be plenty of local contact information there.

Just as in yard sale hunting, it's possible to find "junk boxes" at auctions that have treasures buried in them. If you spot such lots during the preview, try not to shout out "Oh, wow!" Instead, conceal the treasure as best you can without looking too obvious and hope that other clever bidders have not spotted the same item. Then bid realizing that you will need to dispose of some junk to get the item(s) of value.

Storage Company Auctions

Here's another hit-and-miss, but fun possibility. Folks who run those private storage locations auction off the contents of entire storage lockers when customers don't pay their rent.

The auctions are advertised several weeks ahead in local papers, and some places have online calendars and email notification options. The big chains seem to have auctions virtually every week somewhere in town.

You will generally only be allowed to peek inside, which is often not very helpful. (If you are nice to the location manager, he or she might have a better idea of the contents to share with you.)

You will be expected to pay for and move the entire contents pretty quickly. (Although I bet you could rent the locker and leave it there if you choose.)

One last caveat: The owner can swoop in at the last minute and pay the bill and rescue his stuff only moments before the auction starts. I told you it could be fun. Look for announcements in the paper, or just pop into the office of a storage company or two and ask for the schedule.

Remember, you will be unloading and carting off the contents of a container of who knows what if you win, so use some common sense and a little caution. Although the chances are slim, you might be the proud owner of some toxic waste, poisons, explosives, and maybe a black widow spider or two.

Law Enforcement Auctions

Local law enforcement sells confiscated goods, unclaimed property, old crime-fighting gear, and who knows what all. Once only traditional auctions were used; now the stuff's finding its way online. Check out the local scene. You could get lucky.

Call your local city and county's non-emergency phone numbers (you can find them in the phonebook). Ask how, where, and when they dispose of unclaimed property. If they have a mailing list, find out how to get on it. If they post notices in the paper, ask which paper(s) and which sections, and about when the notices usually come out.

With a Little Help from Your Friends

I have a friend who buys and sells trains, many of them on eBay. Whenever I go garaging I look for trains for him. He looks for radios for me. We haven't found much for each other yet, but ya never know.

Networking is an important part of any business endeavor. Tell your friends at church that you are an eBay seller, and let them know what you are looking to sell. Join local organizations—the Chamber of Commerce, volunteer work at the police department, and so on. Do more than show up. Do good work and make friends. Friends are always your best source of business connections. Be sure you are a source of help to them as well. That "Karma thing" really works. It just takes forever sometimes.

Direct Solicitation

Don't be afraid to go looking for items. I rent some display cases in a collectibles consignments shop. On one of them I've placed a sign that simply says "I Pay Cash for Vintage Electronics," with photos of the stuff I am interested in purchasing.

Direct mail can work, too. Use a postcard program to reach out to potential sources. Do you specialize in beads? Send a postcard to 500 bead shops. Maybe one or two of them are getting ready to close or trim their inventory.

Want It Now

Clever eBay store sellers are using the new "Want It Now" feature to troll for wholesale lots. This is a little-known eBay feature, but it is catching on and costs nothing to try. Sometimes we get ahead by trying things others don't. This could be one of those times!

The link for Want It Now was in the upper-left area of the main eBay screen last time I looked, or you can just visit http://pages.ebay.com/wantitnow/.

Figure 4.7 shows the posting process. Here you can use specific brands and other terms without being accused of keyword spamming, so be specific. You can even add a photo representing the stuff you are looking for.

Requests run for 60 days. If you are lucky, you will get emails from potential sources of store merchandise.

You can also look for potential buyers this way, and direct them to your store by entering search terms to find buyers who have posted Want It Now requests. Figure 4.8 shows a typical search result. In this example, I used the search term "wholesale lot."

FIGURE 4.7

Posting a Want
It Now request.

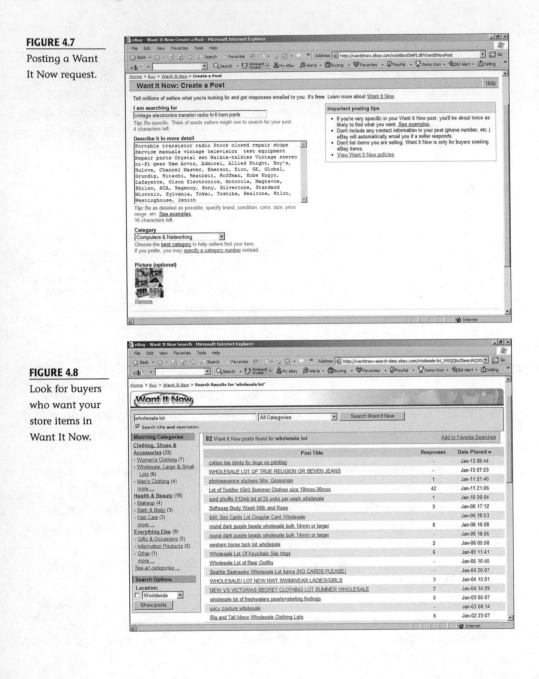

FIGURE 4.8

Look for buyers
who want your
store items in
Want It Now.

Designing and Building a Brand

When someone says "Starbucks," what comes to mind? Can you see the round green logo in your head? Do you think of words such as *Grande* and *caramel macchiato?* We've all pretty much been programmed by Starbucks thanks to its "branding" efforts.

Your eBay store can benefit from this brainwashing technique as well. The best time to think about branding is when you start a business, but it's never too late to tweak your image. HP was once commonly referred to as Hewlett-Packard, for example. The name, logo, official company colors, and other identifiers have evolved over decades.

Your Company Name

Your company name can be different from your eBay seller ID, and the moniker doesn't need to match your eBay store name either. But it's much nicer if it all ties together somehow.

For instance, HP now calls itself "HP" or "hp" everywhere rather than Hewlett-Packard (although this company seems a little schizophrenic where capitalization is concerned). The logo is a white rectangle with *hp* in a circle, all on a solid rectangular background (see Figure 5.1).

FIGURE 5.1

HP's logo in its eBay store.

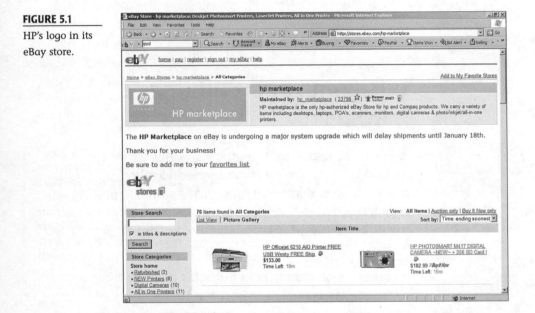

This look is consistent on its products, printed materials, and websites. (Visit www.hp.com, for example.) You can do something similar.

Your eBay ID(s)

If you have the luxury of starting from scratch, or decide to change your eBay ID, choose a meaningful store name, business name, and compatible eBay selling ID if possible. Back in Chapter 2, "Examples of Stores, Plain and Fancy," you saw two sellers of reproduction maps, one with the seller ID Euriskodata, the other called maps-of-the-past. Both sellers appear to be doing fine, but think about how nicely "maps-of-the-past" tells the whole story at a glance.

Try to use the same or a similar name for your business, eBay seller ID, off-eBay website, and your eBay store. If you can't do that, come close. For example, HP uses hp_marketplace as its seller ID and "hp marketplace" as its store name.

Don't Get Sued!

Be careful not to misappropriate someone else's logo or brand or create confusion. Calling your store "Starbucks" and using the coffee giant's corporate colors and other design elements might get you some unwanted attention from the legal profession.

Even the appearance of an affiliation can cause grief. Think twice before you call your store "The Gucci Outlet" or "The Starbucks Cafe," or even "Ron's HP SuperStore." When in doubt, ask an attorney for a legal opinion. And don't think that just because some folks are getting away with this on eBay at the moment they won't eventually get caught and shut down. Many eventually will.

Do a URL Search

Before settling on a name, be sure someone else hasn't gotten there before you. Do a URL search to see whether the name you want (or something so similar that it will confuse people) is already owned by someone. One convenient place to do such a search is www.register.com.

> **note** You might want to do other searches in addition to eBay IDs and domain names. It varies from state to state, but businesses can and do register their names, protecting them from use by others. You can also search many state's databases. Again, an attorney can help get you started.

The "Look and Feel" of Your Store

As you saw back in Chapter 2, stores can look remarkably different. The goal is to make your store accessible and fun for your audience.

If you are aiming at computer-savvy folks in their 20s or 30s, make the place flashy and intriguing. Consider tricks such as mouse hovering to reveal products or categories.

If you are wanting to reach an older crowd, don't get too carried away with technical wizardry, no matter how smokin' a codehead you are. Use large, easy-to-read type on a nice, uncluttered, high-contrast background. Make it obvious what to do next and how to get from place to place. Do the searching and revealing for them (you'll learn how in Chapter 6, "Setting Up Your

Store"). If you hire someone to set up your eBay store for you, make sure that person understands this.

Use Color and Style to Identify Your Store

Pick a color scheme and design style that fits your company and tells viewers something about you. If the business is modern and trendy, use today's bright color pallets and images. If you sell mid-century items, use the colors and typefaces that were popular back then, and so on. Browse the category or categories you plan to sell in and see which stores jump out at you. When thinking about a color and style for your store, ask yourself why each color and style is the right choice.

Pay for a Logo

Develop a visually strong logo and use it everywhere, including in your eBay store, on your eBay listings, business cards, and so on. Tie things together in such a way that people begin to recognize you.

You can even plunk your logo into each of your auction photos if you like (see Figure 5.2). If the logo is big enough, it will stand out in the gallery photos when people search. Those unconscious repeated impressions can sink in. Doubt this? Next time you watch television, count the Coke and Pepsi logos in the backgrounds of virtually everything you see.

FIGURE 5.2

Some sellers include bold logos in their photos.

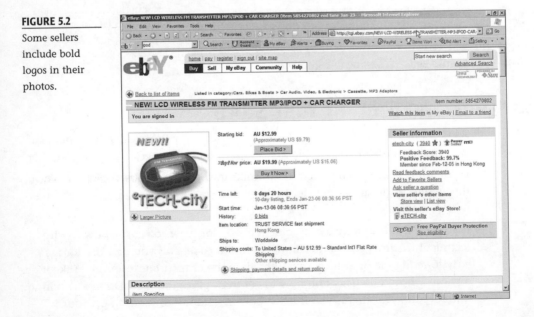

Resist the urge to use eBay's "free" logos and color schemes if you can afford to do otherwise. So many other sellers are using those same logos and color combinations in their listings that you risk getting lost in the clutter. Figure 5.3 shows a free eBay store logo that probably appears in hundreds, if not thousands of store headings.

FIGURE 5.3

"Hey! We sell, umm, antiques and stuff...."

If you are not a graphics designer, and don't have design talent on staff, spend a few dollars for your own logo and corporate look. Shop locally, or Google "logo design" or even "eBay design." These services have become quite affordable.

Follow Through

Once you have the basics in place, keep working on brand recognition. You can add your logo to many eBay communications—automatically generated emails, invoices, business cards, and so on. For example, you can place your logo in checkout screens and emails using eBay's Store Builder. Figure 5.4 shows an example of a logo in a checkout screen.

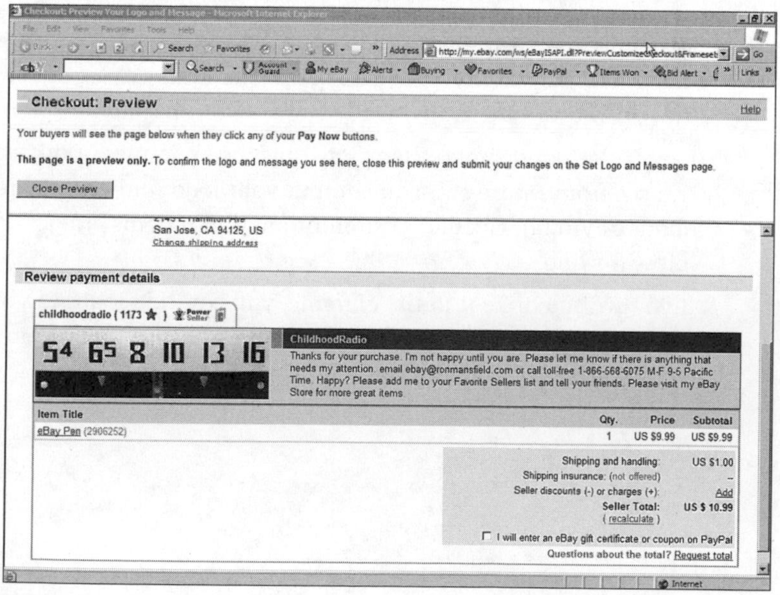

FIGURE 5.4

eBay's Store Builder can help you insert your logo into emails, checkout screens, and more.

You will learn more about these features in Chapter 15, "More Promotional Help from eBay."

You can imprint your brand on peoples' minds in other ways, too. Consider giving away small items containing your logo. Put these promotional items in with products you ship as free gifts to your customers.

At the end of the year, to thank my best customers, I send nice limited-edition custom calendars that I write, photograph, and print. Figure 5.5 shows an example.

FIGURE 5.5

I send free custom calendars to favorite customers.

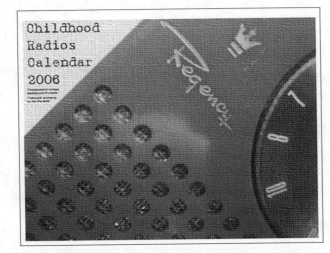

Hopefully they will think of me every day next year, and stare at my store URL when they check to see if it's Friday or Saturday or ogle a photo of a radio they wish they had in their collection. "Hmmm. Maybe *Ron* has one of those."

Pens, rulers, and similar items are obvious examples of other freebies. As you can see from Figure 5.6, you can put your logo and eBay store URL on just about anything. Google "custom promotional items" to get those creative juices flowing.

If you want to take it to the extreme, you can add logos to your packing tape. Figure 5.7 shows a typical website, www.production-packaging.com. Uline and other shipping supply houses offer similar custom items.

FIGURE 5.6

For a price, you can put your branding just about anywhere.

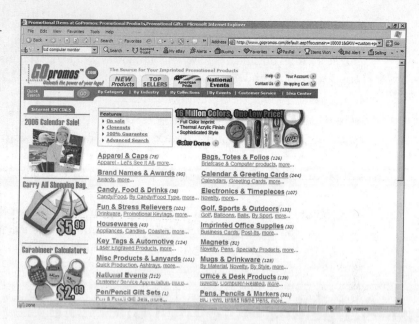

FIGURE 5.7

Even personalized packing tape is available.

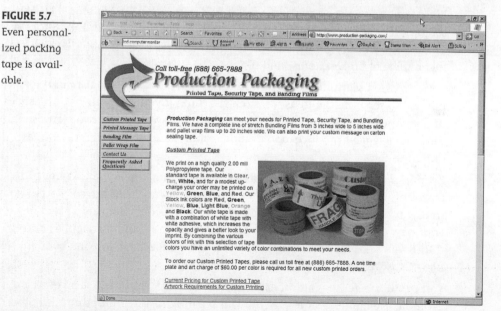

Your Store Has Its Own URL—Use It!

Every eBay store has a unique web address (or URL) in the format http://stores.ebay.com/*storename*. So, for example, my store, childhoodradio, can be reached at...anyone? Right! http://stores.ebay.com/childhoodradio.

Plaster your store's URL on everything. And I mean everything. The rulers, the tape, your business cards, emails. Use it everywhere. People will be coming to your store from outside of eBay. And you know what that means, right? Reduced fees for you when they buy store items.

Your Reputation Is Part of Your Brand

Your reputation is a big part of branding, too. How do you want to be remembered? Are you the quick shipping guys? Are you the experts in art glass? The best place on eBay to find things for basset hounds? Find a way to burn this message into peoples' brains.

And you obviously don't want to become known as "those knuckleheads who overcharge for shipping, use recycled peanuts that smell like cigarettes, and only go to the post office once a month." So become known for your good work instead.

Consider Opening More Than One Store

Big companies do it, so perhaps you should, too. Consider opening a second selling account used to unload items that might "tarnish" your brand if sold under your primary ID. This is where you might do your garage cleaning, sell incomplete or broken items, and so on.

You can also use multiple IDs and stores to differentiate great merchandise, not just to separate the treasures from the junk. If you sell both running shoes and computer accessories, for example, consider two IDs and two stores so that the divergent products don't muddle your completely different images and messages.

Keep in mind that your seller feedback, seller rating, and so on, do not transfer to this new ID. If you are a PowerSeller, this means that buyers won't know that you're a PowerSeller and you'll start with a feedback rating of zero on your new account. (Using the new second account to buy the supplies and things you need for your selling will help get the feedback looking good in the new ID as well.)

You can also refer to your other ID and its feedback in listings, and even cross-promote the multiple stores, as you will see in Part III, "Promoting Your Store."

Setting Up Your Store

Okay, let's get to the fun part. If you have not already done so, it's time to sign up for an eBay store. This chapter will get you going. If you already have a store, you can jump ahead to Chapter 7, "Defining Store Categories," but don't skip Chapter 7 because, even if you already have a store, you should give careful thought to either setting up or revamping store categories.

Store Prerequisites

To open an eBay store, you must be a registered eBay seller with feedback of 20 or higher, or be an ID-verified eBay seller, or be an eBay seller with a PayPal account in good standing.

> **note** Because you will want to use PayPal to sell in your store, opening a PayPal account *before* opening your store is the easiest and quickest way to meet the store opening requirement.

Opening a Seller's Account

If you haven't already, you must open a seller's account by logging onto eBay and clicking the Sell button in the header, or visit the eBay home page (www.ebay.com) and click the Sell button near the top of the page. You'll be taken to a screen similar to the one in Figure 6.1.

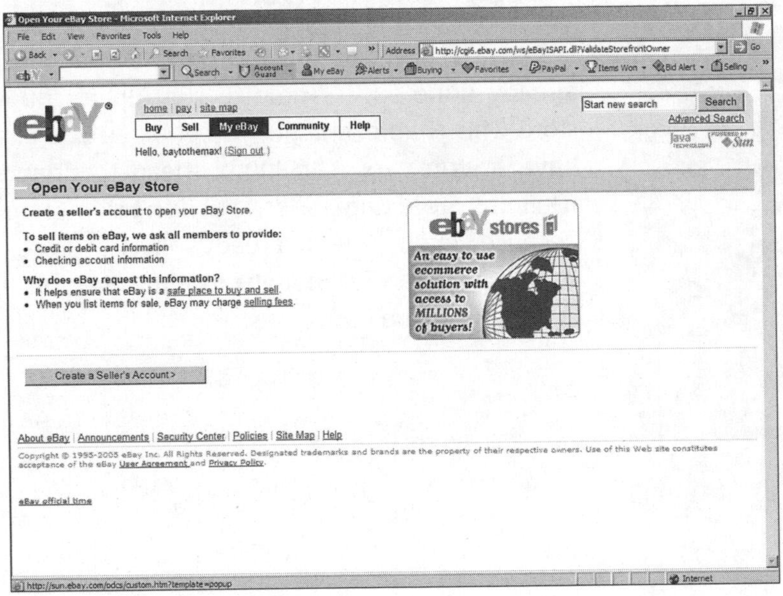

FIGURE 6.1

If you don't have a seller's account, click the Sell button and sign up before trying to open a store.

Be Sure You Have a Store Plan

Once you have your seller's account, but before logging onto the Stores page and diving into the actual store setup steps, be sure you have done the following:

- Given some thought to what you will sell in your store, both now and in the future

■ Picked a great name for your store with both the present and future in mind

■ Looked at enough eBay stores to have some idea of what styles, colors, and layout features you would like to start with

■ Collected some items to begin listing if you don't already have live listings

■ Obtained a logo and some help with color choices if you won't be doing this yourself (although you can always make these cosmetic changes later if you are in a rush to start selling)

■ Set aside about an hour to go through the initial store setup process

Creating Your Store

Begin by visiting the Stores home page (http://stores.ebay.com) and clicking the Open a Store button, as shown in Figure 6.2. eBay will lead you step by step through the process.

FIGURE 6.2

Getting started on the road to a store.

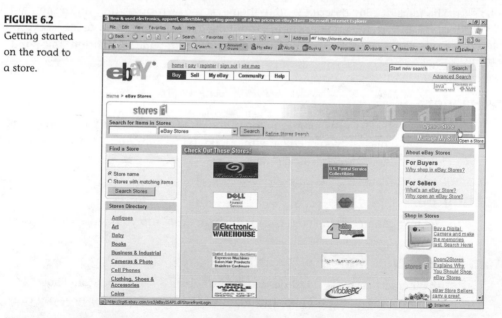

Choose a Theme and Color Scheme

The next major step is to choose from eBay's stock themes and color schemes, or design your own. Refer to Figure 6.3 as you review the elements of a theme.

FIGURE 6.3

Themes all
have common
elements.

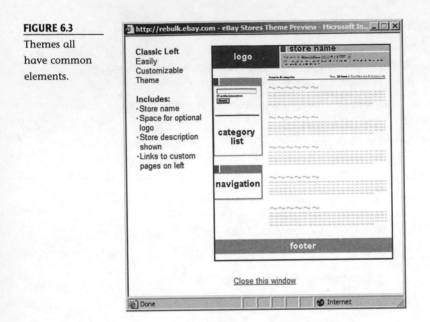

The folks at eBay describe a store theme as the "wrapper" around the content of all your store's pages, creating a unique look and feel for your store. Every theme has a store header, navigation bar, custom page navigation links, and store footers.

Store Header

The store header runs along the top of the page and displays your store name. You can embellish your header with a logo, HTML, and/or text. You will learn how to design yours in this chapter.

Navigation Bar

The navigation bar includes a search box and links to your store's categories.

Custom Page Navigation

If you create custom pages (described in Chapter 8, "Custom Store Pages"), a portion of the navigation bar includes links to those pages. For now you can ignore this feature.

Store Footers

Store footers run (where else?) across the bottom of the page and display standard information such as your user ID. You have no control over them.

Predesigned vs. Customizable Themes

You have two basic types of themes from which to choose—predesigned and customizable themes. Predesigned themes offer eBay-provided, color-coordinated background graphics, fonts, and color combinations. Although they save time, they are all in use by many other sellers, so these won't give you the most unique look and feel.

Customizable themes (eBay calls them "Easily Customizable" themes, and they are) lend themselves to creating a more unique store look. They do take extra time, and some trial and error will ensue.

You will learn more about custom pages and links in the next chapter, but for now it's worth noting that the links for custom pages can either appear as part of the left navigation bar or in the header across the top, depending on the theme you choose. This is easy to change even after your store is up and running, so don't lose any sleep over this or any other "first stab" at theme choices. You can edit the colors and fonts of a theme, change to a different theme, or pick different options within a theme at any time.

Most themes include a designated slot for a 310×90-pixel or smaller logo. The only exceptions are the Minimal Header themes.

note Virtually all graphic design programs have a way to determine the size of the images you create, measured in pixels. The exact process, of course, varies with the program you use. If you are unfamiliar with how to determine the current size of your graphics and resize them, refer to your program's help features or ask someone knowledgeable for assistance.

If you chose an Easily Customizable theme, as shown in Figure 6.4, be sure to choose a color palette from the drop-down list the theme. Don't forget to do this, or eBay will not let you proceed and will scold you.

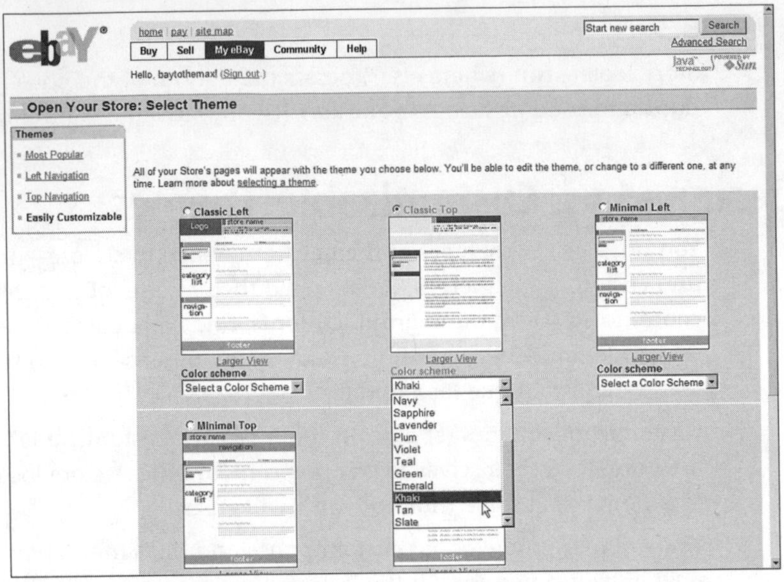

FIGURE 6.4

Customizable
themes require a
color combina-
tion choice.

FIGURE 6.4

Customizable
themes require a
color combina-
tion choice.

Store Name, Description, and Logo

After settling on a theme and color combination, you will be taken to a screen
like the one in Figure 6.5, where you choose a store name, enter a description,
and specify an optional logo.

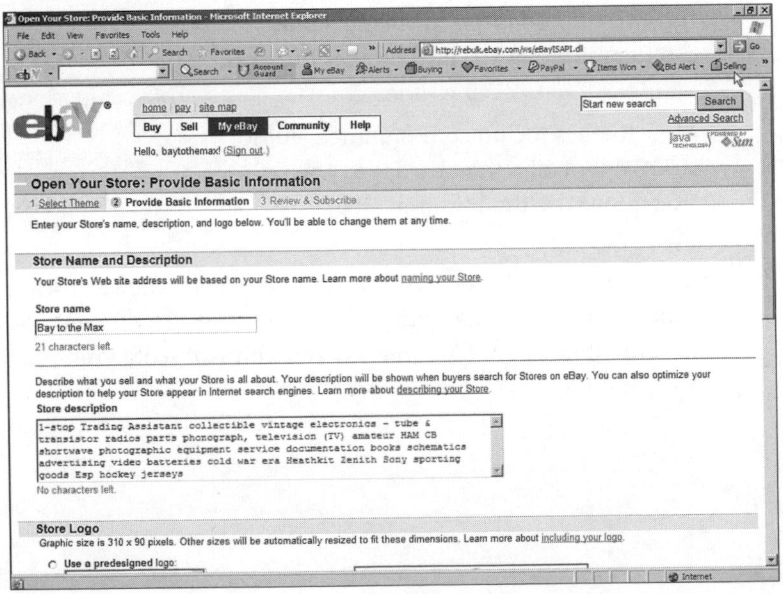

FIGURE 6.5

Enter your
store's name
and description
here, and specify
an optional logo
if you like.

Store Name

Your store name, in addition to describing your store's identity and purpose to visitors, determines your store's web address, or URL. For example, if your store's name is "Bay to the Max," your store's URL is http://stores.ebay.com/bay-to-the-max.

That's because eBay will automatically take out special characters (apostrophes, spaces, &, !, $, and so on), add hyphens between words, and make all letters lowercase. To meet eBay's requirements your store name

- must start and end with a letter or number
- can't start with four or more consecutive letter *A*'s
- can't start with an *e* or *E* followed by a number
- can't contain the characters <, >, and @
- can't be the username of another user on eBay
- can't contain "www" anywhere in the name
- can't contain two or more consecutive spaces or nonalphanumeric characters
- can't end with a top-level domain abbreviation used on the Web (.com, .net, and so on)
- can't be a name that is identical or confusingly similar to another company's name that is protected by trademark law

Also, you may not use a name that contains *eBuy*, *Half.com*, or *PayPal*, or anything confusingly similar to those names. See eBay's Trademarked Items and Domain Name policies in the eBay Help Center.

Your store name can be your eBay user ID, as long as it meets the requirements previously stated.

Store Description

After picking a name, spend some time developing a store description in the Store description box, shown in Figure 6.5. This description will be searchable both on eBay and the Internet, so pack it with useful keywords, even at the expense of grammar. You can enter a maximum of 300 characters including spaces.

For example, the following eBay store description is not a sentence, but it is crammed with searchable words:

"1-stop Trading Assistant collectible vintage electronics - tube & transistor radios parts phonograph, television (TV) amateur HAM CB shortwave photographic equipment service documentation books schematics advertising batteries cold war era video Heathkit Zenith Sony sporting goods Esp. hockey jerseys"

Logo

As you learned in Chapter 5, "Designing and Building a Brand," creating a unique logo can help with branding your operation. The logo must be a maximum of 310 pixels wide by 90 pixels high. If your graphic does not fit or is not proportional to these dimensions, it will be reduced or stretched. You can preview graphics before committing to them. As you can see in Figure 6.6, stretching usually is not a good thing.

FIGURE 6.6

Specify one (and only one) logo source.

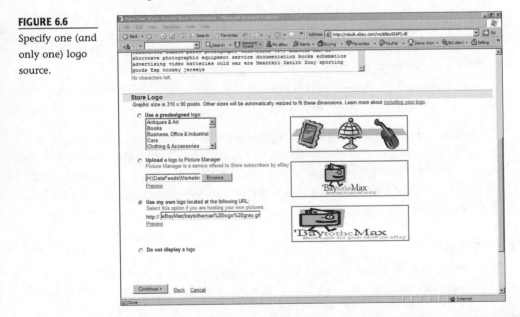

You can use eBay's "clipart" logos, upload graphics to eBay's Picture Manager, or host your own and point eBay to the URL of the logo. The logo file must be in one of the following graphic formats:

- JPG
- JPEG

- GIF
- BMP
- PNG

So, either choose one of the free logos eBay offers or specify the location of your own. When you have looked over your title, description, and other elements on this screen, scroll to the bottom and click the button to submit them. You should see a screen similar to Figure 6.7.

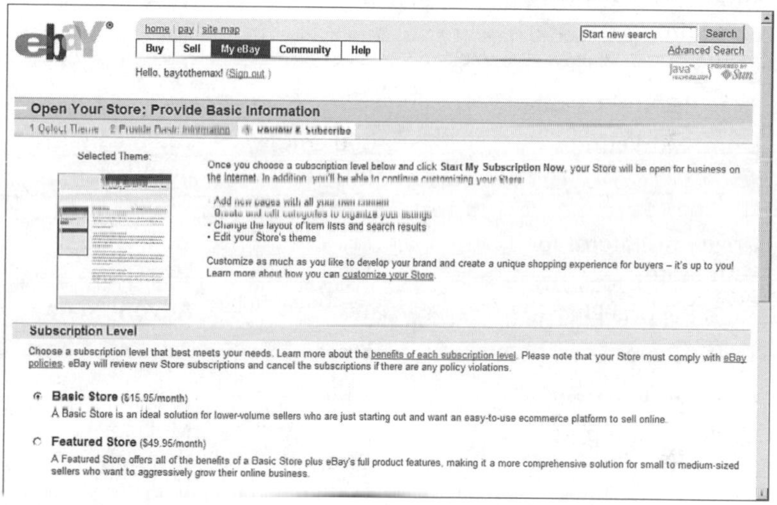

> **note** You can store your logo on eBay using their Picture Manager feature, or store it on an outside website of your own choosing. We'll deal with these options in more detail in Chapter 10, "Creating Listings and Templates."

FIGURE 6.7
Pick the right subscription level for your businesses.

Picking a Subscription Level

The next big choice is how much to spend for which features. Most typical eBay sellers (if there is such thing) should start with a Featured store, because this choice gets you Selling Manager Pro for "free" and gives you extra custom pages and some other goodies. Table 6.1 summarizes the differences.

Table 6.1   Overview of Store Levels and Features

Features Provided	Basic	Featured	Anchor
Additional Pages in Your Store	5 pages	10 pages	15 pages
Promotion Boxes	Yes	Yes	Yes
Store Inventory Format	Yes	Yes	Yes
Vacation Hold	Yes	Yes	Yes

Table 6.1   (continued)

Features Provided	Basic	Featured	Anchor
Online Sales Management	Selling Manager	Selling Manager Pro	Selling Manager Pro
Promotion on eBay Cross-Promotions Tools	Yes	Yes	Yes
Custom Listing Header	Yes	Yes	Yes
Free eBay Keywords (see Chapter 14, "Cross-promoting Your Store on eBay")		$30/month allotment	$100/month allotment
On eBay Increased Exposure		Yes	Yes
Off eBay Store Referral Credit	Yes	Yes	Yes
Email Marketing	100 emails/month	1,000 emails/month	4,000 emails/month
Create Collateral for Your Store	Yes	Yes	Yes
Sales Reports Plus	Yes	Advanced data	Advanced data
Traffic Reports	Yes	Advanced data	Advanced data
Accounting Assistant	Yes	Yes	Yes
Customer Support	Monday through Friday 6 a.m.– 6 p.m. PST	Monday through Friday 6 a.m.– 6 p.m. PST	Dedicated 24-hour support
Store Price	$15.95	$49.95	$499.95

All three levels provide promotion boxes, the store inventory format (items organized by categories), vacation hold (great for solo sellers), a subscription to Selling Manager or Selling Manger Pro features, and cheaper final value (FV) fees if shoppers come from non-eBay sites.

The primary differences in the plans are the number of free eBay keywords you get, the number of free marketing emails you can send, and the depth of sales reporting. Anchor stores get 24/7 tech support, whereas other levels can get answers from 6 a.m. to 6 p.m. PST.

Featured stores also let you minimize the size of the eBay header in your store (see Chapter 10). You can use the Display Settings page in Manage My Store to reach this option at any time if you have a Featured or Anchor store.

You get more detailed reporting if you choose a Featured store, and the most comprehensive reporting as an Anchor store (see Part IV for details).

Pick the store level you've chosen on the screen shown in Figure 6.7. You can always upgrade or downgrade later. Featured is a safe bet for starters.

Although it might be tempting to save a few dollars each month by picking a Basic store, in my opinion, a Featured store is a better choice for a variety of reasons. First, you will get greater exposure in the various promotional rotations (discussed in Part III, "Promoting Your Store"). If you plan to use the keyword features (also discussed in Part III) you will get more "free" keyword clicks with a Featured store ($30 worth at this writing). In addition, you get to use Selling Manager Pro, a superior selling tool compared with the non-Pro version. Moreover, the improved depth of sales and traffic reporting alone might be worth the price difference. But if you are on a very tight budget, the $34 monthly savings obtained with a Basic rather than a Featured store might be worth it. You can always upgrade.

When you click the button at the bottom of the screen to continue, you should see a Congratulations screen similar to the one shown in Figure 6.8.

Notice the URL that has been created for my new store. As promised, eBay has put hyphens between the words.

In about 24 hours, any active listings you have will appear in your store. However, because you have not set up any custom categories yet (which is covered in the next chapter), existing listings will be categorized by eBay category. But you don't need to wait 24 hours to see your store.

It's time to click the Go to Manage My Store button and take a look around. Or, if it's dinner time, you can just quit at this point and manage the store via your My eBay store link (found on your My eBay page) any time you choose. Figure 6.9 shows the Manage My Store screen.

Whenever you visit the Manage My Store page, eBay will make some suggestions about ways to improve your store. If you have not added custom listing headers, for example, it will suggest that you use them.

FIGURE 6.8

Hey, ma! Come look. I opened my eBay store.

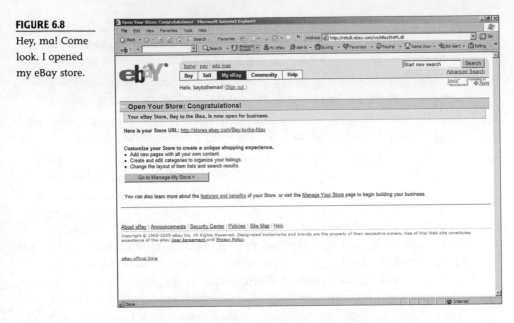

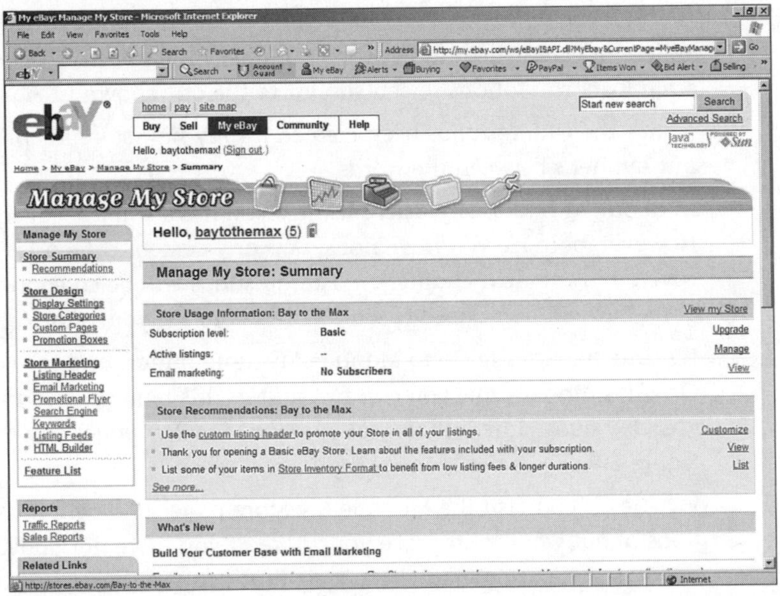

FIGURE 6.9

Managing your eBay store starts here.

Custom Headers

Store listing headers can help drive traffic to your store, by appearing at the top of item descriptions in all your listings. They will show up in any listings you have running when you open your store, and in new listings from here on out. These are designed to drive traffic from your live listings (auctions and so on) to your store. Figure 6.10 Shows an example.

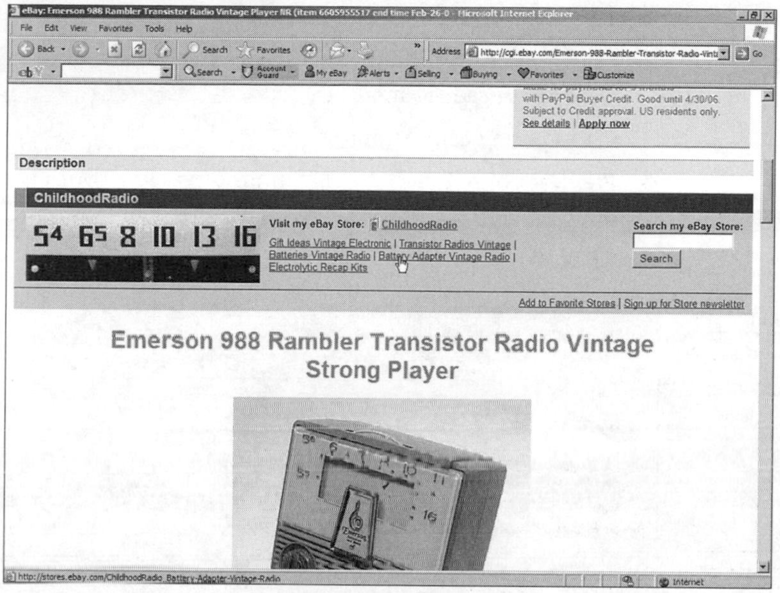

FIGURE 6.10

A typical custom listing header.

Listing headers include your store name and a link to your store's home page, and they match the store's theme colors. You can also add the following items:

- Your store's logo
- That custom store-specific search box we discussed earlier
- A link used by shoppers to add you to their favorite sellers list
- A link enabling shoppers to sign up for your email marketing newsletters
- Links to your custom categories, custom pages, and About Me page (up to a maximum of five links)

You cannot edit your store name, store link, and store colors in your store listing header, meaning that they must match what's found on your storefront.

By the way, eBay suggests that you only include the search box if you always have a large number of items in your store. I suggest that you always have a large number of items in your store. As I mentioned in earlier in this book, one of the cool things about running an eBay store is that it provides you with your own personal search engine, producing search results from your items alone. This is that search box, and you should display it everywhere you can. It's like having "your own little eBay."

Creating and Editing Listing Headers

To create listing headers, follow these steps:

1. Visit the Manage My Store page.

2. Click the Listing Header link under the Store Marketing section of the Navigator (see Figure 6.11).

3. Choose the desired options.

4. Preview your choices by clicking the Preview Your Listing Header link near the bottom of the setup page. (See the next topic for details.)

5. Click the Apply button when you are satisfied.

FIGURE 6.11

Choose and preview your header options.

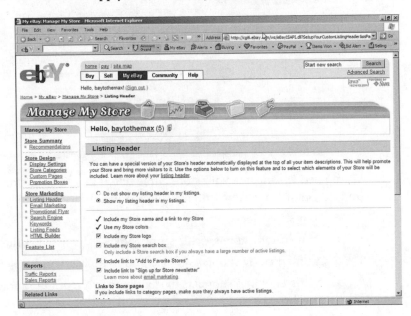

Header Options

The options are pretty self-explanatory. Because you want your store header to be displayed in your listings, click the radio button next to "Show my listing header in my listings." If you have designed a store logo (or have chosen one of eBay's clipart logos) and want the logo to appear in your header, click to enable this. You want the store search box, so be sure that option is checked (and thus enabled as well). You want people to be able to add you to their favorite stores list, and there's an option to enable an Add to Favorite Stores link to your header. Enable it. If you plan to collect names of eBay shoppers to mail your store newsletters (discussed in Chapter 15, "More Promotional Help from eBay"), enable that option as well. If you don't want to create newsletters, or want to wait a while, uncheck this feature. You can always revise any of these settings later.

Because you have not set up any custom pages yet (this is explained in Chapter 8), don't do anything with the drop-down Links to Store Pages just yet.

Figure 6.12 shows a typical header preview with all the options except custom pages checked.

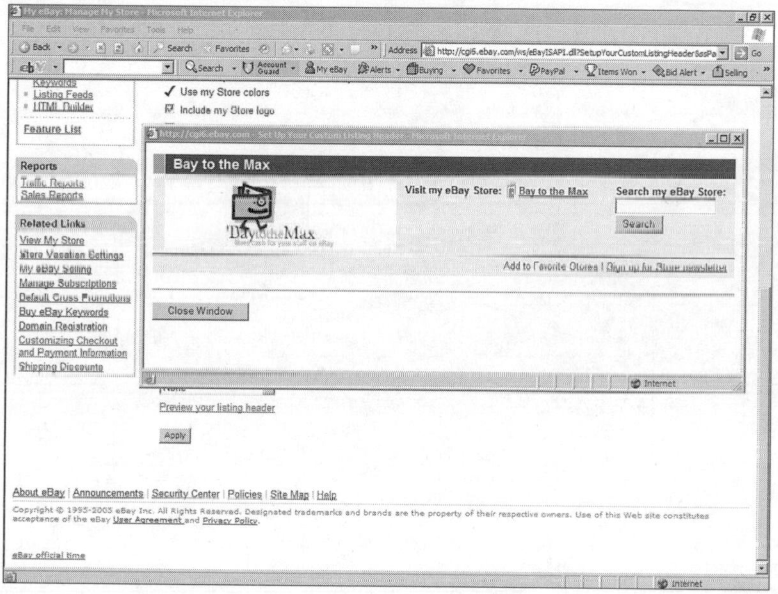

FIGURE 6.12

The beginnings of a new store header that will appear in all listings (including auctions).

After you have looked at some listings containing your new header, you can always come back to the Manage My Store page and click the Listing header link to fine-tune your headers.

First, however, let's get those store categories in order. That's the topic of the next chapter.

Defining Store Categories

Establishing the correct store categories can make shopping a pleasure for your customers, and increase your profits. Store categories are a vital part of any well-run eBay store.

Don't confuse store categories with the eBay selling categories used to organize and locate listings on eBay proper. Instead, think of store categories as the departments, aisles, and/or shelves of your store.

Departments, Aisles, and Shelves

eBay recently increased the maximum number of categories from 20 to 300. You get to name 299 of the 300 categories and eBay assigns and reserves "Other items" as the name for the 300th category. You can use up to two levels of subcategories to organize stores now. For example, you could have a Camera category with Digital and Film subcategories. The total

note Although it is possible to rename categories after you have set them up, this can cause problems if you have a lot of listings running, as you will see later in this chapter. Planning ahead is always better than fixing later.

number of categories and subs cannot exceed 300. For example, you could have 100 categories each with two subcategories each, and so on.

How you name your categories will vary with the kind of store you have, what items you sell, and how you want shoppers to be able to browse or navigate your store. This should be given serious thought before you name all your categories. Therefore, this section discusses a good way to understand the concepts involved in picking category names.

Organizing Narrow Inventories

Imagine a small, traditional brick-and-mortar camera shop in your neighborhood. When you walk through the store door and read the overhead signs, you might see some that say the following:

- Film Cameras
- Digital Cameras
- Lighting
- Film and Processing
- Equipment Bags
- Lenses and Filters
- Photography Books
- Tripods

When you walk up to the digital cameras counter in our imaginary neighborhood store, your will have some decisions to make, such as the resolution of the camera in megapixels, whether it's a point-and-shoot or has lenses you can swap, and on, and on. Perhaps you have a particular brand in mind and want to concentrate on Nikon or Canon or whatever.

Brick-and-mortar stores have ways to help guide you through this maze, and so do you as an eBay store owner. Your task is to help your shoppers narrow their searches and find exactly what they're after. But before we turn to those specific tools, let's consider another "real-world" shopping trip.

Suppose you go shopping for a camera at Wal-Mart. Whoa. Those overhead signs don't have anywhere near the detail of the camera store signs. You walk in and see Women's Wear, Gardening, Music, and so on. Cameras, if they even have their own sign, lurk behind the Music department, and perhaps behind the acres of seasonal merchandise. Heck, cameras might not even be on the same floor where you are standing, or might be located in a small corner of the Electronics department. This big store has more important major item categories than cameras. It needs to use very general signs to get you to the right section of the store, and then draw you to what you are looking for in other ways.

So, how is this accomplished in your eBay store? Because you only have 299 assignable categories, you need to use them wisely. If you have specialized store like that local camera shop mentioned earlier, your categories can be pretty specific. Otherwise, you'll need to set up broad store categories.

If, for example, you specialize in digital cameras, your categories might be broken down mostly by manufacturer the way J&K Cameras (ID jandkcameras) does, as shown in Figure 7.1.

FIGURE 7.1

A specialized store can use fairly narrow categories.

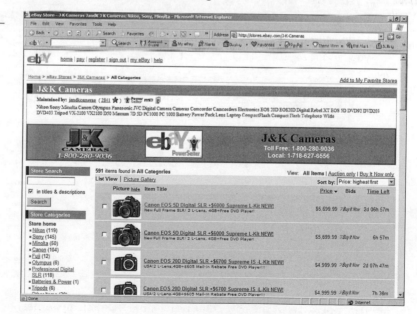

This is an interesting example of the different ways categories can be used, even in the same store. J&K categorizes primarily by manufacturer (Nikon,

Sony, and so on) but has additional categories for accessories—batteries, tripods, and such. This store also has a category called Professional Digital SLR for high-end pro cameras.

This way, if I am a camera shopper, I can easily look at J&K's selection of Nikon cameras or Sony cameras, and so on. If I want a tripod, I know right where to look for that as well.

J&K's store was using fewer than 20 categories when I visited. For example, it sells both still cameras and video cameras, so it could have had a store category called Still Cameras and another called Video Cameras. Because J&K has not created a separate Video Camera category and sells Canon video cameras, if I click the store category for Canon, I will see the Canon still cameras, of course, but I will see the Canon video cameras as well. Not a bad thing, necessarily, but an example of something that could be changed by adding a Video Camera category. The store could further filter what shoppers see by adding categories to segregate its merchandise even more.

There are probably as many ways to categorize inventory as there are eBay stores. Take a look at Figure 7.2, another camera store.

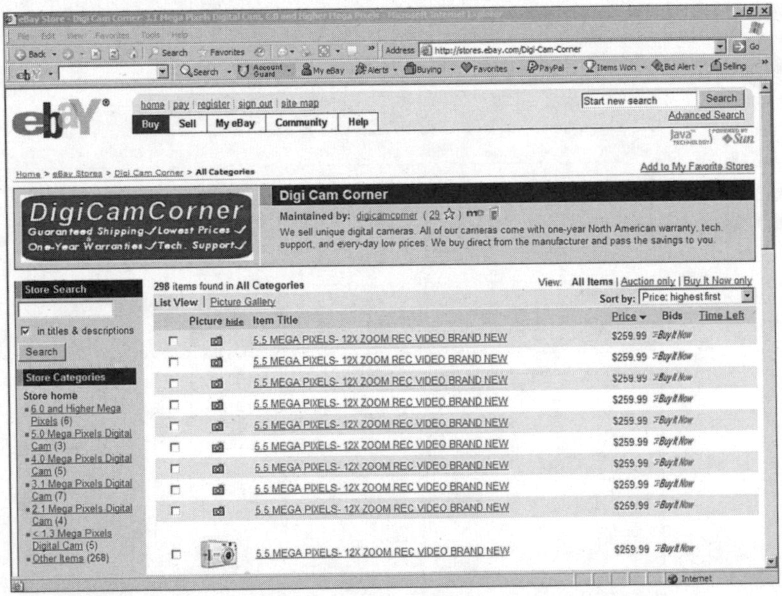

FIGURE 7.2

This camera store organizes by camera resolution.

The operators of the DigiCamCorner store (ID digicamcorner) have decided to organize by the number of megapixels offered in cameras they sell. This makes it easy, for example, to find a 6-megapixel camera if you need one.

Organizing Diverse Inventories

But what happens if you run a general merchandise store, the equivalent of a Wal-Mart? With only 299 assignable categories, you are certainly not going to devote one to "9.0 and Higher Mega Pixels" the way DigiCamCorner did. Suppose you are a Trading Assistant with a Trading Post and sell all manner of items the way AuctionDrop does. Take a look at Figure 7.3.

FIGURE 7.3

Diverse stores, like Trading Posts, use very broad categories.

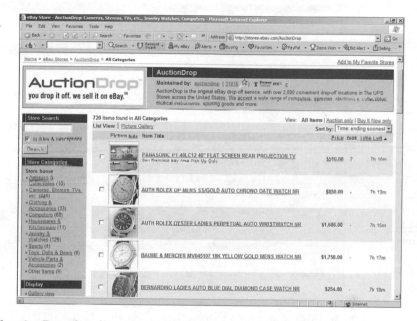

AuctionDrop has its cameras lumped in with stereos, televisions, and other electronics, in much the same way you would expect to see them in a big department store. Other broad categories include Computers, Jewelry & Watches, and so on. In fact, all of AuctionDrop's categories are broad, which makes perfect sense given its product mix.

What's Right for You?

Okay, now's the time to sit down and pencil out up to 299 categories for your store. Then we'll look at setting them up next. Store category names can be up to 29 characters long, including spaces.

> **note** Consider reserving a "wildcard" category that you can use for special occasions, such as having sales, or for seasonal or topical purposes. You can change its name as the need arises. It could be called "Halloween Costumes" one month and "Thanksgiving Decorations" the next, and then perhaps "Fire Sale" when you want to unload those Tom Cruise key chains. Just be sure that the items in the wildcard category belong there after you change the category's name.

Setting Up Your Store Categories

Here are the steps to follow for setting up your store categories:

1. Begin by logging into your eBay account and visiting your My eBay page; then scroll down a bit until you can see the My Subscriptions link(s) in the left navigation area of the screen, as shown in Figure 7.4.

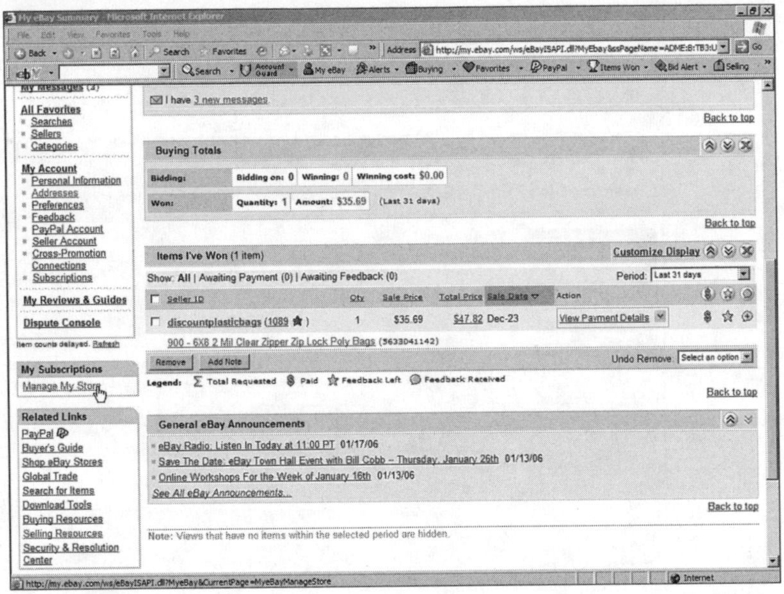

FIGURE 7.4

Visit My eBay to start defining your store categories.

2. Click Manage My Store, and in the resulting screen in the Store Design area of the left navigation bar, click Store Categories, which will provide a page similar to Figure 7.5. This is where you enter and edit store category names. It is also where you define which order categories appear in your store (discussed momentarily).

3. If you have never set up any store categories, you'll see a list of positions (1–300) and generic category names (Category 1, Category 2, and so on). Click the Edit Category names link also shown in Figure 7.5.

4. You will soon see the Edit Store Category Names screen shown in Figure 7.6. This is where you type category names.

note Categories will display in your store navigation bar in the order you type them here, unless you reorder them (also discussed in this chapter). It's no big deal if you type categories in the wrong order here, but it's nice if you get them right at this point, because it will save some time later.

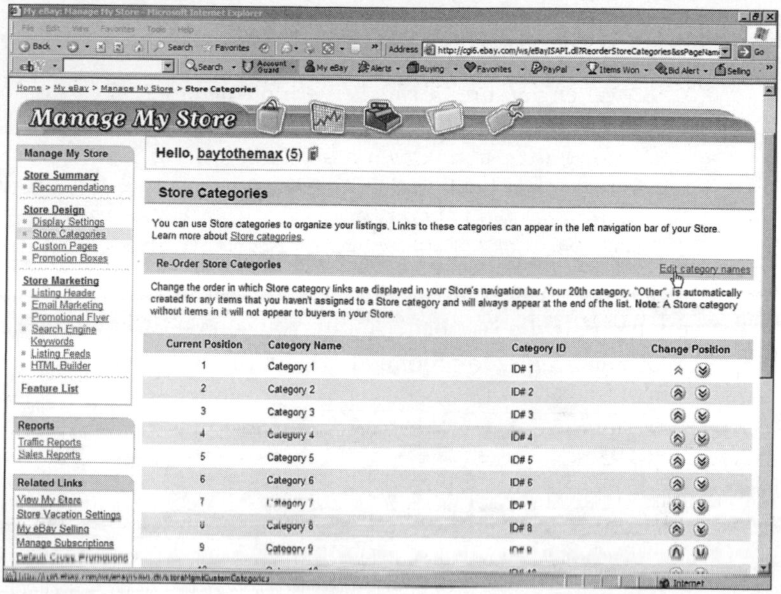

FIGURE 7.5

Add and edit store categories here.

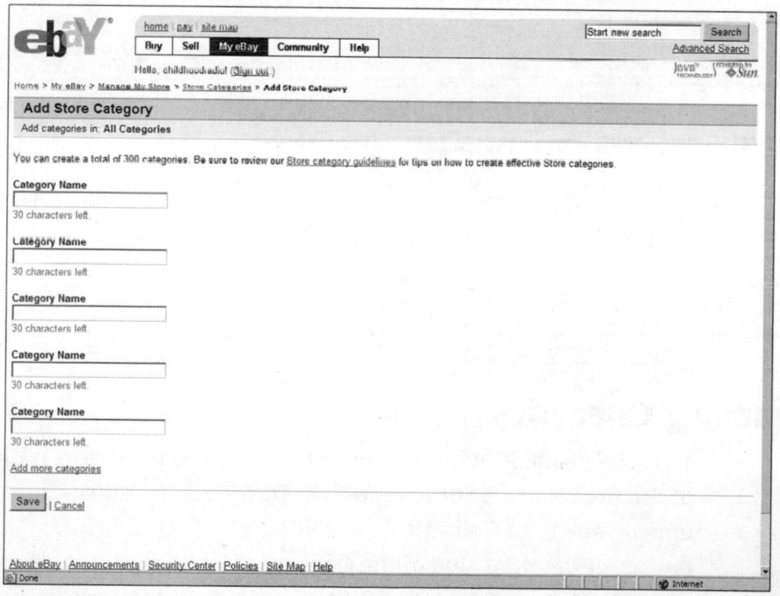

FIGURE 7.6

Type up to 299 category names here. Click the Save Settings button when done.

5. Either drag or "triple-click" to select the entire contents of a category name field (Category 1, for example) and then type the desired category name. Repeat this operation in other fields as necessary to enter

all your categories. Spelling counts! In Figure 7.6, I am using broad categories for this "Trading Post" store.

6. When you are finished entering categories, click the Save Settings button.

You will be taken back to the Store Categories page, which will now be populated with your store categories in the order you entered them. It will look something like Figure 7.7 now. Look these over carefully and either use the back arrow in your browser or click the Edit category names link to correct any typos, if you see them. Again, you can do this any time, but now is a great opportunity to proofread and fix things before moving on.

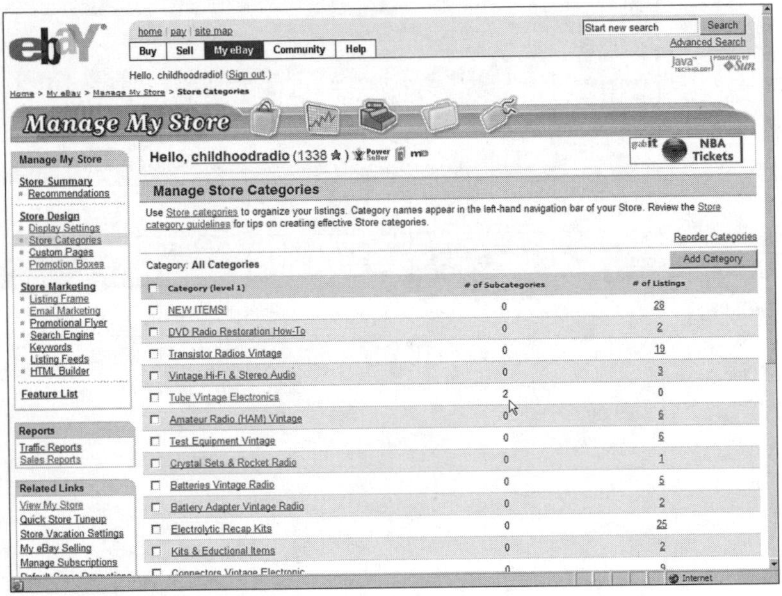

FIGURE 7.7

Proofread and perhaps reorder your categories here.

Rearranging Categories

To move a category up or down in the list, use the arrow buttons at the right of the item names. For example, in Figure 7.7, to make Consumer Electronics appear ahead of Collectibles & Antiques, you could either click the up-arrow button at the right side of the Consumer Electronics line or use the down-arrow button to the right of the Collectibles & Antiques line.

Only Stocked Categories Show

By now you are probably excited to see your store with its categories displayed along the left edge, just like the big dogs, right? Well, ya can't. Check out Figure 7.8.

FIGURE 7.8

Store categories only appear when you have listings in them.

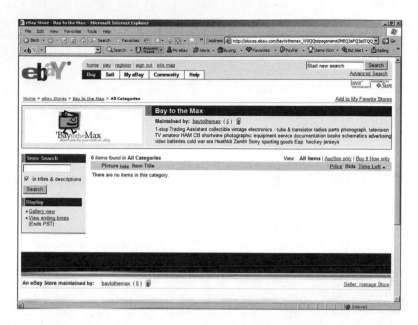

No categories are showing in this store because no items are associated with store categories. In the case of Figure 7.8, this is a new selling account with no active listings, so there are no listings of any kind.

If you set up a store for a selling account that has active listings (active auctions, Buy It Now listings, and so on), these listings will all show up in the Other Items category eBay creates by default for you. Cameras will not automatically show up in your store's Cameras category, for example. You need to tell eBay what to put where. This is a good thing, actually, as you will soon see.

Put another way, you need to tell eBay which listings you want to display when shoppers click the specific store category links in your store. Let's deal with creating category referrals in new listings first.

Store Category Referrals in New Listings

Suppose I want to sell copies of my *eBay to the Max* book in the new store. I would start the listing process as usual, but I have a new question to answer (see Figure 7.9).

> **note** It would be a good idea to set up your store categories now, if you haven't already, and get your listings organized into the correct general categories before continuing on to the next chapter.

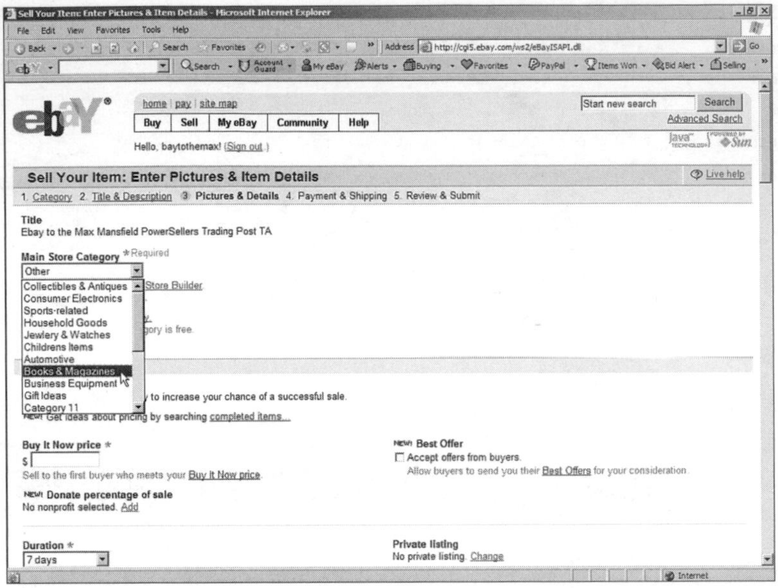

FIGURE 7.9

When creating new listings, be sure to specify store categories.

Because I now have a store, eBay will always ask which store categories I want my newly listed items to appear in. As shown in Figure 7.9, you select categories from the Sell Your Item: Enter Pictures & Item Details screen.

I want my item to show in my store's Books & Magazines category, obviously, so I use the drop-down list of my store categories to pick Books & Magazines. If you don't pick a store category, eBay relegates your new listing to the Other Items category by default.

note Don't be frustrated if your items don't display in their newly designated categories right away. Have patience, grasshopper. It takes eBay a little while to display your new items and categories in your store view (just as it sometimes takes a while for new listings to show up in eBay's main search engine). The delay time varies with eBay's workload, among other things, but is usually just a few minutes.

Listings Can Appear in Two Store Categories

But wait! You can showcase a single live item in two store categories, rather than just one. After selecting the first, required category, click the Add a second Store category link (see Figure 7.10).

Figure 7.11 shows my store with two categories visible—Books & Magazines and Gift Ideas—both made visible by my creating one listing and specifying two store categories for it.

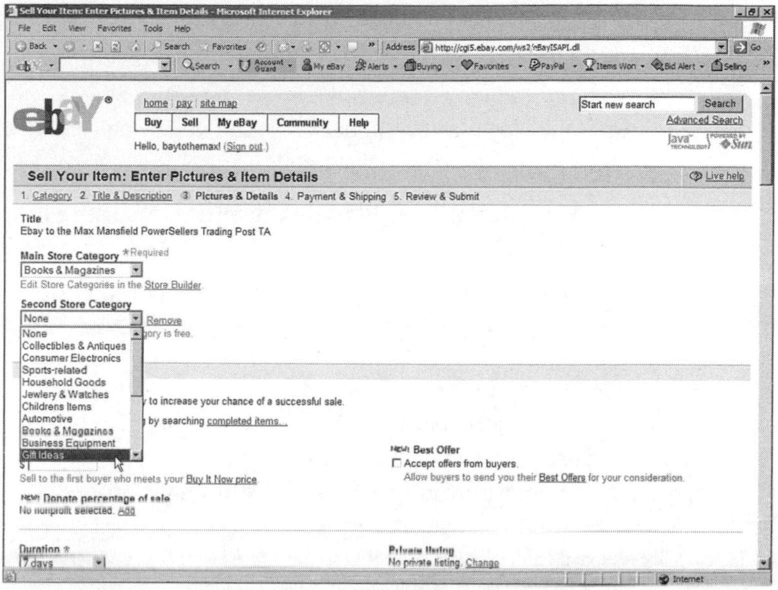

FIGURE 7.10

Add a second store category if you like.

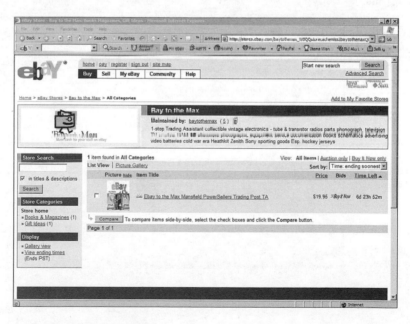

FIGURE 7.11

After a brief delay, categories and items show up in your store when you launch new items

Changing a Listing's Category

Suppose you wish an item was in a different category, or you have just opened a store and found all your items in the Other Items category, or you want to add a second store category to an active listing so that the item shows up on two of your store's shelves. You can change categories by using eBay's Revise Your Listing feature. Here are the steps to follow:

1. Log onto eBay. (If you have more than one eBay ID, be sure you use the one containing the active listing you wish to revise.)

2. Find the listing you want to re-categorize.

3. Click the Revise your item link near the top of the listing (see Figure 7.12).

4. Scroll to Pictures & Details and click the Edit pictures & details link shown in Figure 7.13.

When you get to the Revise Your Item: Pictures & Item Details page, you will see the store categories at the top. Pick new categories or remove the second store category here (see Figure 7.14). Then remember to scroll down and click the Save Changes button as with any listing revision.

FIGURE 7.12

Visit listings and click Revise your listing to change store categories.

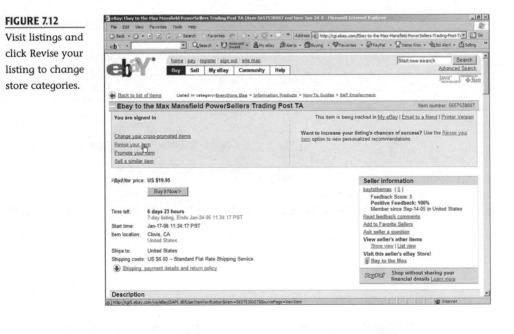

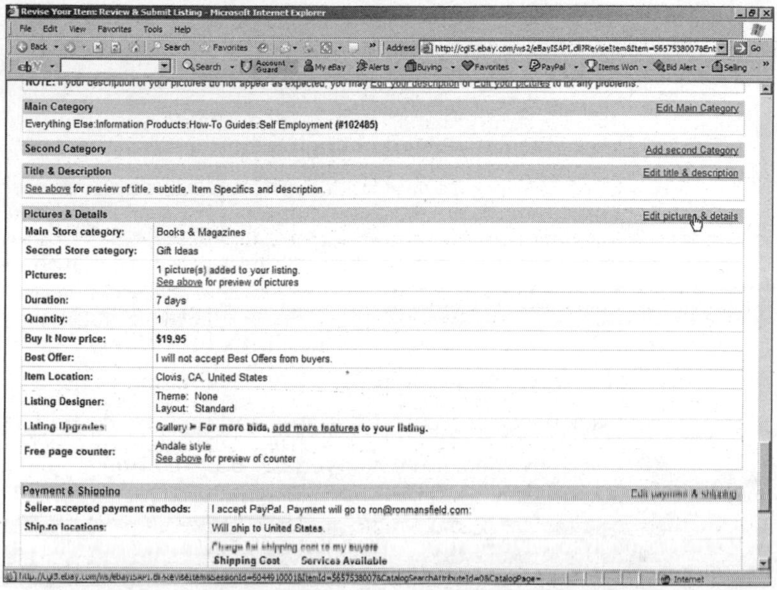

FIGURE 7.13
Change cate-
gories with the
Edit pictures &
details link.

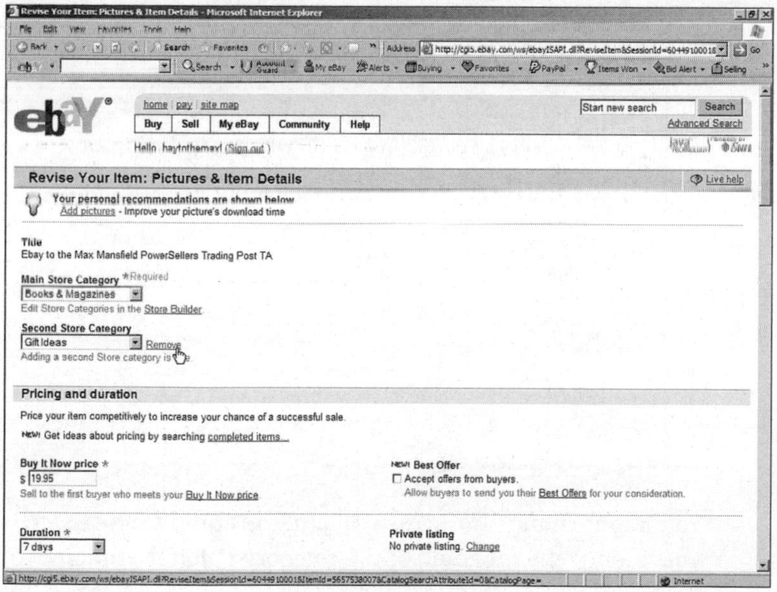

FIGURE 7.14
Change or
remove store
categories for a
live listing here.

Modifying Category Names

By revisiting the category list, you can rename your categories (see Figure 7.15). Here are the steps to follow:

1. Visit My eBay to start changing your store categories.

2. Click Manage My Store, down in the Subscriptions area of the left navigation bar.

3. In the resulting screen in the Store Design area of the left navigation bar, click Store Categories.

4. Click the Edit category names link at the right of the Store Categories section of the Manage My Store screen.

5. Click to select a category name and replace or revise it.

6. Click Save Settings when you are done editing store category names.

FIGURE 7.15

Edit, add, or remove store categories here.

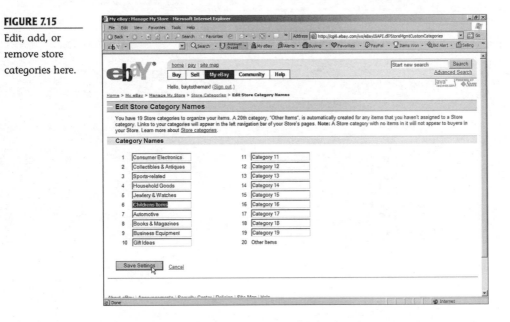

You might change Cameras – Digital to Digital Cameras, for example. But if you change the meaning of the category (Digital Cameras to Garden Hoes, for example), visitors will see digital cameras in your Garden Hoe department unless you also revise the store category assignments.

Overcoming Category Limits

By now you are probably wishing you could have more than 299 definable store categories, or at least store subcategories. Until eBay provides them, you'll need to use some of the searching tricks described in the next chapter.

I'll leave you with a hint. It has to do with embedding search terms that only you know about in each listing.

Custom Store Pages

Do you remember the first very basic stores we looked at in Chapter 2, "Examples of Stores, Plain and Fancy"? And do you recall the really fancy ones? If not, flip back there now and look at Figures 2-8 and 2-12. The first, Africa Direct, is a perfectly fine store without any custom pages. It simply employs the easy-to-use eBay tools (promotion boxes and such) discussed throughout this book to create an attractive, well-organized store anyone would be proud to call their own.

The second example, Period Paper, is a beautiful store. I know for a fact that the owner paid a professional to create it for him. It's stunning and fun, and is also well organized and easy to navigate.

This second store uses custom pages. The first does not. You do not necessarily need them either. In fact, if you are not comfortable with HTML, Flash, and other web-creation playthings (and especially if you don't have an eye for design), you should probably either stay away from custom pages completely, or pay for expert help setting them up.

If you are a brand-new eBay seller, or still trying to get a regular clientele established, you might want to skip this chapter and come back to it later. That said, let's plunge ahead.

Why Use Custom Store Pages?

Custom pages can be used to set your store apart and improve navigation. They can also help visitors find exactly what they need. Custom pages will give you the opportunity to explain your policies, offer advice, brag about your company's history, and much more. Figure 8.1 is an excellent example of an advanced custom "landing page" that has other custom pages linked to it.

FIGURE 8.1

This custom landing page also refers to other custom pages and helps shoppers do very narrow searches without even realizing it.

This Designer Athletic store at http://stores.ebay.com/Designer-Athletic (ID designerathletic) shows a great use of graphics to create what is basically a catalog cover, table of contents, and index all rolled into one storefront, or landing page. This is the first thing shoppers see when they enter the store.

eBay Store Category links appear on the left side of Designer Athletic's landing page. Study them for a moment.

The store categories are pretty broad, sometimes spanning five or more shoe sizes. Now look down at the bottom of the store page in Figure 8.1, where you see all the available shoe sizes listed separately. It's as if there were 33 categories just for shoes of specific sizes. This is accomplished by using either subcategories or those "behind-the-scene searches" I alluded to in Chapter 6, "Setting Up Your Store," and will show you how to create in this chapter.

The upper-right area of the page contains a list of links by manufacturer, which is also accomplished with in-store search tricks.

Clicking those photos in the upper-right area takes you to lists of all men's shoes, all women's shoes, and so on. Before moving onto the "how-to" in this chapter, take one last look at Figure 8.1. This time check out the lower-left corner of the screen. There is a list of custom page links for each of the custom pages in this eBay store. In this case, the "Size Chart" and "Christmas Delivery Schedule" pages are custom; the rest are links to standard eBay pages.

You can create pages to accomplish just about any purpose, as long as they don't violate eBay policy. Most stores create a Store Policies page, an About the Seller page, maybe an FAQ page, and from there the sky's the limit. For example, Figure 8.2 shows part of the Designer Athletic Size Chart page, used to help buyers convert between U.S., U.K., European, and CM shoe sizes. It's a handy shopping aid.

FIGURE 8.2

This custom page helps shoppers convert shoe sizes.

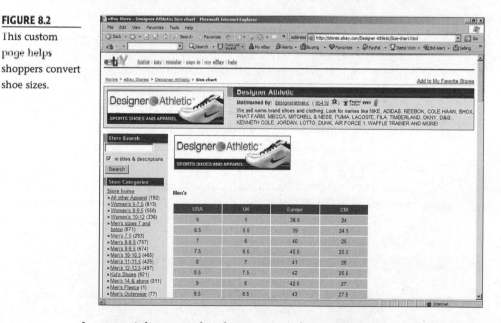

As you might remember from your earlier reading, the level of your store subscription determines the number of custom pages you can create:

- **Basic**—5 pages
- **Featured**—10 pages
- **Anchor**—15 pages

Elements of a Custom Page

Custom pages can be almost completely hand-crafted by computer-savvy store owners, or professional-looking pages can be easily fashioned by nontechies using combinations of eBay-provided layout elements, including item lists, text boxes, promotional boxes, and photos (or graphic images of any sort actually). It's easy to accomplish because eBay walks you through the steps and lets you preview as you go. Here's what you add to your pages:

- **Promotion boxes**—Promotion boxes help cross-promote other items you have listed. They are discussed in depth in Part III, "Promoting Your Store." For now, you should know that when creating or modifying custom pages, you can add promotion boxes and dictate their positioning and content.

- **Item showcases**—Item showcases offer a chance to feature, or highlight particular items on a custom page. This is a great way to promote sale items, new items, seasonal merchandise, and so on. Because we'll go into detail in Part III, you can just stick this concept in the back of your mind for now.

- **Store navigation bar**—When designing a custom page, you will have an opportunity to specify if and where you want special page links to appear on your navigation bar.

- **Text**—Custom pages can have text, of course. You can use eBay's built-in HTML code generator to specify such things as typefaces, colors, styles, and so on, or you can create your own HTML and paste it into the Custom Page text-editing box, as you will see momentarily.

- **Item lists**—Custom pages can have lists of items you sell, but this is not a requirement. One powerful way to use this feature is to create custom pages that display filtered lists resulting from searches you do on behalf of shoppers. You'll see this in action later in this chapter, I promise.

- **Images**—The eBay templates allow you place up to four photos or other graphic items in the predefined formats provided for custom pages. You can specify photo locations within reason, and the photos or other graphics can be used as clickable links if you desire. If you are a code warrior, you can add as many graphic images as you like by designing your own page content and layouts from scratch rather than using the eBay templates.

Creating a Custom Page

To begin creating any new custom page, follow these steps:

1. Log into eBay and go to your My eBay page.

2. Scroll down and click Manage My Store.

3. Click the Custom Pages link under Store Design. You should see a screen similar to the one in Figure 8.3.

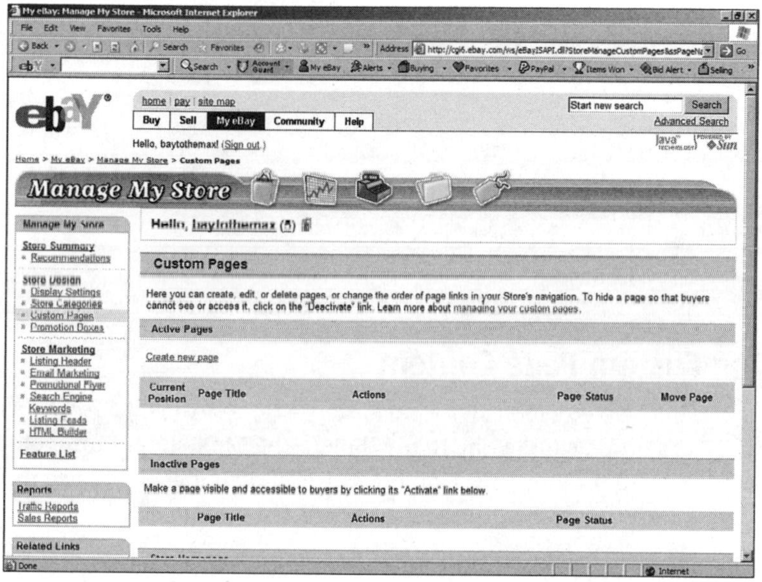

FIGURE 8.3

Begin creating custom pages here.

4. Click the Create new page link under the Active Pages heading and you should see a screen similar to Figure 8.4.

5. Take a moment to look at the predefined layout options, being certain to scroll down far enough to see them all. Click the button associated with the one you like. Don't belabor this step because it's just a place to start. You can explore alternate layout options easily, as you will soon see.

6. If you want your active listings to show on your custom page, pick a layout containing an item list.

7. If you want to display photos or other graphics, pick a layout with the number of pictures you desire.

8. If you want promotion boxes, chose a layout containing them, and so on.

In the next section, we'll build a custom page, step by step.

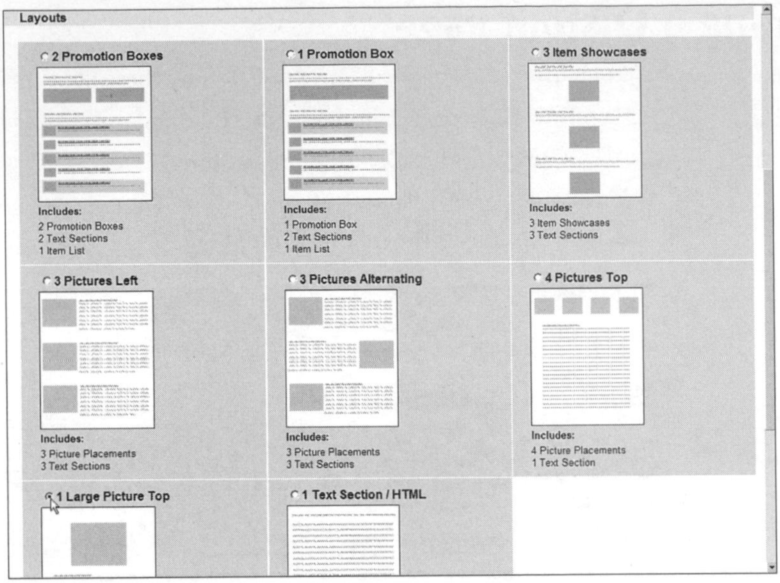

FIGURE 8.4

Scroll down to
see the available
preformatted
layout options
and choose one.

Providing Custom Page Content

The best way to understand custom pages is to watch somebody build one, so
let's add a simple one to my 'Bay to the Max store. I am going to create a
page to promote my Trading Assistant activities. I will use this store to sell
things owned by other people. Here are the steps:

1. I've started with a layout containing one picture holder and room
   for text.

2. I clicked the Continue button and was presented with the next step of
   the process, shown in Figure 8.5.

3. I entered a page title. There are
   some rules, however:

   ■ Page titles must start and end
     with numbers or letters, not
     punctuation.

   ■ You can't use the terms *eBay*,
     PayPal, and *Half.com*.

   ■ The rules vary by page type, and they change over time. But don't
     worry. You won't be allowed to break any rules and will be asked to
     correct your transgressions before being permitted to move on. As
     much as I'd like to name my page "I'll sell for you on eBay," I can't.

> **note** Custom pages are
> indexed by search
> engines, so, if appropriate, use
> powerful keywords in the titles of
> your custom pages. Use brand
> names, model numbers, or other
> hot keywords when appropriate.

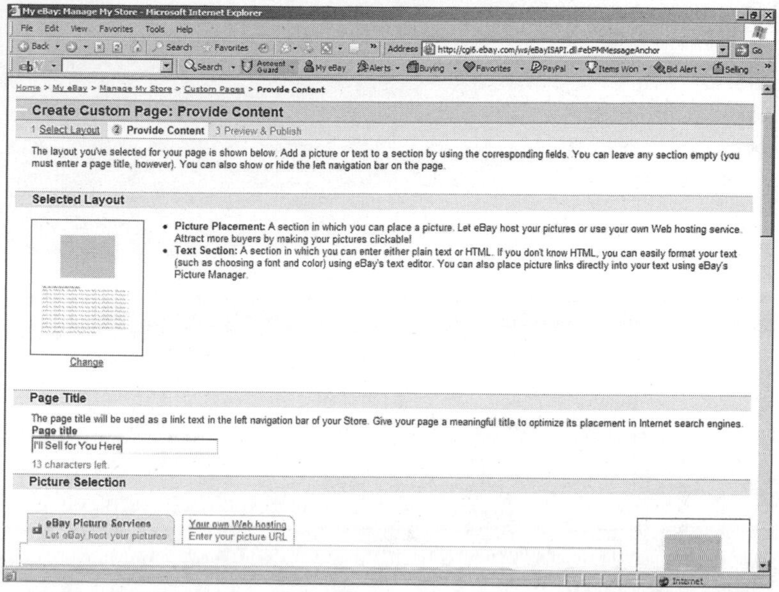

FIGURE 8.5

The beginnings of a custom page with text and a photo.

4. I'm using eBay's Picture Manager in this example to host photos and other graphics, but you can host your own photos on another server and "point" to them in your custom pages. Let's take a quick, but by no means exhaustive look at using eBay's Picture Manager for the task. If you have chosen a layout with picture placeholders, eBay presents you with the Picture Manager entry point shown in Figure 8.6. This is where we upload and wrangle photos and other graphics.

> **note** If you wish to host your own pictures off of eBay, click the Your own Web hosting tab at this point.

5. If you already have pictures stored in Picture Manager, you will see them here. I do not in this example, so I will need to upload them. Scroll down a bit and click the Add Pictures button. Take a look at Figure 8.7. This is where you locate graphics on your computer and upload them to eBay. Pictures should be a minimum of 200 pixels wide.

6. When you locate a photo or other graphic and click Open, it will be sent to eBay, and your screen will look something like what's shown in Figure 8.8. I've uploaded a 400×395-pixel mug shot.

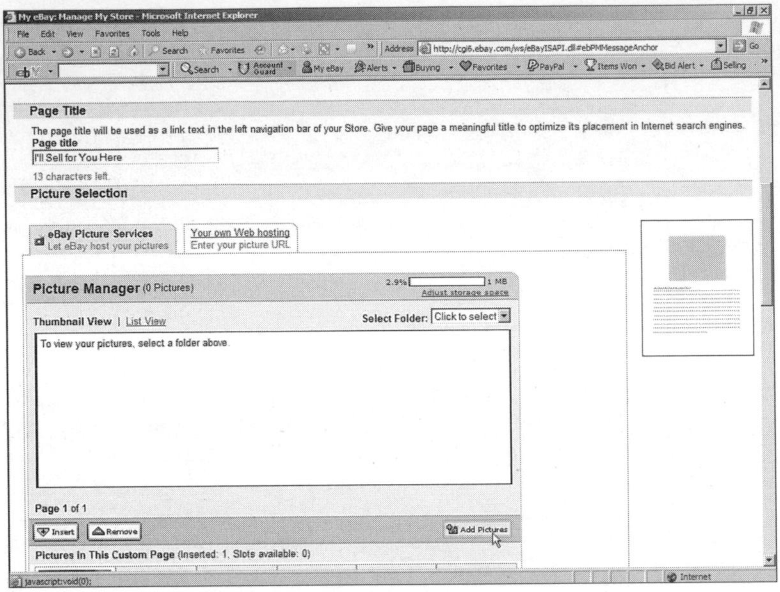

FIGURE 8.6

You can use eBay's Picture Manager for custom page graphics.

FIGURE 8.7

Locate and upload pictures from your computer to eBay.

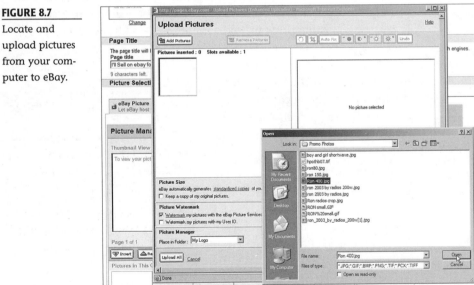

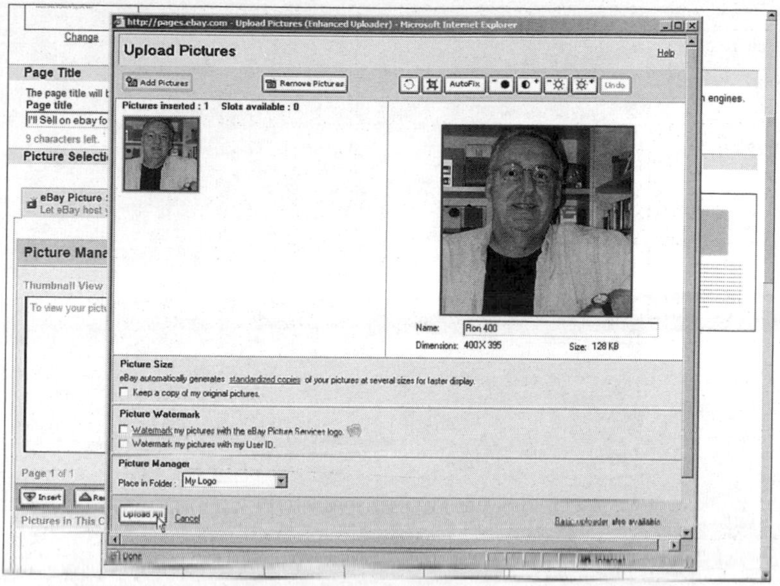

FIGURE 8.8

A picture being uploaded to Picture Manager.

7. We have some say over the appearance of the photo. For example, we can remove the annoying Picture Manager watermark (that little camera in the southeast corner of so many photos on eBay). You can even add your own annoying watermark.

8. It's also possible to create folders to organize your photos—one for logos, another for store items, and another for auction items, and so on. But this is a book about stores, not Picture Manager, so let's plunge forward.

9. Click the Upload All button to send the photo(s) to eBay. You will be presented with a screen similar to the one shown in Figure 8.9.

10. Click the check boxes under the picture(s) to be inserted into the custom page and then click the Insert button.

> **note** To remove pictures, select them and click the Remove button instead. The photos stay in Picture Manager, but are removed from the custom page you are designing.

11. To turn photos or other graphics into links, simply specify the desired destination URL by inserting link addresses in the Make Pictures Clickable section of the screen shown in Figure 8.10. Remember to obey eBay's rules about off-site linking and such.

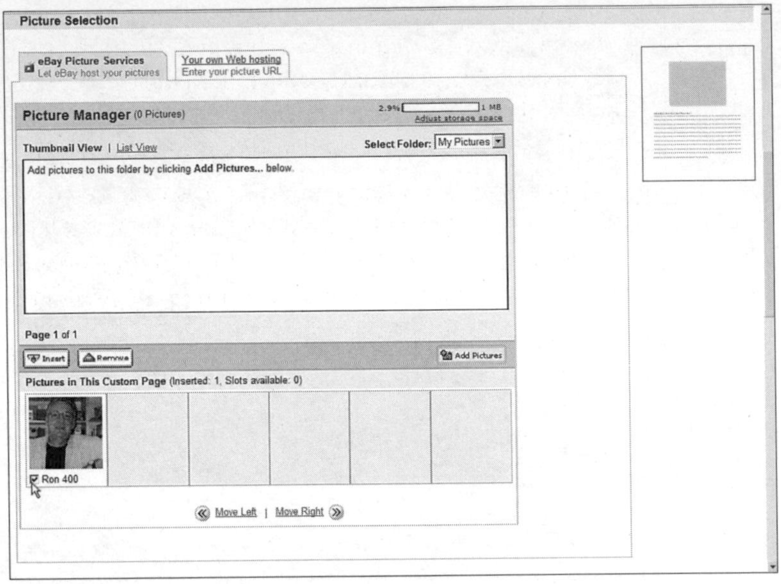

FIGURE 8.9

Photos available
in Picture
Manager can be
added to custom
pages.

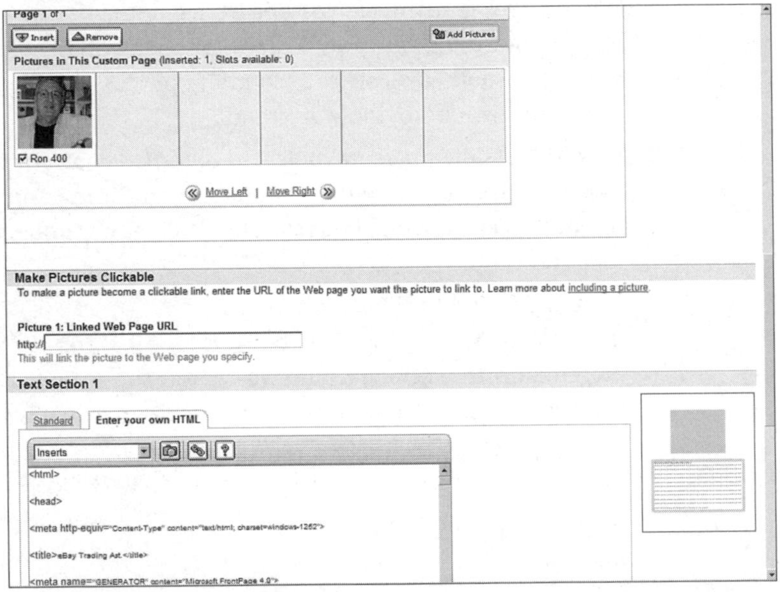

FIGURE 8.10

Photos can be
turned into links
by typing URLs
into the Linked
Web Page URL
box or boxes.

12. Peeking out of the bottom of Figure 8.10 you can see the place to enter
    text for your custom page. If the layout you have chosen provides for
    multiple blocks of text, you will see more than one of these text-entry
    boxes, one for each block.

13. You can either use eBay's "Standard" Description Editor (a collection of standard text-editing features that will remind you of a simple but useful text-editing program) or click the Enter your own HTML tab, as shown in Figure 8.10, and then paste HTML code you have developed elsewhere (using Microsoft FrontPage or Dreamweaver or whatever).

14. After entering your text, scroll (if necessary) to reach the bottom of the screen where you will make a decision about the left navigation bar. Turn the bar on or off (show it or hide it). In Figure 8.11, it has been turned on. Click the Continue button to move along.

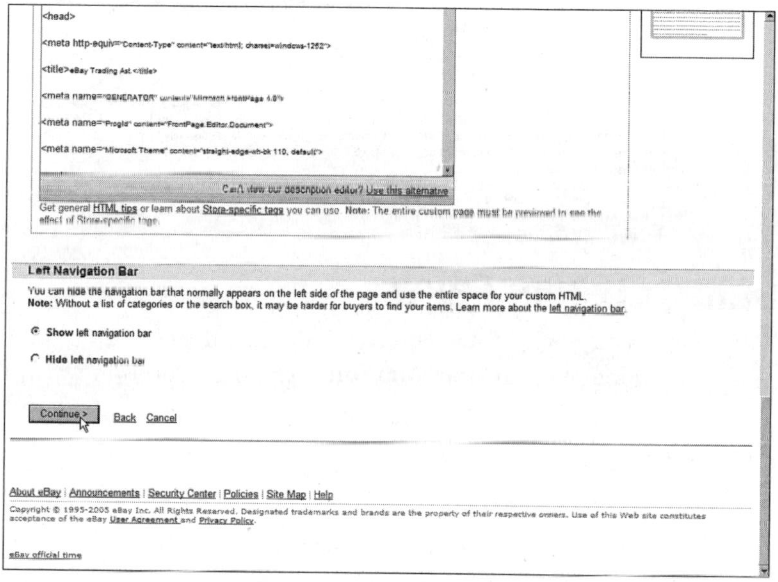

FIGURE 8.11

Turn the left navigation bar on or off and click Continue.

15. You will see a preview of the page so far, as shown in Figure 8.12, and at the bottom of the preview page you will be given a chance to either save and publish or go back to change the options you've used. Scroll down a bit and click Save and Publish if you are happy with the options you've chosen. Otherwise, use the Back link to make changes.

FIGURE 8.12

When you are
happy with the
preview, click
Save and
Publish.

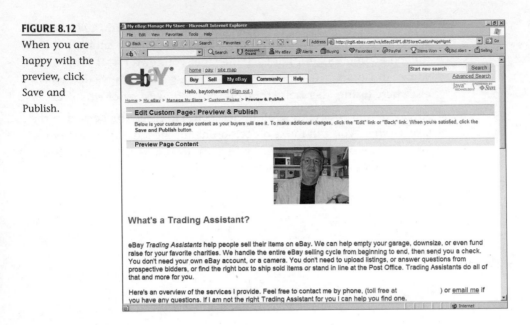

Managing Custom Pages

Once you have created you custom pages, they are automatically activated
and added to your store. You can then do the following with these pages:

- Edit them
- Deactivate them
- Reactivate them
- Change their order of appearance
- Delete them
- Turn them into landing or home pages
- Use them to filter listing displays

All these tasks involve getting to the Custom Pages section of your store. To do
so, follow these steps:

1. Log into eBay and go to your My eBay page.

2. Scroll down and click Manage My Store.

3. Click the Custom Pages link under Store Design. You should see a
   screen similar to the one shown in Figure 8.13.

4. Once you reach the Custom Pages screen, you can use pull-down
   menus to edit, view, deactivate, or delete pages. In Figure 8.13, we are
   about to edit the Policies page.

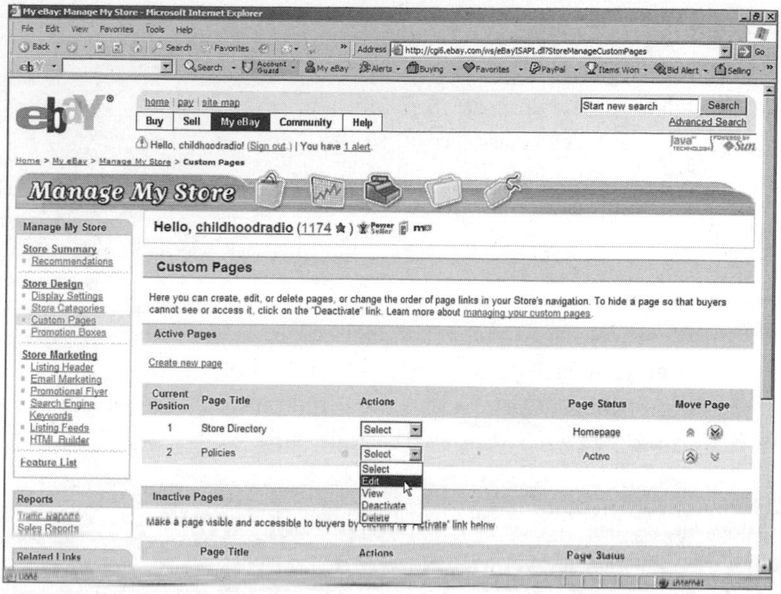

FIGURE 8.13

Begin managing
Custom Pages
by visiting the
Custom Pages
section of the
Manage My
Store feature.

Editing Custom Pages

When you choose Edit from the Custom Pages screen described in the previous section, a pull-down menu presents you with a list of choices corresponding to the type of page you are editing. For example, if you are editing a page containing HTML you have entered, you will be presented with that HTML code.

Deactivating Custom Pages

Choosing Deactivate removes the page from view and stores it in the Inactive Pages section just below the Active Pages list (see Figure 8.13). This turns off the page, but keeps it around for use later. It's a perfect way to store seasonal pages for later reuse, for example.

Activating Custom Pages

To activate any page in the Inactive Pages list, simply choose Activate from its drop-down list.

Reordering Custom Pages

You can change the order in which pages appear in your store's Custom Pages Navigation list with the Move Page arrow buttons at the right of the screen in Figure 8.13. For example, to move Policies up, you could either click its up-arrow button or the Store Directory page's down-arrow button.

Deleting Custom Pages

You can delete custom pages by choosing Delete on the drop-down menu. You will then be asked once to confirm the deletion. If you approve the deletion, your page will be forever gone.

note If you think you might need a page again, deactivate rather than delete it. Deactivated pages no longer appear in your eBay store, but they're not deleted. This is an excellent way to show and hide special pages containing seasonal sale items, special sales events, promotions, and so on.

Creating a "Landing" or Home Page

To control which page visitors first see when they visit your store, scroll to the bottom of the Custom Pages screen and pick a page from the Store Homepage drop-down list, as shown in Figure 8.14.

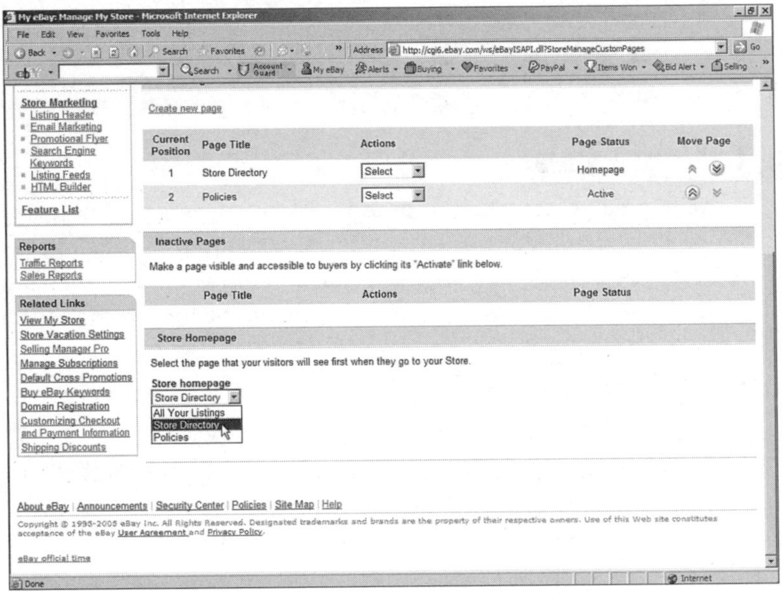

FIGURE 8.14

Choose the page you want shoppers to first see when they visit you.

By default, eBay displays all your listings when visitors first enter. But you can specify a custom page that shows just the items you want to highlight, or custom graphics and a fancy catalog page like the ones you have seen throughout this book.

Creating a "Category Pointer" Page

Here's a quick way to make your store more attractive and easy to navigate. All you need to do is create at least one custom page where you will put links that point to each of your categories. Consider the simple, but fancy-looking example in Figure 8.15.

FIGURE 8.15

Each link in the center of the screen points to a different store category link.

Clicking any of the links in Figure 8.15, such as Gift Ideas for Enthusiasts, Radio Restoration DVD, and so on, will display only items within that particular category. Clicking the Collectible Transistor Radios link (or the picture above it) displays only radios. Clicking Vintage Hi-Fi & Stereo Gear shows only those items, and so forth.

Follow these steps to create a category pointer page:

1. Create a custom page to be used as your "catalog page," perhaps adding graphics.

2. Type the names you want for each link into your catalog page.

3. Open a second browser and click the store category link for the corresponding category. For example, when I click the Transistor Radios Vintage category in my store's Navigator, I am taken to a page with the URL http://stores.ebay.com/ChildhoodRadio_Transistor-Radios-Vintage_W0QQcolZ2QQdirZQ2d1QQftidZ2QQtZkm.

4. Copy and paste the resulting address from the second browser into the catalog page to create a hyperlink. This is more easily done using an HTML tool such as FrontPage or Dreamweaver, but you can hand-code the links if you like.

5. Once the links are in place and the custom page published, whenever a shopper clicks one of those links in the custom page, eBay does the search and presents the search results.

Let me make two more points before moving on. The general technique you have just learned—doing searches and creating links on custom pages from the resulting page URLs that eBay gives you can be used in much more intriguing ways, as you will see in the very next topic. It is, in fact, the way around the 300-category limit. But before going there, I want to point out one last thing.

The Gift Ideas for Enthusiasts link back in Figure 8.15 demonstrates another interesting concept. Clicking that link displays a variety or merchandise from transistor radios to parts to books, seemingly from different store categories, as you can see in Figure 8.16. How's that done?

FIGURE 8.16

One click on the Gift Ideas for Enthusiasts link displays a variety of diverse items.

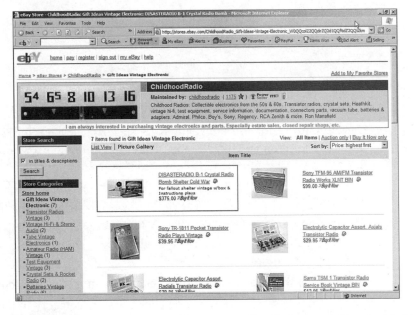

There are two ways to accomplish this actually. In this case, I've decided to use that "wildcard category" I described back in Chapter 7, "Defining Store Categories," as a catchall for items that might make good gifts. As you'll recall, I could just as easily reserved the category for sale items or seasonal goods. But today, it's for gifts.

As you'll also remember, eBay lets you assign two store categories to each item you list. So if a particular transistor radio looks like a great gift item, I assign it to both the transistor radio and wildcard (gift) categories. Any items earmarked as

note If you use these search techniques, be sure to keep your store stocked with active items available in every category that shippers can search. Otherwise, the links won't pull up any items of interest.

gifts show up in that wildcard category and are therefore displayed when shoppers click the Gift Ideas for Enthusiasts link.

Using Fancy Search Filters

Okay, it's time. Do you remember the shoe store from the beginning of this chapter with all those shoe types, brands, and sizes? And do you remember the knitting supply store with all the needles? Custom pages using searches make it possible to point shoppers to exactly what they want to purchase even in stores selling thousands of diverse items.

For example, as my store grows, I am going to have hundreds of relatively inexpensive books and parts, and I want to make them available to collectors, but not clutter up the store so much that they can't see the $500 radios. Fancy searches and custom pages to the rescue. Consider Figure 18.17. It's a hodge-podge of books. There's one about eBay selling, a collectible Sams TSM radio service book, and so on. Eventually there will be hundreds of books to wade through.

FIGURE 8.17

This diverse book offering needs to be organized.

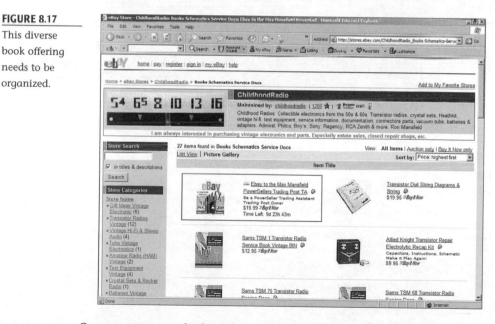

One way to wrangle them is to set up a second custom page with links that help divide up the book inventory. So when you click the Books Schematics and Service Docs link on my landing page, instead of seeing the entire contents of that category, you are taken to a second custom page that looks like Figure 8.18.

On that page are links to different searches I have performed in my store using the store's search feature. For example, to round up all the Sams TSM books, I did the in-store search for "Sams TSM" and then copied and pasted the resulting URL as shown in Figure 8.19.

tip eBay's HTML Builder, discussed in Chapter 16, "Promoting Your Store Outside of eBay," can be used to create code for custom pages.

FIGURE 8.18

Your custom landing page can point to additional custom pages like this one, with search links designed to limit the inventory displayed.

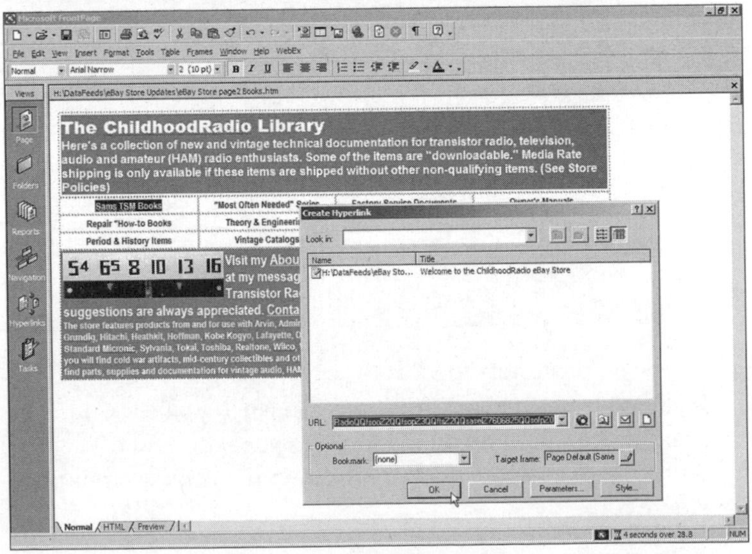

FIGURE 8.19

Creating filtered links for custom pages.

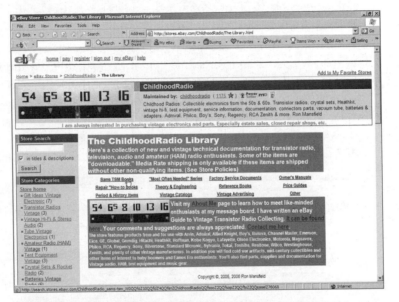

Consider Hidden Search Codes

Use care when setting up custom searches. Be sure that the searches produce the results you want. Suppose, for example, you create a simple search in your shoe store for Nike shoes. Everything works great. But then one day you list an Adidas shoe, and in the description you write, "unlike the Nike shoe of the same style, blah, blah."

When shoppers click your Nike link they will see that Adidas shoe as well. Although this is not the crime of the century (eBay allows competitors names in descriptions, just not in titles), it does clutter your store. It's the electronic equivalent of some knucklehead trying on shoes in a store and then putting them back in the wrong box or on the wrong shelf. It's just not tidy.

Hidden codes are the solution. And you don't need to know HTML to create and use them. All you need to do is place some unique codes (text) in your descriptions and change them to the color of the background so they disappear. The real trick is to design and add codes that are unlikely to appear anywhere else on the Internet, never mind on eBay. For example, I could use the following code for those TSM books:

childhoodradio_books_sams_tsm

Then, I could use this code for Sony schematics and so on:

childhoodradio_books_schematics_factory_sony

Noticed that I have used the underscore character to link the words to turn them into truly unique text strings. Change the font to the color of the listing's background, and shoppers won't even see the codes. But you can search for them when you set up your custom searches.

By giving some thought to the order of these codes, you can create different types of searches starting from the top down. You can also put multiple search codes in the same listing. For example, if I wanted a search link to round up everything about Sony TR-650 radios, I could add the search code child-hoodradio_Sony_TR-650 to the listing for the schematic for that model, along with the search code for the schematic itself. The trick is to develop a scheme and use it consistently. For example "TR-650" and "TR650" are not consistent.

Creating listing templates for each type of search, complete with the appropriate hidden codes, is easy to do using Selling Manager Pro, which is discussed in Part II, coming right up.

Part II

Managing Your Store

Automating with Selling Manager Pro (SMP)

Although a slew of third-party auction management tools are offered by Ándale and others, and even though eBay offers other tools of its own (Turbo Lister, Selling Manager, and so on), as an eBay store owner you should give serious consideration to using eBay's Selling Manager Pro instead.

Selling Manager Pro Features

Selling Manager Pro is a "free" add-on when you purchase a Featured or Anchored store. If you are not a Featured or Anchor store owner, there is a monthly fee of $15.99 (at this writing).

SMP is web-based, so unlike Blackthorne and similar disk-based products, you can access it from just about any browser-equipped computer. You should be able to use it with Microsoft Internet Explorer 4.0 and later versions, Netscape 3.0 and later versions, as well as AOL 3.0 and later versions without regard to operating system. It is also compatible with Apple Safari. However, eBay Picture services are not compatible with Safari.

Selling Manager Pro provides the following helpful features:

- Inventory templates to speed listing and relisting
- Tools to help you process paperwork for multiple buyers at the same time
- Ways to track costs and therefore profitability
- Ways to create and manage automated email messages for such things as payment receipts, shipping notifications, and so on
- Ways to automate feedback if you desire
- Integrated label printing and notification systems
- Reports to help you see how your business is doing and how to improve it

We will be getting into the nuts and bots of Selling Manager Pro throughout the rest of this book as we use it to illustrate the specifics of running an eBay business. For now, let's start with an overview of SMP. Figure 9.1 shows a typical opening screen. Like everything on the Internet, SMP is evolving, and every now and then you will wake up to a slightly different face. Figure 9.1 shows how SMP looks at my place this morning.

Along the left side of the screen you will see links to information about all your buying and selling activities. There's a link to your My Messages page. You can easily reach your favorites and account settings from here as well. In fact, if you scroll down you will also find links on the left of the screen for the Reviews and Guidelines feature (discussed in Part IV, "Reports") and for your subscriptions to marketplace research and other eBay options.

note When you subscribe to SMP, you see it automatically instead of your old "My eBay" page.

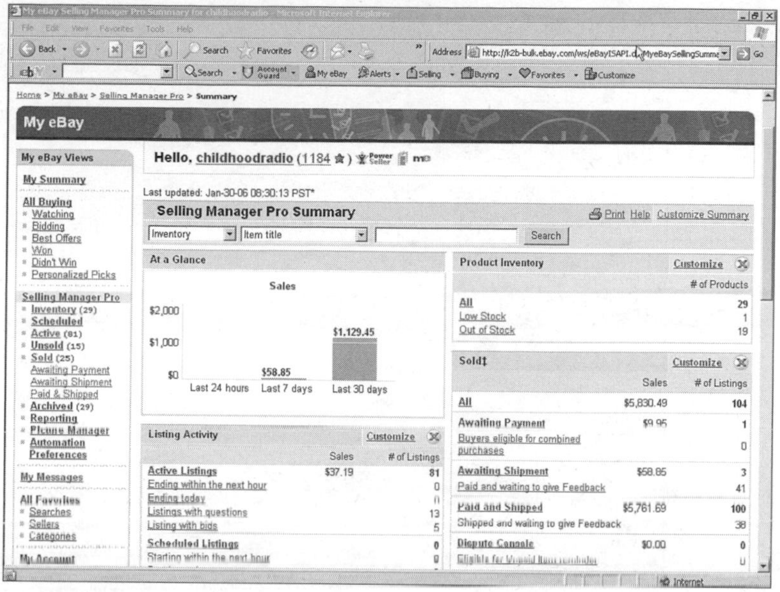

FIGURE 9.1

FIGURE 9.1

The main
Selling Manager
Pro screen gives
you a snapshot
of your business.

Your Store at a Glance

The main section of the of the screen (Figure 9.1) shows recent sales, inventory status, listing activities sales, payments, items awaiting feedback, and so on. This page, and most of the rest in SMP, is customizable. That's what those little Customize links you see scattered around do. You will learn more about this in a moment.

This screen is the jumping-off point for an incredible amount of business detail. For example, clicking the Sold link at the left of the screen takes you to a page similar to Figure 9.2.

Another click takes you to details about specific sold items, including the buyer's name and shipping address; whether, when, and how items have been paid for; if and when they shipped; and so on. You can see just a small part of this detail in Figure 9.3.

You can even create lists of items that have not yet been paid for, need shipment, and so on. For example, Figure 9.4 not only shows an unpaid item, but also provides both the recommendation that I contact the buyer and a link to make that easy to accomplish.

FIGURE 9.2

The main
Selling Manager
Pro screen con-
tains links to
multiple layers
of detail. Here
you see sold
items.

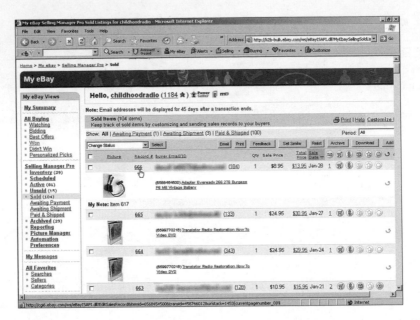

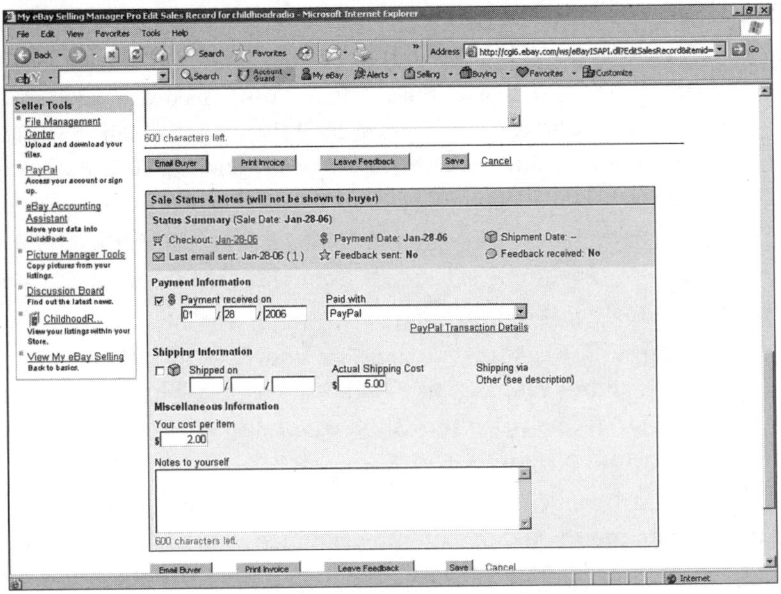

FIGURE 9.3

Sold item
records contain
all the details
you need to
manage them.

FIGURE 9.4

SMP lists help
you know what
to do and pro-
vide helpful
links.

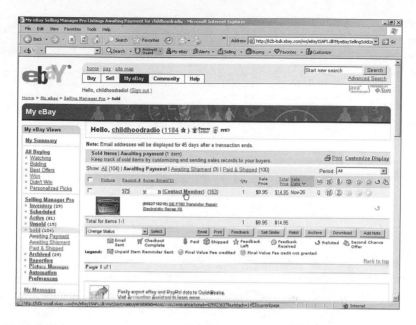

Inventory Wrangling

Because stores often have huge inventories with hundreds or even thousands
of different items, SMP makes it easy to keep track of items and create templates not only for different products, but also for different selling formats
used for the same product. For example, Figure 9.5 shows two inventory templates for the same product, a DVD. The first is for creating Good 'Til
Cancelled listings, and the second is for fixed-price listings. We'll get into this
in detail in Chapter 11, "Managing Your Inventory and Auctions."

Inventory and Template Creation

SMP is also the jumping-off point for creating new inventory items and the
listings themselves. Figure 9.6 shows where this takes place. We'll dig more
deeply into creating new inventory items and listings in Chapter 11.

Automation Preferences

SMP will automate many of your email and feedback tasks if you choose, and
we will look at these features more closely in Chapter 11. For now, Figure 9.7
gives you a glimpse at some of these features. Not all sellers will want to use
these options, and we'll discuss why in Chapter 11.

FIGURE 9.5

Use SMP to manage inventory and listing formats.

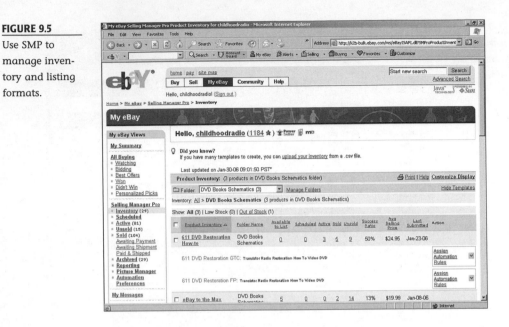

FIGURE 9.6

Use SMP to create inventory items and store vendor information.

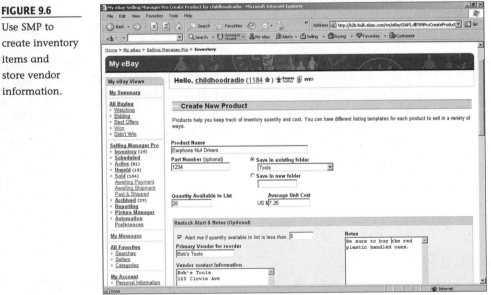

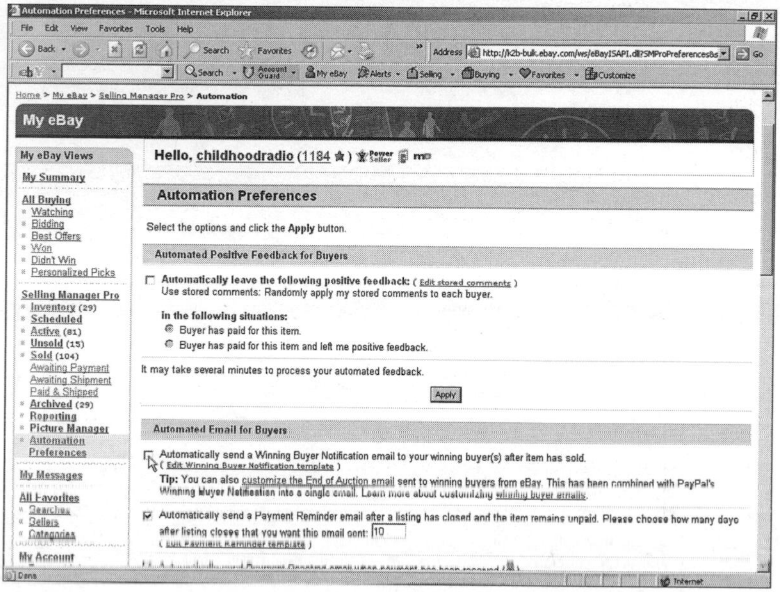

FIGURE 9.7

Use SMP to automate feedback and many email tasks when appropriate.

Other Helpful Links

Now that eBay has become a huge (some would argue unwieldy) place, it's nice to have frequently used links at hand. If you scroll to the bottom of the Selling Manager Pro screen, you will see links for managing auctions, keeping an eye on your eBay bill (yikes!), and even links to do such diverse things as cancel auctions, block bidders, and so on. If you have ever said to yourself while staring at the big eBay map, "Where IS that thing?" you can probably find the link you want at the bottom of the SMP screen shown in Figure 9.8.

SMP Integrated Shipping Tools

Wouldn't it be nice if you could create a shipping label complete with postage, update your shipping records, and email the winner to say the item has shipped, all with just a few clicks. Well, you can, at least sometimes. Figure 9.9 shows part of the process. It's even possible, with some skill and luck, to "batch" your shipping tasks and handle multiple buyers in one fell swoop. You'll learn much more about this in Chapter 13, cleverly titled "Shipping."

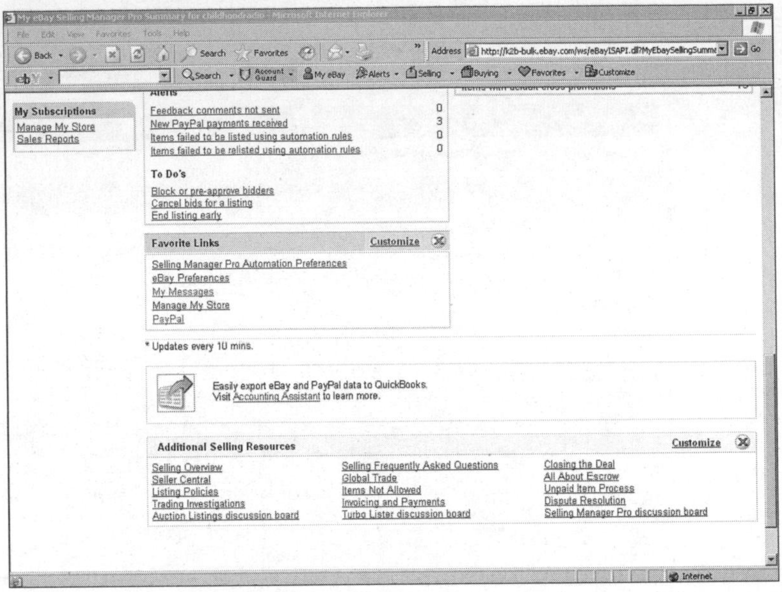

FIGURE 9.8

Lots of useful links appear at the bottom of the SMP page.

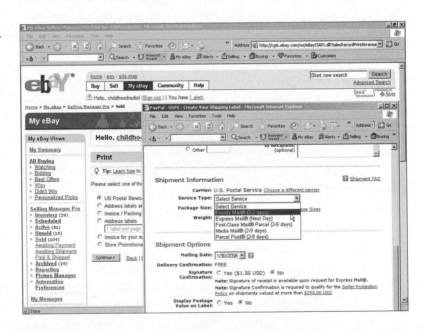

FIGURE 9.9

Selling Manager Pro includes a set of integrated label-printing tools and other shipping tools.

Customizing SMP Views

You can customize both the Summary view and the particulars of specific lists. For instance, Figure 9.10 shows the options I have chosen, including displaying up to 200 items per page and displaying my own notes, which I use to keep track of an item's owner when acting as a Trading Assistant.

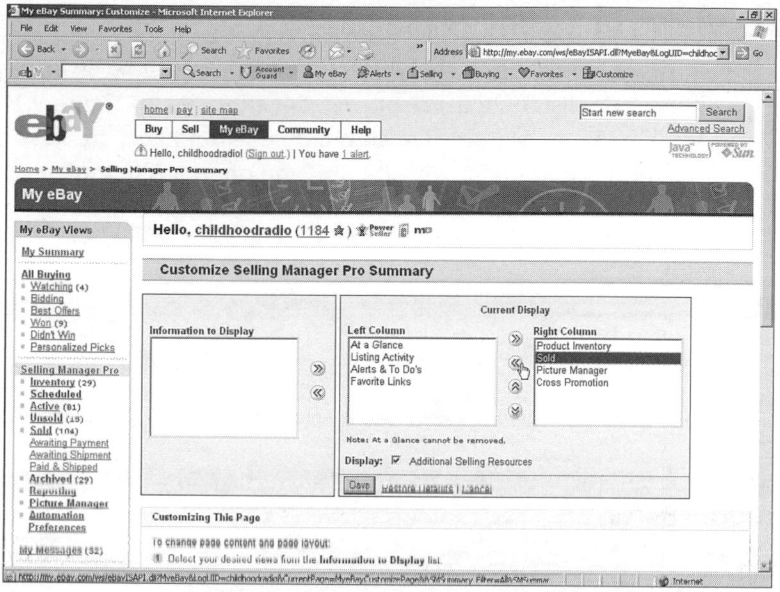

FIGURE 9.10

Customizing Manager Pro's Summary view.

I also have included bidder IDs so that I can quickly keep an eye out for potential troublemakers with bad feedback during live auctions (see Figure 9.11).

FIGURE 9.11

Add buyer IDs to displays so that you can quickly spot bidders with feedback problems. (No problems today.)

Filtering Views in Selling Manager Pro

Throughout Selling Manager Pro's pages, you will be given opportunities to "filter" the lists of items displayed. For example, in Figure 9.12, the activities list is about to be filtered so that only auction items are shown. This will hide fixed-price and store items. Be sure you are not filtering out items accidentally using these features. Get in the habit of looking at the drop-down boxes as you work.

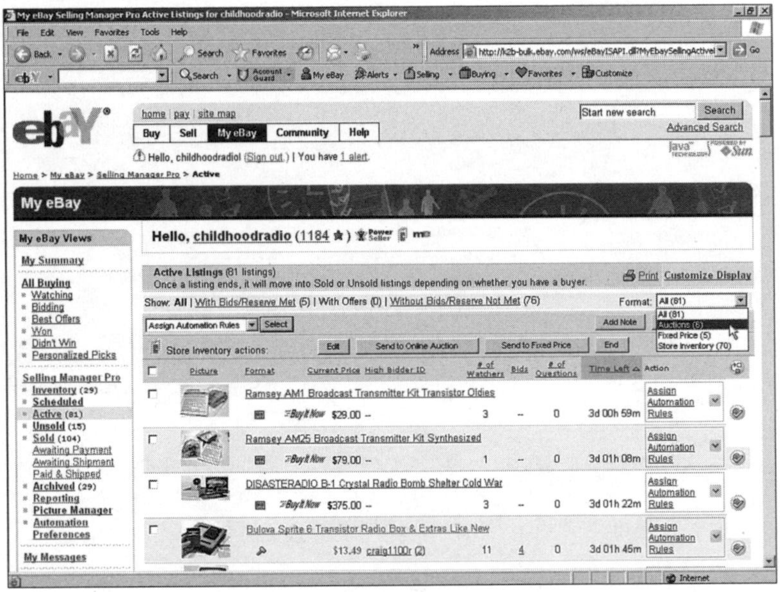

FIGURE 9.12

Selling Manager Pro's screens can be filtered to show selected items.

Viewing Reports Through SMP

Selling Manager Pro is the gateway to a number of useful reports, discussed at length in Part IV. Figure 9.13 shows an example.

note Where reporting is concerned, most of the heavy lifting is actually done using Store Sales Reports, also reachable from SMP, and discussed in Part IV.

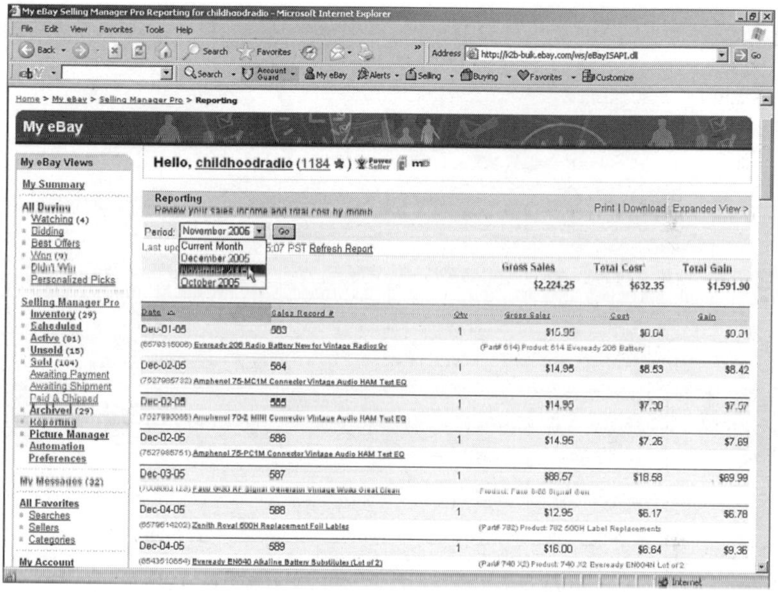

FIGURE 9.13

Selling Manager Pro's reporting can provide insights into profitability, among other things.

Creating Listings and Templates

In small, simple store operations, listings can be a lot like creating regular auction listings. About all you need to do differently is choose Store Inventory as the selling format when beginning a new listing.

But sellers wanting larger stores with many items, and such nuances as seasonal items, will want to create their listings as templates and treat them as inventory. One of the easier ways to do this is with Selling Manager Pro (SMP). Other solutions are available as well, such as eBay's Blackthorne and third-party solutions from ándale and others.

This chapter discusses ways to create simple store items and set up an inventory using Selling Manager Pro. The following chapter will address the managing of active store listings, both with and without Selling Manager Pro. I suggest you read both chapters before deciding whether you want to get started with or without SMP. If you decide to use it, you should create your store listings from within it.

Creating Basic Store Listings

To begin selling the simple way (without Selling Manager Pro), log into eBay and click the Sell button near the screen's top. You will see a screen similar to Figure 10.1. Notice that two versions of the Sell Your Item form are available to me as I write this. We'll use the newer one.

> **note** eBay's tools are constantly evolving. For example, the listing screens changed multiple times as I was writing this book, and will likely change some more. Don't be concerned if things look a little different on your screen.

FIGURE 10.1

Start listing a store item.

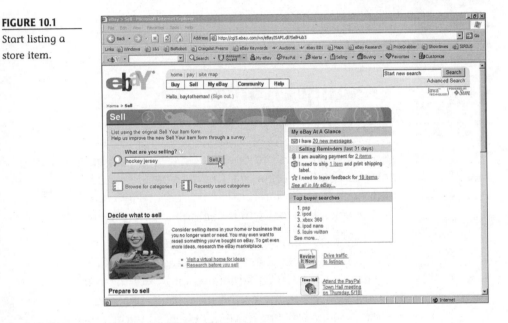

Selecting an eBay Selling Category

Suppose we want to sell some hockey jerseys. If I know the eBay selling category number or have used the selling category recently for other listings, I can pick it from a list of recently used categories.

Alternatively, I can browse the ever-lengthening category list. Instead, I've chosen to use the category search feature.

By typing "hockey jersey" into the search box and clicking the Sell It button, I am presented with a screen similar to the one in Figure 10.2. It's showing me a list of potential categories with what eBay thinks is the best match first. The more specific you are when doing the search, the better the results will be. For example, if I knew this was an NHL jersey, I would have added "NHL" to the search text back in Figure 10.1, and the second choice in Figure 10.2 have been displayed as the top choice. It's not an NHL jersey I'm selling, and the top choice in Figure 10.2 is appropriate, so I will click to select the category I wish to use (Sporting Goods > Ice, Roller Hockey > Ice Hockey > Jerseys, Shirts > Other …) and then click the Save and Continue button.

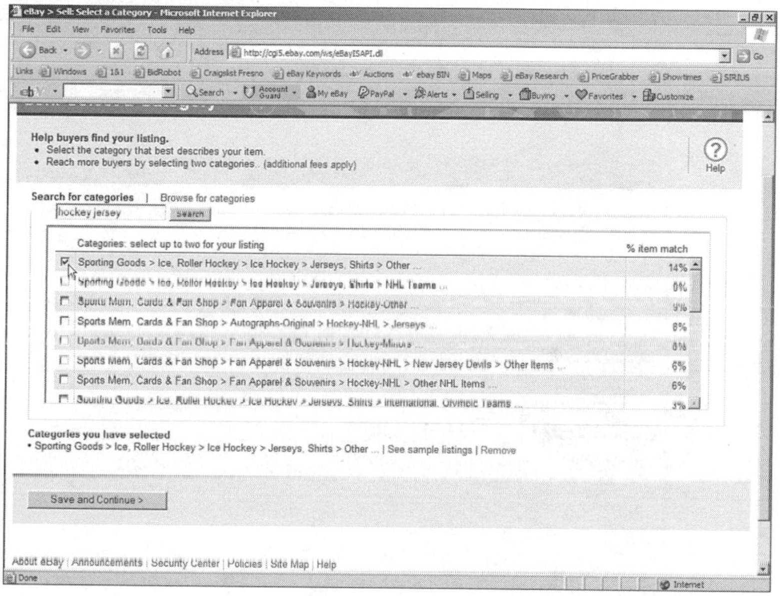

FIGURE 10.2

Choose an eBay
selling category
for the store
item.

FIGURE 10.2

Choose an eBay selling category for the store item.

You will be prompted to add a second category, which will double the listing price and somewhat increase your chances of shoppers seeing your store item. Because store items don't get very prominent billing in category searches (they appear at the bottom of searches and without Galley photos), I seldom list store items in two categories, but the option is available. You can turn off the second category reminder if you like.

caution Don't confuse eBay selling categories with your eBay's store categories discussed in Chapter 7, "Defining Store Categories." You pick those later in the listing process.

Specifying Store Categories

Once you have selected an eBay selling category or two, you will be asked to specify up to two store categories or subcategories. See Chapter 7 if you have not already set up store categories.

Figure 10.3 shows one of the drop-down lists with which you'll be presented. These will contain the store categories you've set up. In Figure 10.3, I've chosen my "NEW ITEMS!" store category (good for repeat visitors) and am about to pick "Sports-related" as the second store category. If you don't choose a second category, eBay defaults to "Other" for the category.

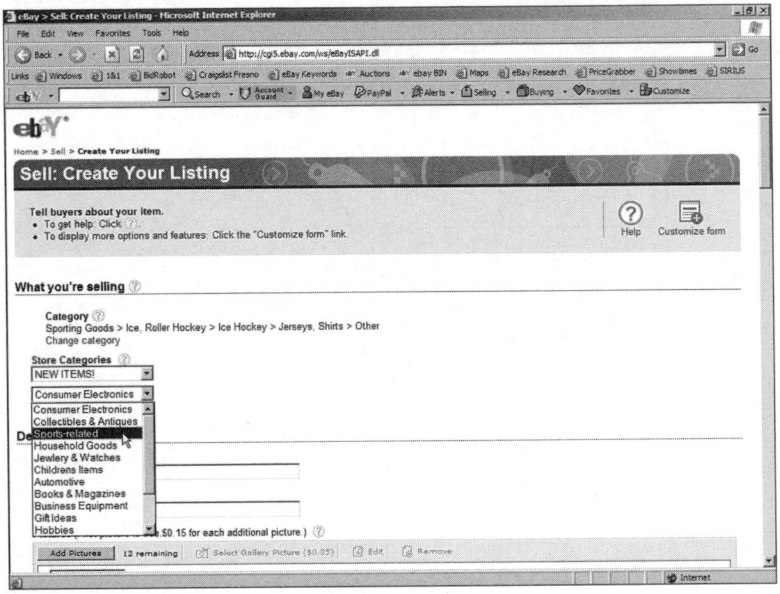

FIGURE 10.3

Specify up to two store categories or subcategories.

Adding a Title, Photos, and Description

Scroll down, if necessary, to reveal the next part of the selling form. Now things will begin looking a little more familiar. We need to add a title, optional subtitle, photos, description, and so on. Enter a good, searchable title, and possibly a subtitle if you think it will help. (Remember, subtitles are not searchable and cost extra, so don't use them with abandon.)

Next, add one or more pictures, as shown in Figure 10.4, using eBay's picture-hosting services.

Alternately, you can host the photos yourself and tell eBay where to look for them. This is a great feature for advanced users because it can save you money. Click the Self-hosting tab in the photo tool instead of the Basic or Enhanced tab and enter the URL of your photo(s), as shown in Figure 10.5.

You can use your own tools to crop, enhance, and otherwise edit photos or work with the tools built into eBay's photo feature, which are perfectly adequate for many store owners.

FIGURE 10.4

Add one or more pictures to your listing.

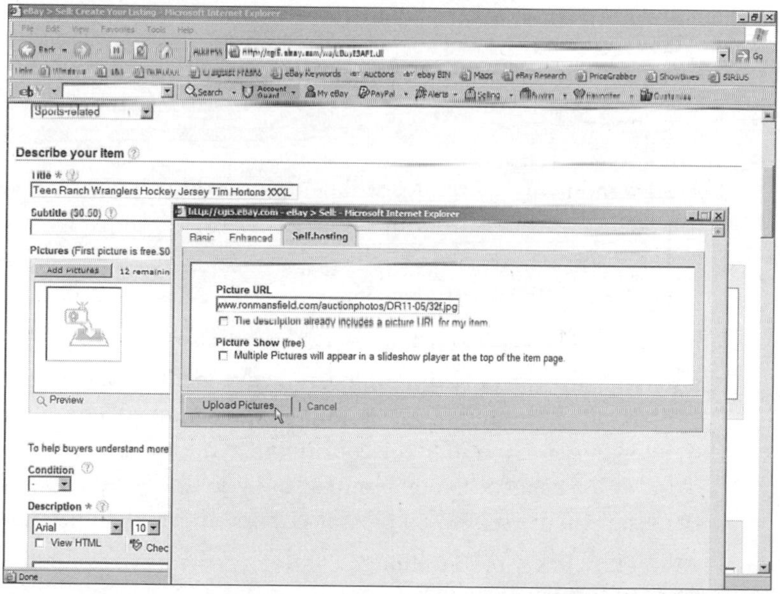

FIGURE 10.5

If you "self-host" photos, specify their web addresses here.

When you have specified the photos you want to include in your store listing, scroll down, if necessary, and opt for the Picture Pack (Gallery, Supersize, Picture Show, and additional pictures) or individual options if you want to spend the extra money. The free picture show is certainly worth trying. Click Upload when you have prepared your photos and selected the desired options (see Figure 10.6).

note At this writing, if you want to use eBay Express (discussed in Chapter 11, "Managing Your Inventory and Auctions,"), you need to have at least one photo hosed by eBay. Like everything else on the Internet, this is subject to change, of course.

FIGURE 10.6

Choose the desired options and upload the photos.

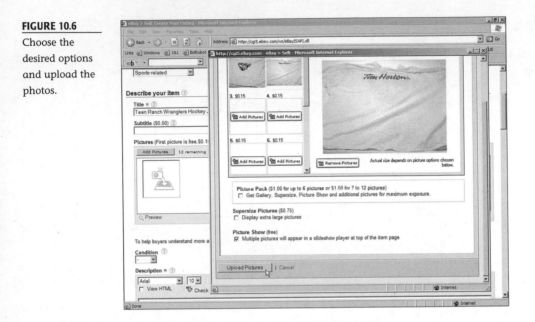

After a moment, the photos will be uploaded to eBay. You'll see thumbnails of the pictures. Scroll further in the Sell Your Item form if necessary.

Specifying the Condition of the Item

Use the drop-down list to specify the condition of the item. The choices will vary with the category, but at least always include New and Used. Sometimes Reconditioned is an option. Certain combinations of condition and eBay selling category are required for your items to appear in eBay Express, so if you want to list items in Express, make sure you understand the rules for items of the type you are selling. Express is covered in more detail in the next chapter.

Also, eBay has some prohibited condition/category restrictions. Used underwear is prohibited, for example.

Entering and Formatting Descriptions

Next, enter your item's description. You can either prepare it offline and paste it into the Description window, or use the eBay editing tools instead. Figure 10.7 shows me using eBay's tools to write and format a description. Notice the text-formatting tools available to change the text appearance, alignment, and so on.

FIGURE 10.7

Enter the description next.

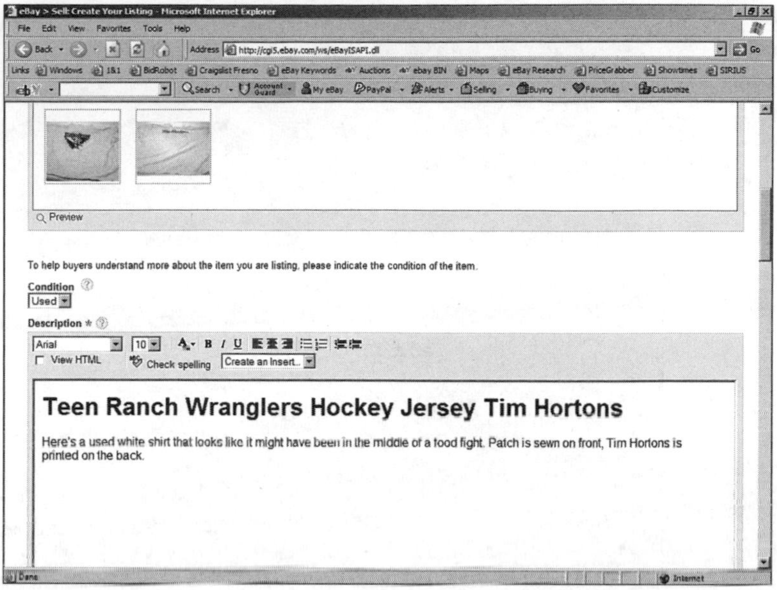

Creating Description Inserts

Especially in a store setting, you are likely to have "boilerplate" text that you will use over and over, perhaps with no variations, or only minor ones. For example, I sell a lot of hockey jerseys for a Trading Assistant client of mine, and always want to mention whether the shirt is game worn and then describe the damage, if any. (Hockey jerseys are often worth more if they are really beat up, by the way.)

Using the (somewhat limited) Insert feature could save me some time doing that for each shirt. Begin by picking Create an Insert from the drop-down list in the description-editing tool. You will see a window similar to Figure 10.8, where you can either type plain text or enter HTML. There is a 1,000-character limit per entry, so if you are doing even simple HTML or have lengthy text, you will need to create multiple inserts. I'm using HTML in Figure 10.8. There's a limit of five insert entries, so using multiple lines is difficult to accomplish. You might also need to manually format the text if you don't use HTML. Hopefully this Insert feature will evolve.

Using Inserts

Once you have created inserts, you can plunk them into your descriptions by simply clicking at the desired location and then choosing the desired insert from the drop-down giving results like those shown in Figure 10.9.

FIGURE 10.8

Create and save boilerplate inserts using either text or HTML.

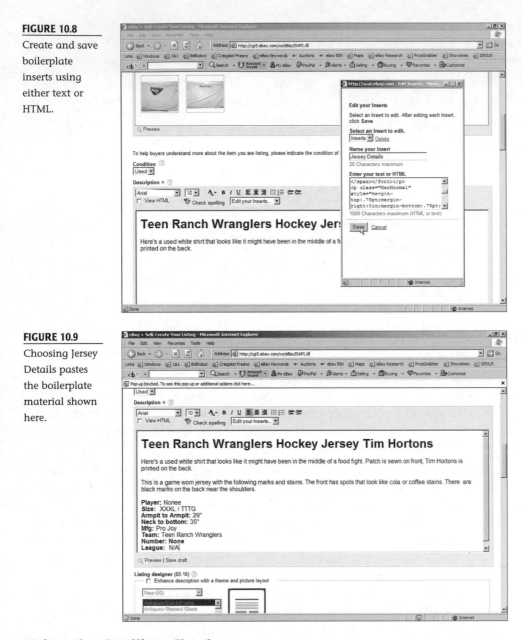

FIGURE 10.9

Choosing Jersey Details pastes the boilerplate material shown here.

Using the Spelling Checker

When you are done entering your title and description, use the built-in spelling checker to find and correct misspellings (see Figure 10.10).

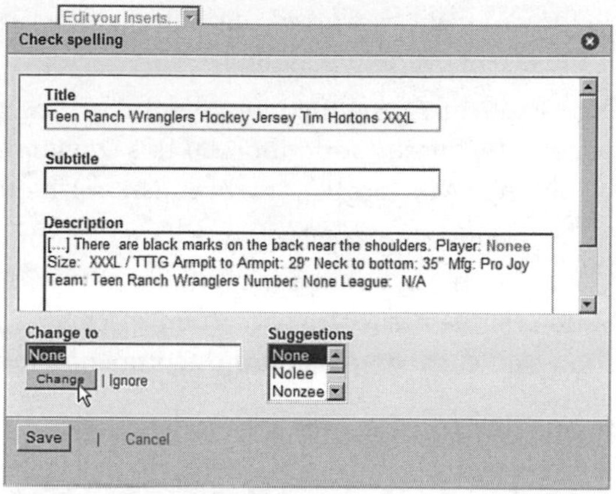

FIGURE 10.10
Spell-check the
title, subtitle,
and description.

Specifying Themes and Counters

After entering and editing the title and description, continue scrolling as necessary to see the next choices, illustrated in Figure 10.11.

Select an optional theme if you like (I'm using "Sports – Activities" for this example). Add a visitor counter if you like. You can control the position of photos with the drop-down list underneath the theme list.

Sellers either love or hate visible counters. One theory holds that they tend to build interest on hot items. Buyers see all the interest and hop on board. The other school of thought is that high counts turn potential bidders off because they think there will be too much competition. Both those views don't necessarily turn into bids, of course. I personally use visible counters. Invisible counters are an option if you want to see the number of visits without making the statistics public.

Setting the Price

Because you are creating a store listing, click the Store Inventory tab shown in Figure 10.11 and then enter a price, quantity, and duration. Optionally, you can also permit best offers and/or a later starting time.

Store items have a unique "Good 'Til Cancelled" duration, which I highly recommend using. It is very inexpensive, makes it unnecessary for you to remember to manually relist things, and helps keep your store stocked.

Donating a Percentage of Proceeds to Charity

Figure 10.11 also shows how you can designate a portion of the proceeds to one of the many charities registered with eBay. You will need to register with

MissionFish to do this. You will be walked through the process online the first time you elect to make a charitable donation.

Tax receipts are automatically generated for you and can be viewed online. If you want to check out the latest information on this evolving service before signing up, check out the FAQs located at www.missionfish.org/Help/help.jsp.

You can search for charities using keywords (I'm using "Fresno" in Figure 10.11) and then click the charity's name to read about it. Scroll to the right to click the Select button for the desired charity. Then specify the percentage you want to donate. You can learn more about this feature at www.missionfish.org.

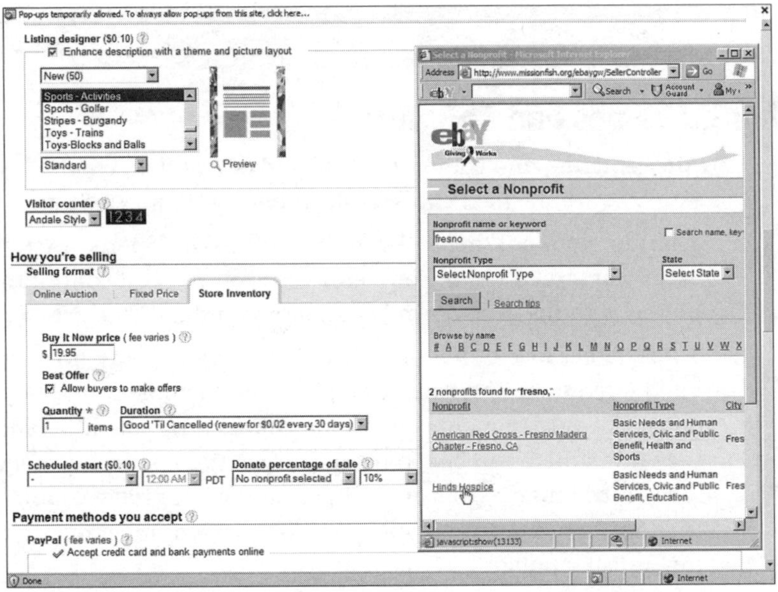

FIGURE 10.11

Specify a theme, counter, selling format, and charity.

Payment Options

Referring to Figure 10.12, choose the payment options you offer and confirm that your PayPal address is correct. You can require shoppers to pay immediately after they buy, if you like. I am not a big fan of this feature, particularly if you offer combined shipping discounts because it inhibits folks from purchasing multiple items in your store. This also makes it seem like you don't trust the buyer to pay

tip If you take money orders and/or personal checks for payment, and if your listings will show in eBay Express, warn shoppers somewhere in your listings that Express shoppers cannot pay by check or money order. Send them to your store by using a link in the listing.

promptly. If you take money orders and checks, click to activate these options. Remember to caution folks in your listings that Express buyers cannot pay you with money orders or checks.

FIGURE 10.12

Specify payment and shipping options.

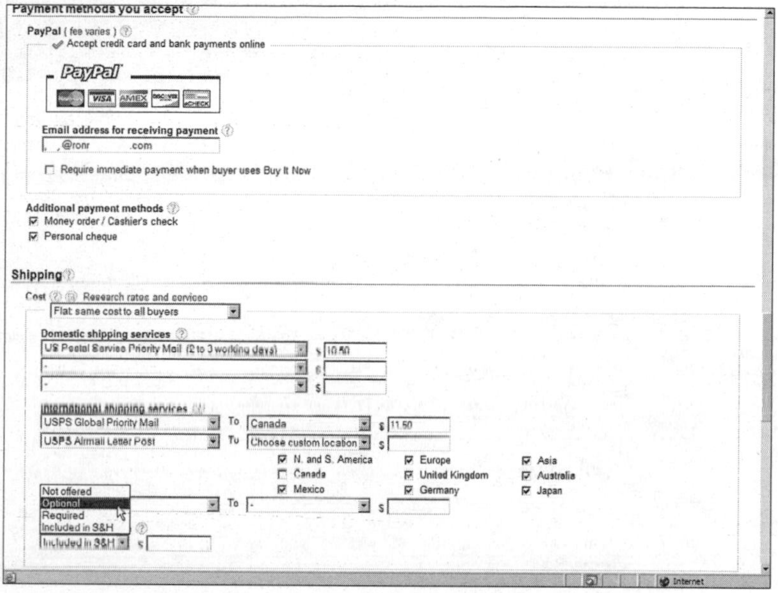

The Shipping Options section of the Listing form is used to specify the shipping choices you want to offer buyers. You can choose flat rates, calculated rates, and special rates for freight items over 150 pounds. If you offer a combined shipping discount, check the associated box. Figure 10.12 shows this area of the Listing form.

Buyer Requirements, Sales Tax, and Return Policy

Scrolling to the end of the Listing form, enter or edit the buyer requirements, sales tax settings, and refund policy (see Figure 10.13). Add any special checkout instructions you desire. Click Save and Continue. With any luck, you will be taken to a screen similar to Figure 10.14. If you have made errors or omissions, eBay will prompt you to make corrections before proceeding.

I recommend that you block bidders in countries to which you do not ship, and that you block folks with two or more unpaid items in the last 30 days.

Consult with your accountant or local tax agency to learn the correct tax percentage to collect, because it varies from place to place, even in the same state. At the moment, eBay does not break out local, county, and other taxes, so you will need to manually wrestle with these on the odd day that you sell something to someone in your same city or county or whatever. For the majority of in-state sales, the setting you choose in Figure 10.13 should be appropriate if you get the right advice.

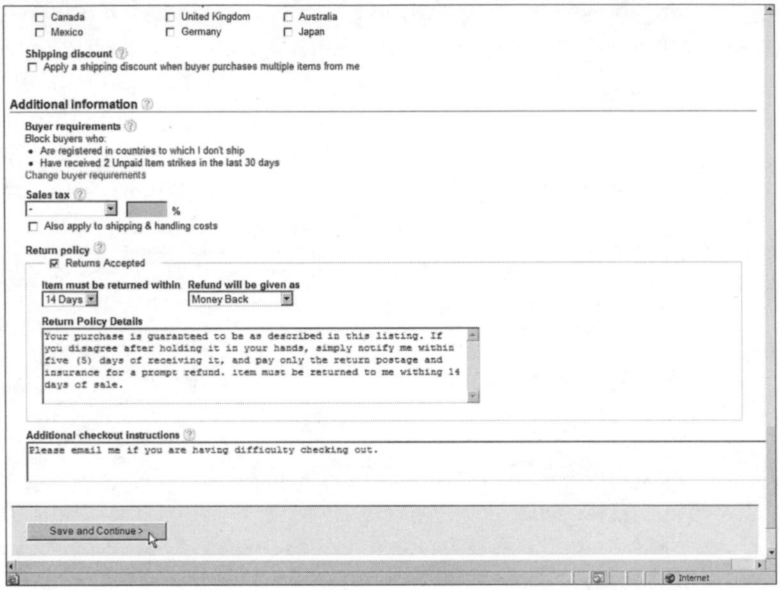

FIGURE 10.13

Buyer requirements, sales tax, and return policy.

A few states require sellers to charge tax on shipping and handling fees. If you live in one, check the "Also apply ..." box.

You can choose not to have a return policy, of course, but this will inhibit bidders, and when things turn ugly you will end up either processing a refund, or watching PayPal give your money back to the buyer anyway, so you might as well have a fair, generous refund policy.

> **note** If you sell valuable stuff, it might be worthwhile to warn buyers that you will check security marks, serial numbers, and so on before issuing the refund. Invisible security marking kits are sold on eBay. Simply search for "invisible security marker."

I offer a 14-day money back guarantee. I have sold thousands of items and have had only three come back as of this writing.

Writing something along the lines of "Email me if you are having trouble checking out" is a good idea because things do break down occasionally.

Search Result Appearance Options

Once you have successfully specified the selling details described earlier, you will see a screen similar to the one in Figure 10.14 titled "Make Your Listing Stand Out."

Here you will get a chance to purchase and specify a gallery photo (which I recommend) and other options such as placing search results in bold type, highlighted type, and so on. Below these options you will see a preview of how your listing will look in search results compared to another standard listing. Notice in Figure 10.14 how different our listing looks with the added (and expensive) border and highlighting. The top item is plain. The second item has both a border and a highlight.

These embellishments are sometimes useful for expensive items, especially in crowded categories, but not recommended for inexpensive commodity items because they won't pay for themselves. I'll remove the border and highlight choices by unchecking them before continuing to list this inexpensive item.

FIGURE 10.14

Choose and preview search result appearance options.

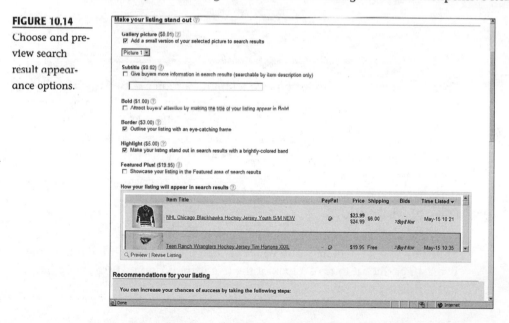

Next, eBay will make recommendations designed to improve your selling price and, of course, eBay's bottom line. Consider their suggestions (and the source).

Scroll in the Preview box to review the listing. Revise it if necessary, and then scroll the main window until you see the Fees section. Make sure you have not picked expensive options by mistake. You can also estimate the final value fee here and see your current eBay account balance by clicking the links. Figure 10.15 shows this.

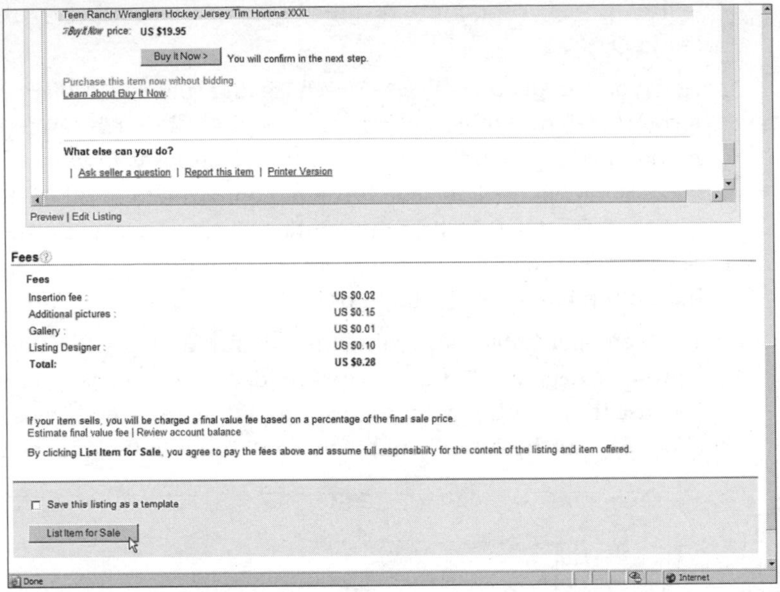

FIGURE 10.15

Review the fees.

There's a way to save this listing as a template for later reuse, as you will see in Chapter 11, but we are not going to use that feature in this example. If you want to create templates, I think you should use Selling Manager Pro, Blackthorne, or a third-party tool instead. Because we will be looking at Selling Manager Pro's templates next, let's just click the List Item for Sale button and move along.

Double-checking Your Work

Unless you've scheduled the item to launch at a future date or time, it will go online almost immediately and you'll be taken to a screen with a link to the live listing. Click it to take a look at the live listing. Figure 10.16 shows our sample listing on eBay.

FIGURE 10.16

Review (and possibly revise) the live listing.

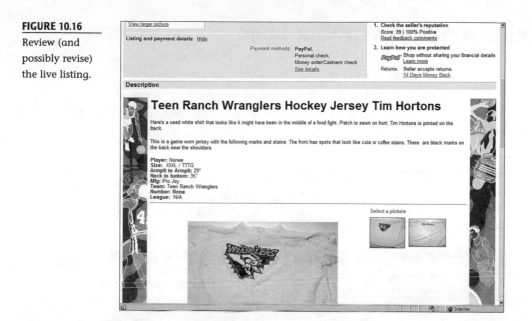

Review (and possibly revise) the live listing.

Revising Live Listings

It's always better to get things right the first time, of course, but sometimes you'll want to change something in a listing. To revise your listings, use the Revise Your Item link near the top of the listing. Obviously, you must be logged into eBay as the seller of the item to see the Revise Your Item link.

As you probably know from your non-store selling, when you revise a listing it will display a revision date thereafter. If none of the items in a store listing have sold yet, you can revise any information, including the price, description, the photos, and so on. You can also remove optional features (such as borders) and add or change the Gallery picture.

However, once even one of the multiple items in a store listing sells, you can only revise its price, change the available quantity and store category, add or remove optional features, or add to (but not edit) the description.

Auction item rules are a little different. For a refresher course on the rather complex subject of when you can revise what, visit http://pages.ebay.com/help/sell/edit_listing.html.

Seeing New Items in Your Store

Don't panic if you visit your store and don't find the new item there instantly. It takes a while for the store index to catch up with live auctions, so it's best to wait 10 minutes or so before looking for recently listed items in your store.

The new listing I created in this chapter is now shown in my BaytotheMax training store, shown in Figure 10.17. Incidentally, it can take even longer for the "New Arrivals" promotional boxes to update, so chill.

FIGURE 10.17

It takes a few moments for new listings to appear in your store.

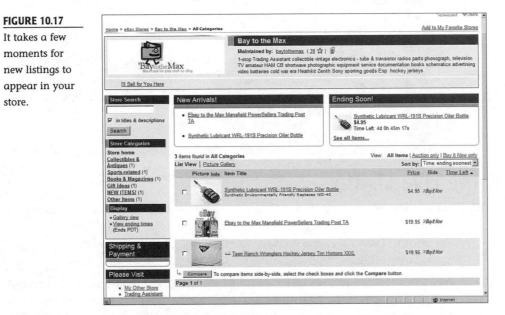

Creating New Listings with Selling Manager Pro

As you know from reading Chapter 9, "Automating with Selling Manager Pro (SMP)," I am a big fan of Selling Manager Pro (SMP), particularly for small-to-medium-sized stores. If you use SMP, you will want to start creating new listings from within SMP itself, using the Create Product feature. How you arrange things in SMP is up to you, and can be a bit confusing especially if you organize things in folders, which is an SMP option.

We need to get a couple of key concepts out of the way before I show you how to create a new listing from within Selling Manager Pro.

Products vs. Listings

In SMP terminology, you can have multiple listings and different selling formats for the same product. For example, suppose I want to sell a new type of battery. I might want to list it as a Buy It Now item, and as a store item, and I might even want to auction a few off to test the pricing waters.

In each case, it would be the same battery from the same vendor, at the same cost. And, I would have a finite inventory of the batteries—10 in stock to start, for example. I might also have an in-house part number for the battery that is different from the manufacturer's number. I'll also want to make some notes to myself about these batteries.

Suppose I have 10 batteries and create three separate listings for that same battery. I might offer three in a Buy It Now listing, put six in my store inventory, and offer one as an auction to test the pricing.

Whenever a battery is sold, either from a Buy It Now listing, out of the store inventory, or via an auction, I would want the available inventory to be decreased as a result of each new sale. Selling Manager Pro will keep track of that for me if I launch the listings through it.

So, doubling back for just a moment, this is one product that could be used to create multiple listings in different selling formats (Buy It Now, store, and auction listings, let's say).

Templates

Using SMP, I can create three slightly different templates to make it easy to launch this product in any of the different selling formats. This saves a lot of reinvention because I can simply copy a listing I like as a new template with a different selling format. For example, I could start by running a test auction. Then, after determining the right price, I could copy the auction template but save it as a Buy It Now listing and/or store inventory template. Obviously, you can use templates to save other variations besides the selling format. You could create holiday versions of listings, slightly different descriptions of a product for different audiences (selling categories), and so on.

So far so good? If this doesn't make sense yet, it should in a moment.

Organizing with Folders

SMP product folders can offer organization (or add confusion) to your inventory. The best way to use them is to create a new folder for each product. Then you can store up to 20 templates within each folder. Therefore, I could use one folder for the new battery, containing three templates for the different battery selling formats, and maybe another template for the same battery but using a Christmas gift theme, and so on.

Creating a New Product Record in SMP

Open My eBay and click the Inventory link in the left navigation panel. You will see a screen similar to the one in Figure 10.18. Create a new product by clicking the Create Product button.

FIGURE 10.18

Start creating a new product in SMP.

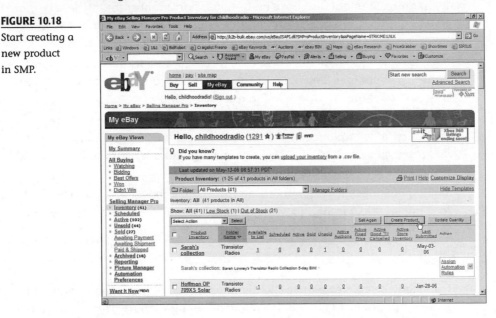

Enter the details of the product using the form shown in Figure 10.19. Start by naming a new folder. Folder names can only include simple alphanumeric text. Do not use periods, asterisks, and so on.

I like to name folders beginning with my in-house part number, and I repeat that part number in the optional Part Number box. This improves reporting somewhat.

Enter the starting quantity, a product name (visible only to you), and your average unit cost. (Don't forget to include the costs of having items shipped to you, any labor costs you add to the product, and so on.)

Enter vendor contact information and notes to yourself if you like. Again, none of this stuff shows up in your listings. It's for in-house use only.

Click the Save & Create Listing button.

Select a selling site from the resulting screen (eBay US, for example). Click Continue. You will be presented with selling format choices shown in Figure 10.20. Let's start with an auction.

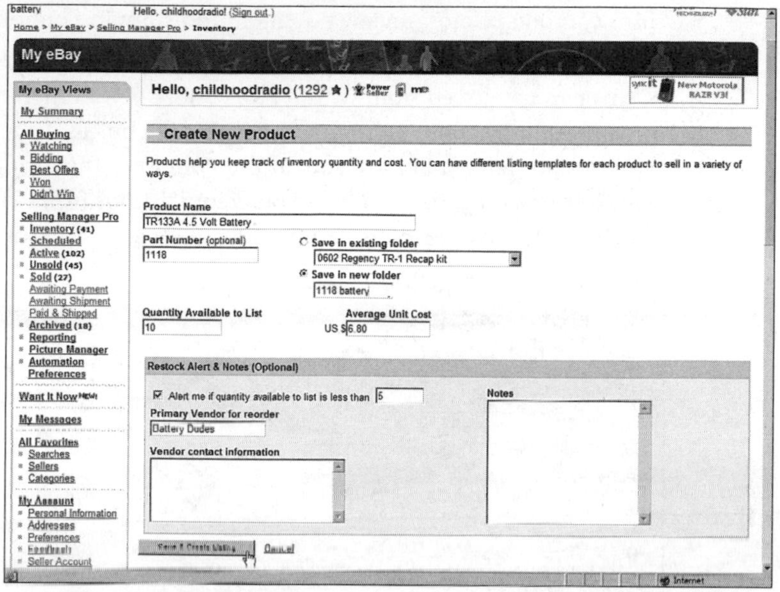

FIGURE 10.19
Enter product details for in-house use.

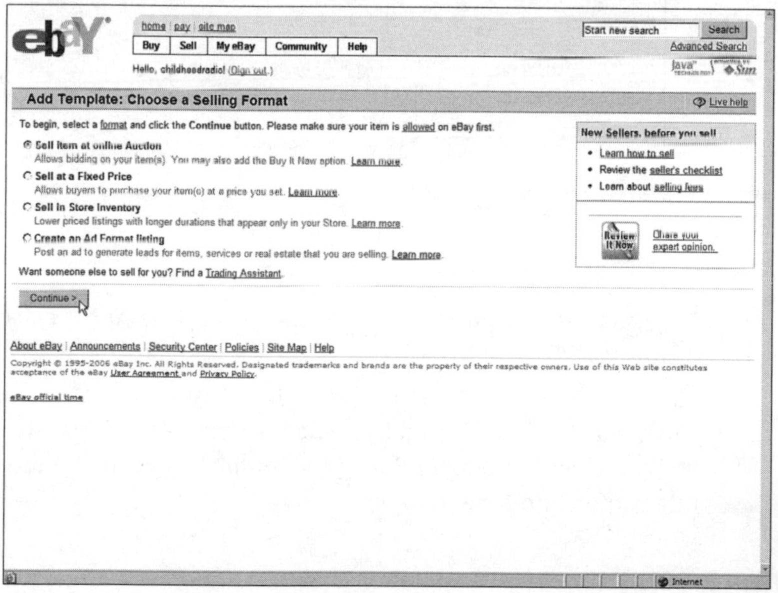

FIGURE 10.20
Select a listing format.

From here, the listing-creation procedure continues in a way that should be familiar to you now, so I'll just mention the steps. You pick an eBay selling category or two, create a title and description, specify the desired store category or categories, enter a starting price if it's an auction, add a BIN price if there is one, and specify the duration information.

You also can add photos, review payment and shipping options, state your refund policies, and so on.

All of this can be altered from within SMP before you launch the listing, by the way, because you will be saving this series of choices. When you get to the Review stage, a new option appears at the bottom of the form. You can see the new buttons in Figure 10.21. When you create listings from within SMP, you are prompted to save them and, optionally, both save and launch them. For this exercise, let's just save.

FIGURE 10.21

SMP asks you to save listings as templates.

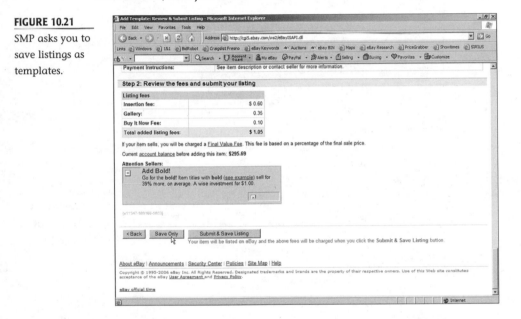

The listing is saved as a template, and you will see a screen similar to Figure 10.22.

The new listing template appears with the listing title that will appear online when you make the listing live. The new template is titled Template x, with x being the next incremental template number. You can change the template title, which I find useful to do.

Renaming Templates

Click the check box next to the template(s) you want to rename and choose Edit Template Name from the pop-up list. Click Go. When asked, name the template. I use my in-house product numbers, a short description, and the selling format (Auction, Store, BIN, and so on). You will see the method to this madness in a moment.

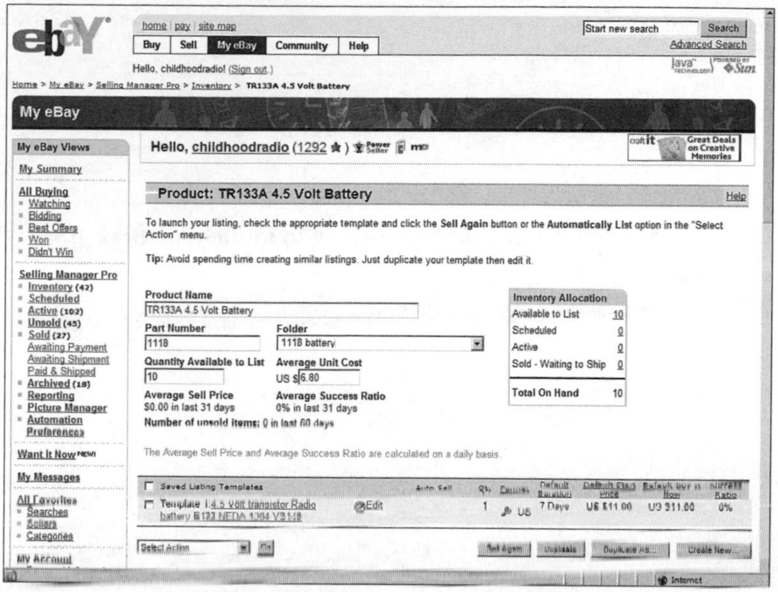

FIGURE 10.22

An inventory
item and
template.

Creating Different Selling Formats for the Same Item

Once you have a template for a new product, you can duplicate it quickly by making only the necessary changes. For example, I could have a second battery template for Buy It Now selling and a third for store stock. All I need to do is copy the template and change the selling format options.

To duplicate a template, follow these steps:

1. Click the check box next to a template and then click the Duplicate As... button shown in Figure 10.22. You'll be presented with a screen like the one in Figure 10.23.

2. If you want to use a different selling format (and we do here), click the Selling Format button, pick the new format (fixed price, in this example), and then click Continue.

3. Cycle through the rest of the choices, making any necessary alterations.

4. When you click the "Save Only" or "Submit & Save Listing" button, the new template will be saved with the name template 2 (or whatever). As I mentioned, I like to use more meaningful names, so I've changed them. Figure 10.23 shows this. Notice the Format column. One template has a little hammer icon, indicating the auction format, the second template has a keyboard-like icon for fixed price, and the third icon is for stores.

FIGURE 10.23

Three templates
for one product.

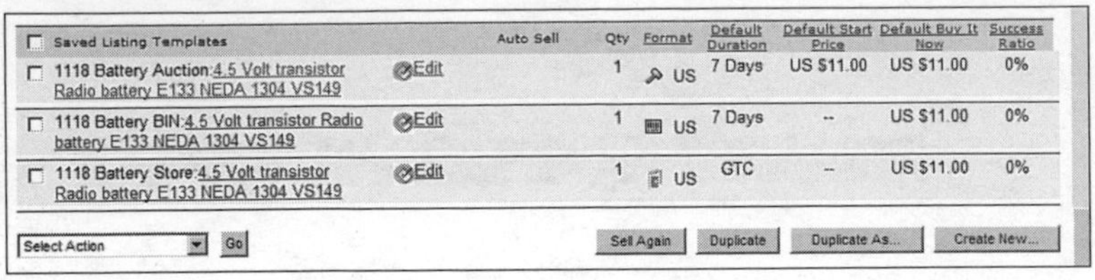

Saved Listing Templates		Auto Sell	Qty	Format	Default Duration	Default Start Price	Default Buy It Now	Success Ratio
☐ 1118 Battery Auction:4 5 Volt transistor Radio battery E133 NEDA 1304 VS149	⊘Edit		1	🔍 US	7 Days	US $11.00	US $11.00	0%
☐ 1118 Battery BIN:4 5 Volt transistor Radio battery E133 NEDA 1304 VS149	⊘Edit		1	▦ US	7 Days	--	US $11.00	0%
☐ 1118 Battery Store:4 5 Volt transistor Radio battery E133 NEDA 1304 VS149	⊘Edit		1	▤ US	GTC	--	US $11.00	0%

| Select Action ▾ | Go | | | | Sell Again | Duplicate | Duplicate As... | Create New... |

In the next chapter, you'll see how to launch auctions from within SMP and
monitor your inventory.

Managing Your Inventory and Auctions

Because your store might have hundreds or even thousands of items, you will need to find a way to efficiently keep track of inventory, costs, orders, ended listings, shipments, and, of course, profit or loss. Many of us run auctions and Buy It Now listings as well. Store sellers often like to automate the relisting of items after batches have sold as well.

Wouldn't it be nice if there was one place on your computer where you could get an overview of how things are going, and then drill down for additional details? Well, there can be such a place. Selling Manager Pro is one solution to this challenge.

Launching Items

Managing store item sales and auctions without Selling Manager Pro is no different from what you have probably already done as a casual eBay seller. You log into My eBay and see something like Figure 11.1. This is a very simple summary screen, where you can click the various links to see items awaiting payment, things that need to be shipped, feedback that needs to be left, and so on.

FIGURE 11.1

A My eBay summary without Selling Manager Pro.

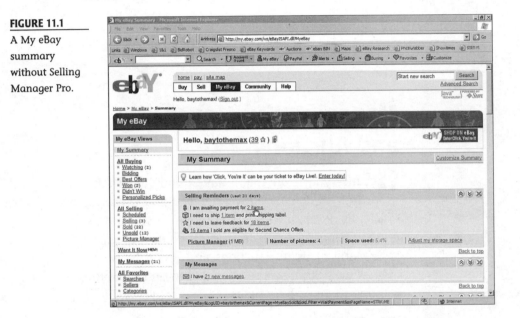

The good news is, this simple, uncluttered presentation is easy to navigate and is self-explanatory. The bad news is, it lacks the automation and features many busy store owners need.

Figure 11.2 shows the different presentation you will get when visiting the My eBay page in a store that subscribes to Selling Manager Pro. It's like comparing a Cessna to a 767.

Because you can customize this page, yours might look different, but the significant things to notice are all the extra links on the navigation tab at the left. This chapter looks at how to use many of these features. Some of the others are discussed in other chapters. Shipping, for example, is covered in Chapter 13, "Shipping."

Perhaps the biggest change for many new users of SMP is the way items are launched. This is best done from the Inventory screen shown in Figure 11.3.

FIGURE 11.2

A My eBay summary using Selling Manager Pro.

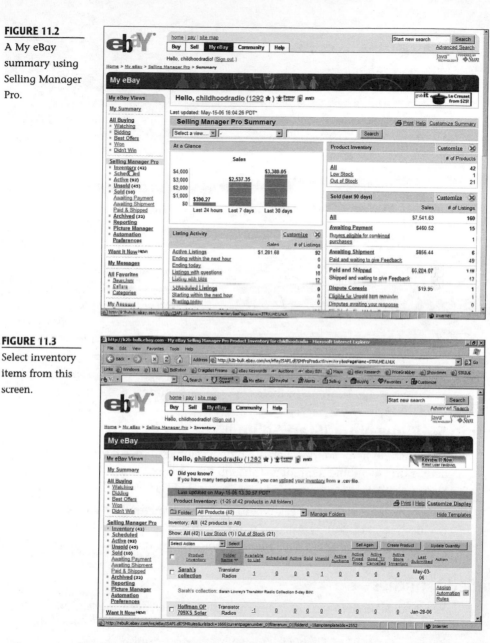

FIGURE 11.3

Select inventory items from this screen.

You can display information about an inventory item as well as see and use its templates simply by displaying its folder using the drop-down list. For example, Figure 11.4 shows the new battery product and its three templates created in the previous chapter.

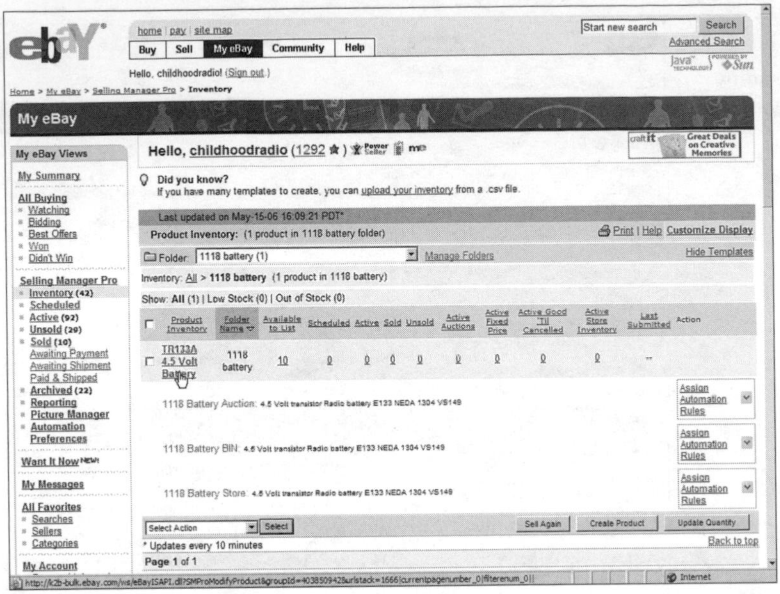

FIGURE 11.4

View and manage an inventory item and its templates.

FIGURE 11.4

View and manage an inventory item and its templates.

From here, you can see the status of the inventory as well as what, if anything, is active. In Figure 11.4, we have a quantity of 10 batteries, none scheduled to be listed or live yet. If there were active listings, the appropriate quantities would show up in their appropriate columns.

Activating SMP Inventory (Start Selling)

To launch an item, simply click the product name to reveal the product's details and available templates. Clicking the "TR133A 4.5 Volt Battery" link in Figure 11.4 reveals the screen you see in Figure 11.5.

To list an item, click the check box to the left of the template you want to use (we use the 1118 Battery Auction template in Figure 11.5). To start selling immediately, simply click the Submit Listing button and away you'll go.

Scheduled Launches

To schedule an item to start selling at a different date or time, click the "Scheduled to start on" radio button shown in Figure 11.5 and specify the desired launch time. Then click the Submit Listing button.

FIGURE 11.5
Launch or
relaunch your
items here.

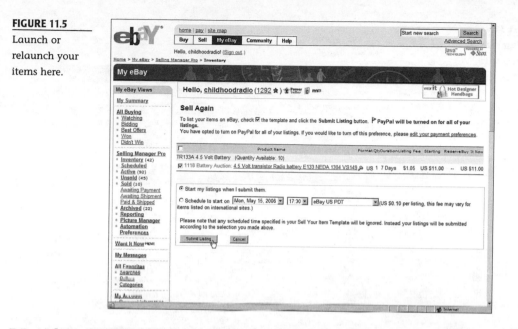

Monitoring Bidders, Sales, Payments, and Shipments

It's a good idea to keep an eye on things, particularly auctions. Although auctions are not strictly store items, as you can see in Figure 11.6, you can use SMP's Format filter drop-down list to display just your auctions. Not only can you watch how the bidding is going, but if you customize the display (using the Customize Display link in the upper-right corner), you can see the eBay ID and feedback rating of the high bidders. This is a great way to get an auction snapshot.

Monitoring Sales

SMP makes easy work of seeing what has been sold, paid for, needs to be shipped, as well as what has already been shipped, by using links along the left navigation bar. Figure 11.7 shows part of a list of things needing to be shipped.

FIGURE 11.6

Monitor auction progress with SMP (IDs intentionally disguised).

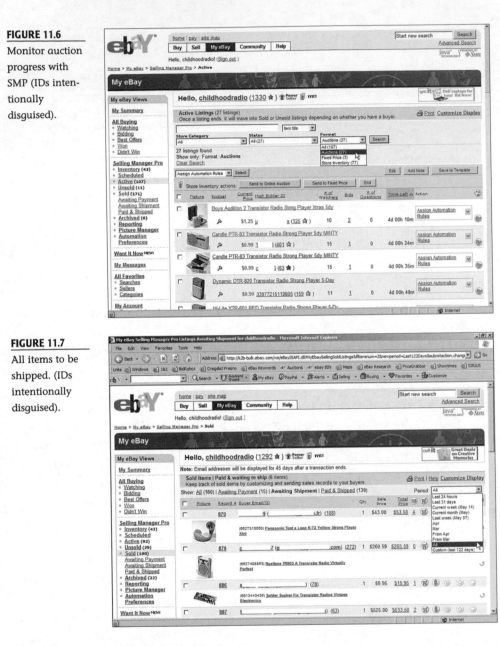

FIGURE 11.7

All items to be shipped. (IDs intentionally disguised).

Viewing the Correct Period

Because you can tell SMP to display data over specific date ranges (Last Week, Last Month, All, and so on), be sure you are looking at the right information. Always choose All, as shown in Figure 11.7, when looking at items to be shipped. Look at Figure 11.8 to see what happens when I choose Last 24 Hours instead. As you can see, it looks as though there's nothing to ship, when in fact there is plenty to do.

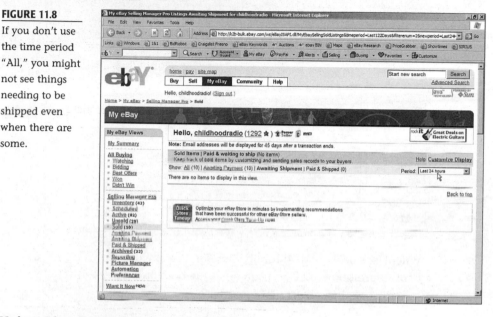

Using the Awaiting Payment Lists

The SMP Awaiting Payment lists work the same way as the Awaiting Shipment and similar lists. Click the left navigation bar's link and see who owes you what. In cases where a winner has purchased multiple items, they will be combined and a combined total will be displayed for you. Automatic payments from PayPal, for example, will move items into the Awaiting Shipment bucket automatically.

If someone pays by check or via some other "outside of eBay/PayPal" payment method, you will need to manually mark the items paid. Do this by finding the items in the Awaiting Payment list and clicking the corresponding record numbers. You'll see a sales record similar to the one in Figure 11.9.

The top part of the form (not shown in Figure 11.9) contains the buyer's address. You can see the purchased item details for a single item or combined items and any shipping fees and perhaps combined shipping discounts that have automatically been computed. You can use this part of the screen to change and apply discounts or extra charges, and you can recalculate the total as well.

FIGURE 11.9

Wrangle manual payments, fee adjustments, and more in this area.

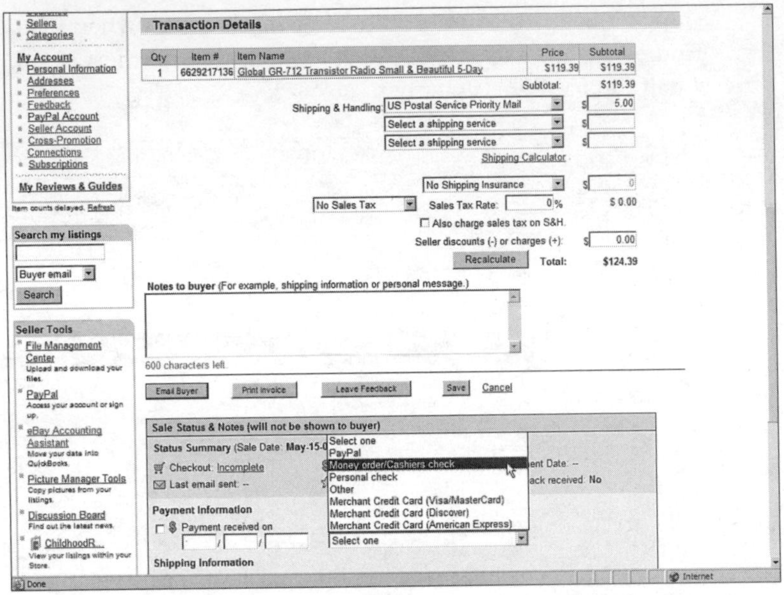

If payment has been made through eBay/PayPal, the date will show in the payment information area. You can enter the date and type of manual payments here as well, as shown in Figure 11.9.

Shipments, Invoices, and Emails

The information shown in Figure 11.10 was revealed by scrolling further down the buyer's record screen and shows the shipping information area and buttons used to print optional invoices and postage labels, send and track emails to the customer, and leave feedback.

This is also where you record your actual cost for the item(s) sold, which is useful in profitability reporting. You can also make notes to yourself here.

Saving Changes

There's a little Save button at the bottom of the screen, and it's important to click it whenever you make changes to a customer's record (see Figure 11.10).

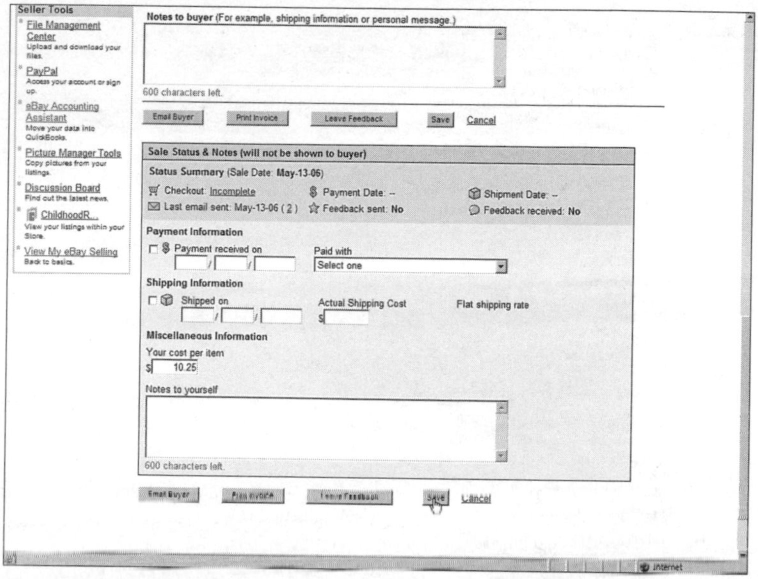

FIGURE 11.10

Scroll to see and change shipping dates, costs, and so on.

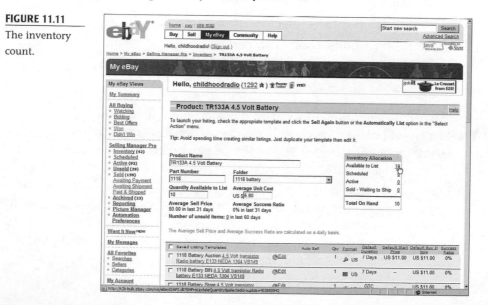

Adjusting Inventory Counts

You can manually adjust inventory counts by visiting a store item's record and clicking the Available to List link, as shown in Figure 11.11. You'll then see something like the screen shown in Figure 11.12. Use the Remove choice in the Action drop-down list to decrease the available inventory and the Add choice in the drop-down to restock. Specify the quantity in the Quantity box and click Update Qty to save your work.

FIGURE 11.11

The inventory count.

FIGURE 11.12

Adjust the
inventory up
or down.

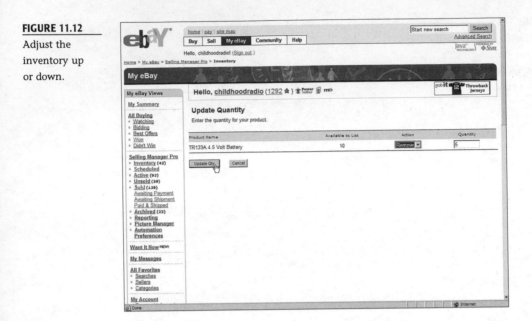

Inventory Control and Automated Relisting Options

You can tell eBay what to automatically do with your inventory under a variety scenarios. For example, you can have eBay take the following actions:

- Keep a fixed number of listings active
- List according to my schedule
- Relist once if an item does not sell
- Relist in my store if an item does not sell
- Relist continuously until an item sells
- Relist continuously whether an item sells or doesn't sell
- Take no automatic actions (No Rule)

You can accomplish this by visiting a product's record, as shown in Figure 11.13, and putting a check mark next to the applicable template. Then, choose Assign Automation Rules from the pop-up list and click Go, also shown in Figure 11.13.

Suppose, for example, that the new battery we offer at auction does not sell and we want to put it in the store inventory automatically. When the automation screen (like the one in Figure 11.14) appears, we pick that option from the drop-down list and click Assign. If the auction ends unsuccessfully, the item will move to the store inventory.

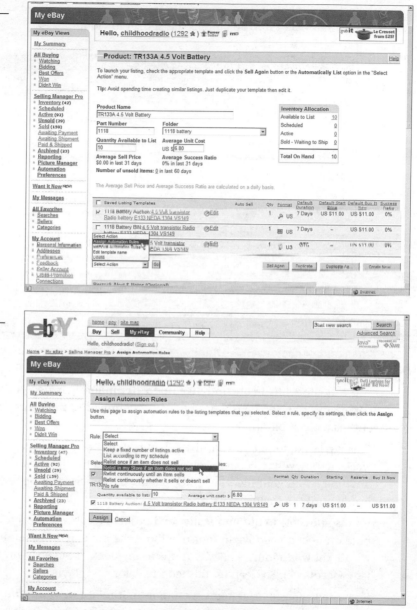

Automating Emails and Feedback

You can have eBay send email on your behalf and even leave feedback when buyers pay. Reach the settings for these features by clicking the Automation preferences link that appears in your My eBay screen if you subscribe to Selling Manager Pro. The options are shown in Figure 11.15.

FIGURE 11.15

Automation options for SMP users.

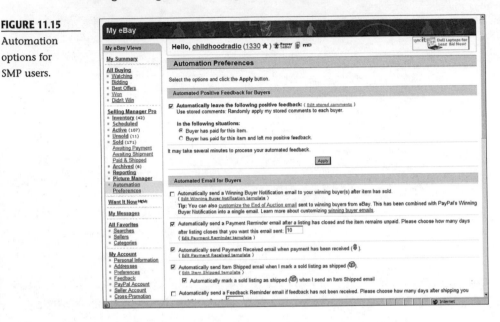

Automating Feedback

You can choose to create and save up to 10 randomly issued positive feedback comments. They obviously need to be fairly universal in nature, and not too enthusiastic or bland.

This type of automation runs the risk of rewarding some bozo who took two weeks to pay with feedback like "Wow! Lightning fast payment. Come again anytime." And your favorite, quick-paying customer could be rewarded with just "Thanks. A+ eBayer."

It's also possible to automatically send positive feedback as soon as you get paid and get a negative in return without the buyer fearing retaliation (which we all know is against policy, but it is in the back of buyers' minds when they leave feedback). So sleep on this feature before employing it.

If you sell thousands of items each month, it might be worth automating your feedback, or at least giving it a try for a while. Click the Edit Stored Comments link to reveal the entry/editing screen shown in Figure 11.16. Click the Save Comments button to preserve your prose.

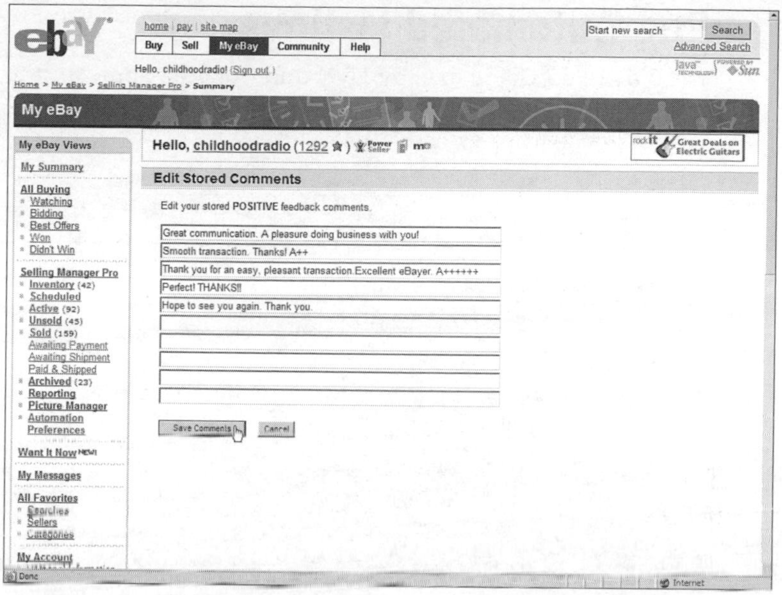

FIGURE 11.16

Create up to
10 automatic
feedback entries.

You can have eBay send the feedback when you get paid or not until feedback is left for you. The latter is obviously less risky, but will annoy some buyers.

Automating Emails

Automated emails, on the other hand, can be a real godsend if you set them up properly. You can have an email sent when the purchase is consummated. You can have eBay send automatic payment reminders. My favorite is automatic shipping notification, which really impresses buyers. There is also an email you can send if you don't get feedback. I personally don't like these emails when I get them and they can backfire on sellers.

Make your email automation choices in the area of the Automation Preferences screen.

Suspending Automated Listings

Need a break? Going to eBay Live! and won't be home to ship your items? You can suspend automatic listings and relistings at the bottom of the screen shown in Figure 11.17.

FIGURE 11.17

Vacation hold.

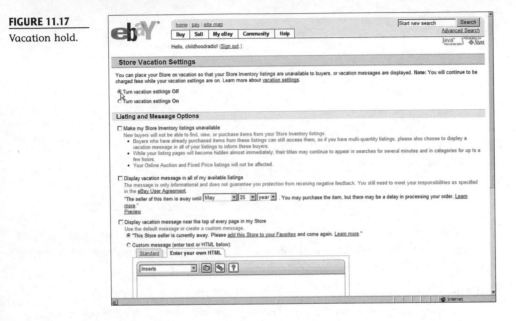

Reach this screen by visiting Manage My Store and choosing Store Vacation Settings from the left navigation area.

12

Store Bookkeeping and QuickBooks

In Part IV, "Reports," you will read about eBay's sales-reporting tools that can give you quick snapshots of how well your business, and even specific store items, are doing. But many eBay businesses need a deeper level of detail. They need to know how much each and every item costs and then sells for, the value of their inventory, supply costs, advertising costs, payroll expenses and associated payroll taxes, vehicle costs, rent, insurance costs, and on and on and on.

Trading Assistants face another layer of complexity because they need to compute check amounts for their customers and issue those checks.

It gets even trickier if you have third parties involved, such as franchisors who "sweep" the payments from your PayPal account for items you've sold and send checks to the items' owners, then move additional funds in and out of your bank, PayPal, and credit-card merchant accounts for you.

The Tools at Hand

Some tools are available that you and your accountant or bookkeeper can use to simplify the bookkeeping process somewhat, but they are far from perfect. Most mid-sized eBay sellers use one or another version of QuickBooks, along with eBay's Accounting Assistant, and perhaps invoice detail exports from eBay and PayPal.

You'll get an overview of that process here. But to get a bookkeeping system that works well for you and that satisfies your accounting needs, you will need to go beyond the contents of this chapter with the help of an accountant and perhaps a tax advisor. You will need to obtain help setting up the specific charts of accounts, sales tax records, payroll systems, and other tools necessary to let you understand your financial situation and remain compliant with federal, state, county, and local laws.

For example, many businesses with employees decide to use payroll services to ensure that salaries are properly paid and withholdings are correct. You will not learn everything you need to know here, but this chapter should give you and your CPA or bookkeeper an overview and a good place to start.

We Need to Do What?

Selling a few things of your own from the garage requires pretty simple record keeping, and you can probably use your eBay and PayPal invoices along with a business checking account and QuickBooks, or even Quicken Premier Home and Business, to get the job done.

But running a full-scale eBay business with thousands of items and literally tens-of-thousands of line items describing listing fees, final value fees, PayPal shipping fees, refunds, eBay fee reversals, and so on, will require you to take your accounting tasks to the next level.

Don't be surprised if, even after employing the tools described in this chapter, you find yourself using Excel spreadsheets or perhaps needing to download eBay and PayPal details into a custom database designed to get the results you want.

For people who think accounting is a science where everything should tie-out to the last penny at the click of a mouse button, eBay can be a pretty frustrating place. There are a number of reasons why eBay bookkeeping is a challenge, even when you employ the available tools and professional accounting help. Some of the frustrations include the following:

- The fact that it takes days to move funds from PayPal and your credit-card merchant accounts to your bank account(s), putting the funds in limbo and causing things to look out of balance when they are not

- The fact that eBay's systems sometimes treat multiple purchases made by the same person as one transaction

- The fact that there's no good way to automatically track the cost of items you *purchase* on eBay for resale on eBay

- The challenges created by city, state, county, and local sales tax entities on those rare occasions when a buyer picks something up or you ship it to a local destination falling into your own state, county, or city jurisdiction

- The need to use multiple programs and multiple steps to do your bookkeeping

QuickBooks

Although by no means a requirement, many eBayers use one or another version of QuickBooks for their accounting tasks. Figure 12.1 shows one of the screens from the online version displaying data imported via eBay's Accounting Assistant (described in a moment).

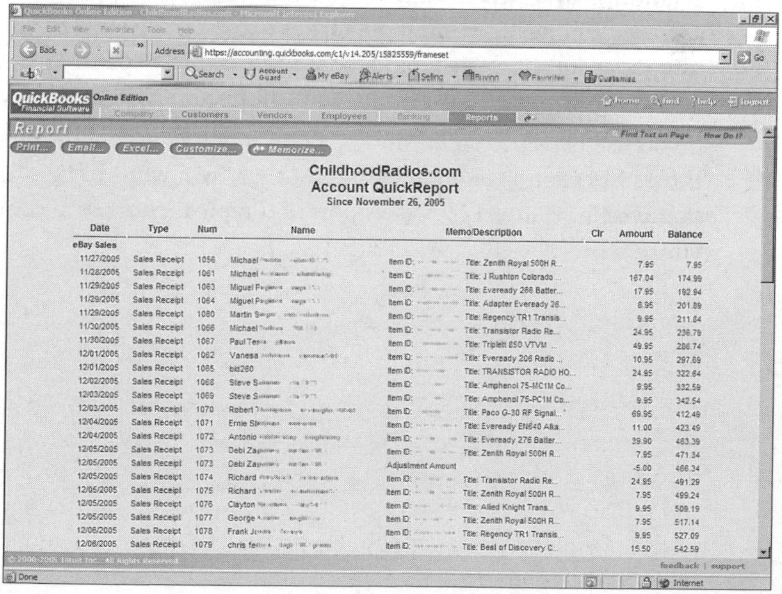

FIGURE 12.1

A typical QuickBooks report using data imported using eBay's Accounting Assistant.

Because there are a number of versions of QuickBooks, you should consult with your accountant or bookkeeper to pick the one that's right for the both of you. Be sure it is compatible with eBay's Accounting Assistant because that's probably the easiest way to get the eBay and PayPal transaction data into QuickBooks. One of the following QuickBooks 2004, 2005, or 2006 products must be installed on the same machine as eBay Accounting Assistant.

note If you don't yet have an accountant or bookkeeper, or are shopping around for a new one, try to find someone who has experience with eBay's Accounting Assistant. It might make things easier and cheaper for you.

- QuickBooks Pro®
- QuickBooks Premier® (including all industry-specific editions)
- QuickBooks Enterprise®
- QuickBooks Online Edition
- QuickBooks Simple Start Desktop Edition
- QuickBooks Simple Start Online Edition

Setting Up Your Chart of Accounts

Regardless of which version of QuickBooks or other accounting software you use, you will need to set up a chart of accounts, or a list of categories and subcategories for the variety of income sources and expenses associated with your particular business. Most likely, you will need a CPA to assist you with this.

If you use eBay's Accounting Assistant, it will help you set up a bare-bones chart of accounts for eBay selling that you will want to fine-tune with professional help. Figure 12.2 shows part of a typical chart of accounts for an eBay business.

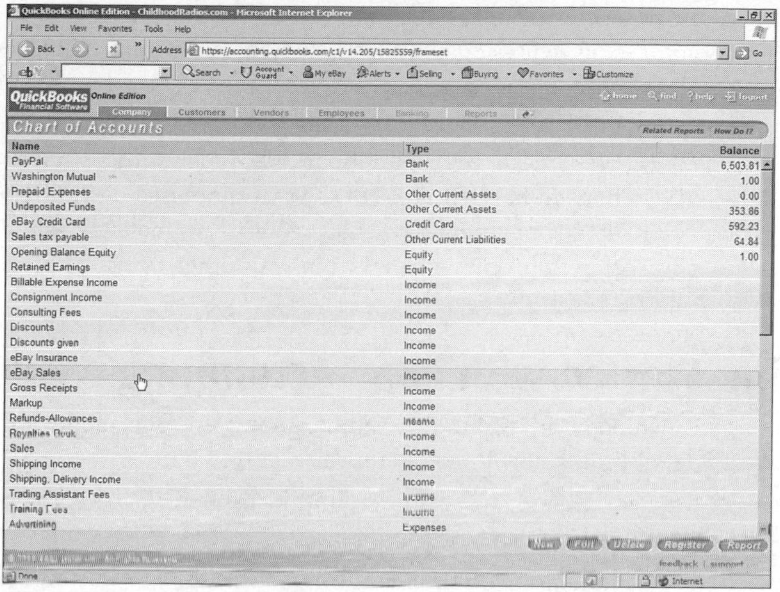

FIGURE 12.2

Part of a
QuickBooks
chart of
accounts for an
eBay business.

eBay Accounting Assistant

eBay Accounting Assistant is a program you download to your computer that helps you import your eBay and PayPal data from eBay, store the data on your local computer's hard drive, and then import it into your QuickBooks company file. This can reduce data-entry time and minimizes transcription errors for many users.

Accounting Assistant is free to download and use, but you must have a subscription to Selling Manager, Selling Manager Pro, Blackthorne, Blackthorne Pro, and/or run an eBay store. Because you are reading this book, you either have or are about to have a store.

You can try any these subscriptions (Selling Manager Pro, for example) free of charge for 30 days. Here's what you can do with Accounting Assistant:

- Download up to 60 days of historical eBay and PayPal fees and details for sales transactions (but not for purchases you've made).

- Specify exactly which categories you want to use in QuickBooks for incoming eBay and PayPal data for QuickBooks.

- Map (assign) eBay sales transactions to existing QuickBooks customers and items.

■ Minimize data-entry time with automatic matching of eBay sales transactions to existing customers and items in QuickBooks. Over time, eBay Accounting Assistant gets smarter about matching this data and further reduces your time spent doing data entry.

■ Use QuickBooks' optional "classes" to separate your eBay sales transactions from other types of sales (if supported by your QuickBooks product). For example, you can separate online eBay sales from physical storefront sales or sales from your other websites.

Getting Started with eBay Accounting Assistant

Download and read the Accounting Assistant users guide. It goes into more detail than you will read here. You can find it at

http://download.ebay.com/accounting_assistant/us/Accounting_Assistant_User_Guide.pdf

You should also read the Accounting Assistant FAQs before spending the time and money to set things up because there are limitations to what can and cannot be tracked. This is evolving over time, so bookmark the Assistant's FAQs and refer to them occasionally. You can find them at

http://pages.ebay.com/help/sell/accounting-assistant-faqs.html#8

Your accounting computer must meet the following minimum requirements to run eBay Accounting Assistant:

■ Microsoft Windows 98, Me, 2000, XP, NT

■ 100MHz processor

■ 30MB free hard disk space (100MB for high volume sellers)

■ RAM for Win 98/Me: 64MB (128MB highly recommended)

■ RAM for Win 2000/XP/NT: 128MB (256MB highly recommended)

note eBay Accounting Assistant currently supports only U.S. versions of QuickBooks' products.

Downloading the Accounting Assistant

After reading the PDF and FAQ files, and determining with the help of your accounting pro that eBay Accounting Assistant really is for you, you can download it for free at http://pages.ebay.com/accountingassistant/.

Getting QuickBooks Ready for the Accounting Assistant

If you have not already done so, you will need to set up your QuickBooks product to work with eBay Accounting Assistant.

In QuickBooks, select Edit, Preferences, Integrated Applications, Company Preferences. Then uncheck the option labeled "Don't allow any application to access this company file."

Installing the Accounting Assistant

Run the downloaded installation program as you would any other. Before using eBay Accounting Assistant for the first time, you will be asked to complete a brief, one-time setup wizard. Install eBay Accounting Assistant on the same Internet-connected computer that has your QuickBooks product. Then follow the general steps, reading the screen choices carefully as they are presented to you.

Alternatives and Embellishments

You might want to consider downloading eBay invoice data and PayPal transactions instead of (or in addition to) using the Accounting Assistant. These types of data won't import directly into QuickBooks, but they might give you more detail and flexibility. For example, Figure 12.3 shows part of a PayPal detail download displayed as an Excel worksheet.

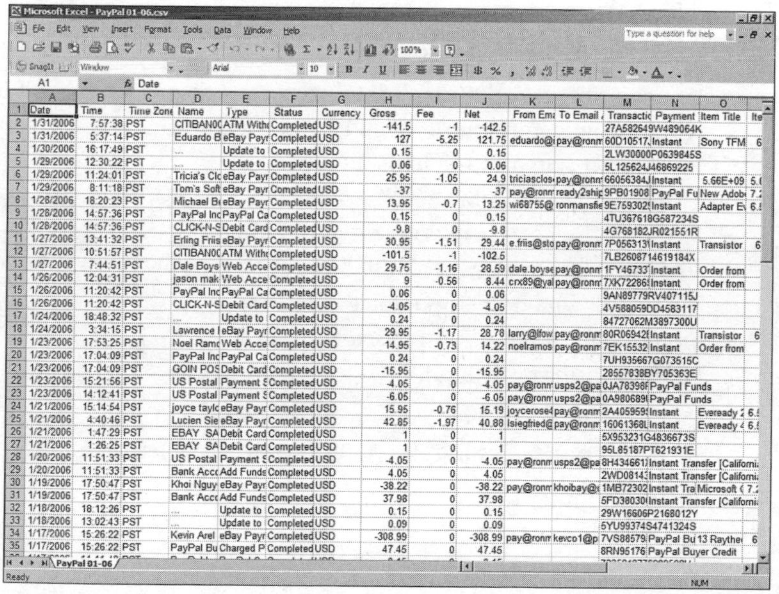

FIGURE 12.3

PayPal details can be downloaded and then used in your own spreadsheets or database programs.

You can download data like this by logging into PayPal and visiting the My Account tab and then clicking the Download My History link. As shown in Figure 12.4, you then specify a date range and file type. File formats include comma-delimited, tab-delimitated, and several Quicken formats. You can also specify the type of data to be downloaded (all activities, payments only, and so on). The data file will be emailed to your PayPal email address of record.

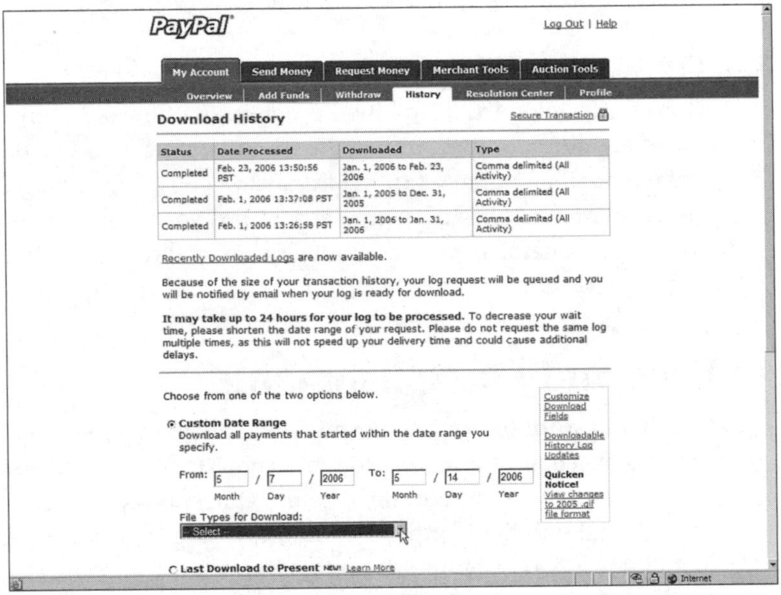

FIGURE 12.4
Download
PayPal history.

Downloading eBay Invoice Data

You can harvest additional data from your downloadable eBay invoice detail reached by logging into My eBay and clicking the Seller Account link in the My Account area of the left-side navigator. This will reveal the My Seller Account Summary page, where you can click either View Invoices or View Account Status to see and download eBay invoice details. Figure 12.5 shows a sample screen prior to beginning the download.

Figure 12.6 shows a typical spreadsheet created by simply opening the resulting eBay invoice detail CSV file with Microsoft Excel.

note Because both the PayPal and eBay data contain auction ID numbers, database designers can match or "relate" them using relational databases.

FIGURE 12.5

Download eBay invoice details.

FIGURE 12.6

View and use eBay invoice details in Microsoft Excel.

High-volume eBay sellers might also want to consider using Developers Tools to gather accounting details. Learn more about the Developers Program and Tools at http://developer.ebay.com/index_html.

13

Shipping

Shipping eBay store items is no more difficult than shipping auction items. In fact, Selling Manager Pro can actually make it even easier to ship all the things you sell on eBay (including non-store items) by telling you when to ship what. It also can help you print invoices, shipping labels, custom documents, and postage if you like.

Shipping with SMP

Selling Manager Pro has a host of features designed to help organize your shipping chores. First and foremost, it can tell you when things have been paid for and are ready to ship, as shown in Figure 13.1. Clicking the Awaiting Shipment link shows you what's been paid for and is ready to go. It will even combine multiple paid items from a single buyer.

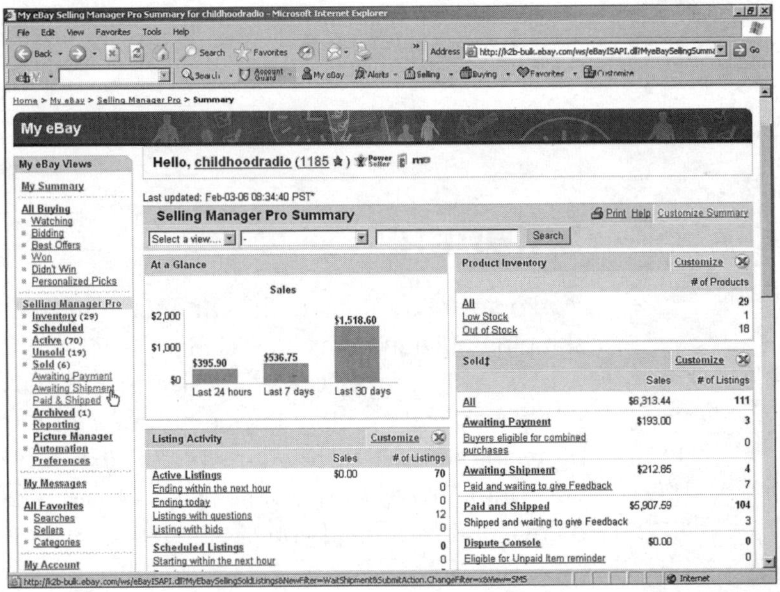

FIGURE 13.1

Click the Awaiting Shipment link to see paid items in SMP.

Clicking the Awaiting Shipment link in your Selling Manager Pro–equipped My eBay page will show you a list of items ready to ship. Figure 13.2 shows an example.

Once you have displayed the ready items, you can either print just address labels or a complete set of shipping documents, including postage you purchase online and customs forms for international shipments. Let's start simply and work up to the more advanced features.

You can choose to work on one shipment or multiple shipments at the same time, and the approach you take will vary with your staffing level, the types of things you sell, and other factors. In the beginning, I suggest you start with one addressee at a time.

note Be sure you are looking at the "All" period when checking the "Paid & waiting to ship" screen. Use the drop-down list to choose All. Shorter periods (such as Last 24 hours) will hide things paid for earlier.

FIGURE 13.2

The Awaiting Shipment page shows paid items that are ready to go.

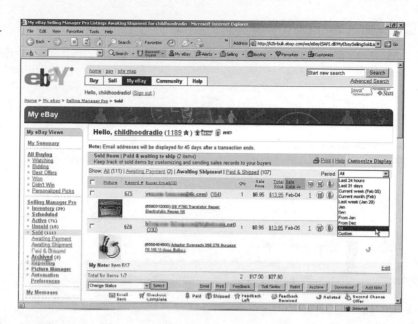

To do this, simply click the box at the left of an item (or group of items going to the same buyer) and then either click the Record # link (675 in Figure 13.2, for example) or click the Print button at the bottom of the Paid & waiting to ship screen.

Either way, you will be taken to a long Sold Listing Sales Record page containing the buyer's ship-to information, the details of the transaction, and the status of the item (typically showing as paid but not shipped at this point). Figure 13.3 shows an example of the middle of this page. Click the Print Invoice button to continue.

The next thing you will see is a screen like the one in Figure 13.4, asking if you would like to print any of the following items:

- Postage
- Carrier-specific shipping labels (USPS, UPS, and so on)
- Generic shipping labels
- Combined labels and invoice/packing slip pages
- Single or multiple address labels
- Invoices for your own recordkeeping
- A store promotional flier (discussed in Chapter 14, "Cross-promoting Your Store on eBay")

FIGURE 13.3

A portion of a
Sold Listing
Sales Record
in SMP.

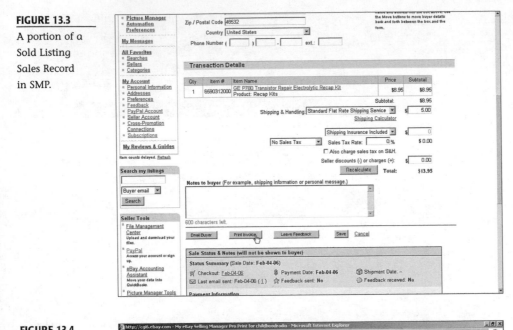

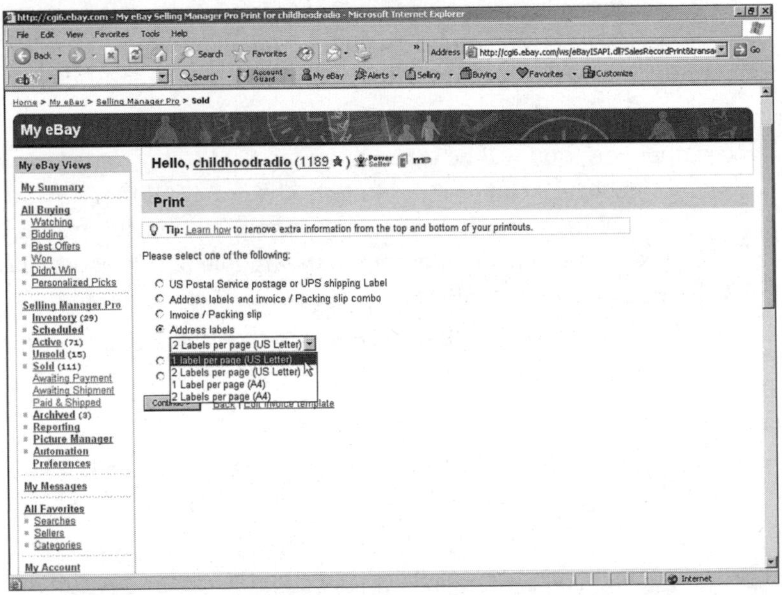

FIGURE 13.4

Shipping paper-
work choices in
Selling Manager
Pro.

Printing Address Labels Alone

The simplest option is to print a plain shipping label. Selling Manager Pro will
use your address as the default origin and will insert the buyer's shipping
address. You get to pick the desired paper size, and what *looks* like single or

multiple copies of labels from a drop-down list, as shown in Figure 13.4. In actuality, the "2 labels per page" choice won't print two labels for the same addressee (for multibox shipments). Instead, this option prints shipping labels for more than one buyer if you have decided to batch your work rather than click on individual record links.

So, unless you are working on multiple buyers simultaneously, pick "1 label per page." These labels are large, and mostly composed of white space. You can get a sense of this from Figure 13.5.

FIGURE 13.5

Labels print either one or two to each 8.5"×11" or A4 sheet. Shipper and recipient addresses are intentionally blurred.

It is possible to purchase 8.5"×5.5" label paper or its European equivalent, or you can buy full-sized sheets and have them cut in half by a printer or in the printing department of many office supply stores if your computer printer will work with these shorter sheet sizes.

note Another option is to use a label printer such as the widely available and popular Eltron/Zebra printers.

Printing an Address Label and Invoice/Packing Slip Combo

The problem with printing out only labels (especially batches of multiple labels for numerous buyers) is that you then need to somehow match the labels up with the winners' items.

A better approach might be to print the address label and invoice/packing slip instead. This makes it easy to pull, pack, and ship accurately. You can fold this paperwork and insert it in a plastic pouch on the outside of the box to serve as the shipping label as well. Figure 13.6 shows an example of a combined label and invoice/packing slip.

FIGURE 13.6

Use the combined shipping label packing slip by folding and placing it in a plastic pouch on the box. Shipper and recipient addresses are intentionally blurred.

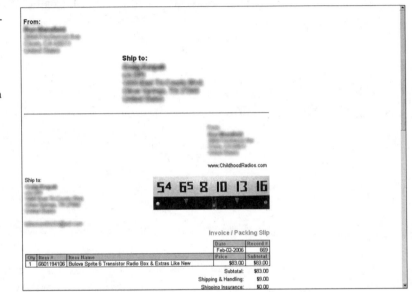

Printing an Invoice/Packing Slip

Another alternative is to print a combination invoice/packing slip with no shipping label. This doesn't work as well in plastic pouches as a shipping label because the Ship To information is on the left of the page. This is best placed inside the box or in an "Invoice Enclosed" pouch.

Printing Invoices for Your Records

If you don't yet work in a paperless office, or if your bookkeeper just wants to see and be able to file "real records," you can print a separate in-house invoice. Alternatively, you can select a quantity of 2 when printing documents like the one in Figure 13.6 and keep one for yourself. It will be quicker to print two copies at once rather than executing the Print command twice.

The advantage of using the "Invoice for your own records" page is that it shows a status box at the bottom. So if you chose to print these invoices, wait to print them until after the items have been shipped, feedback has been left, and so on. Figure 13.7 shows an example.

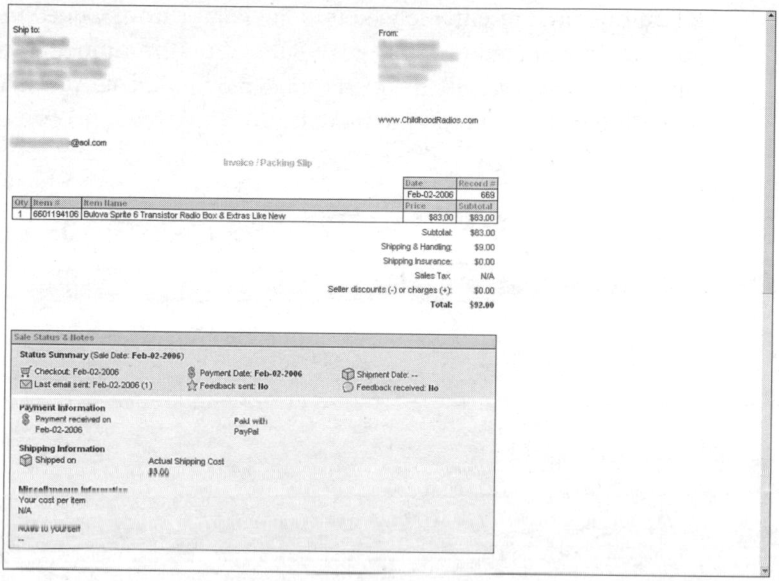

FIGURE 13.7

The "Invoice for your own records" format includes status info. Print an invoice after shipping and leaving feedback. (Shipper and recipient addresses are intentionally blurred.)

Automating USPS and UPS Labels with PayPal

Recently PayPal, UPS, and the U.S. Postal Service have teamed up to make it possible to, as mentioned earlier, purchase online postage from the post office or shipping services from UPS, pay for them from your PayPal account, and then print the labels, postage, and even customs forms from your computer.

There is only one drawback. If you have an employee doing your shipping, this person will need to know your PayPal login information because one must log into PayPal to use these services.

If that doesn't bother you, then keep reading this section. If it does bother you, you might want to skip on down to the "Third-party Shipping Solutions" section.

> **note** To use any of the PayPal shipping features, you need to have a current version of Java installed and not completely block pop-ups in your browser. If you can't see labels on your display when it's time to print, check to be sure Java is installed and pop-ups are not blocked.

Printing Domestic USPS Mail Labels with Postage

After selecting an item or items to ship, choosing the "US Postal Service postage or UPS shipping label" choice from the Print screen (shown earlier in Figure 13.4) gets you started.

If you have not recently logged into PayPal, or have logged in but timed out, you will be required to log into PayPal before continuing. Once logged in, you will see a long page titled "U.S. Postal Service – Create Your Shipping Label." A portion of it is reproduced in Figure 13.8.

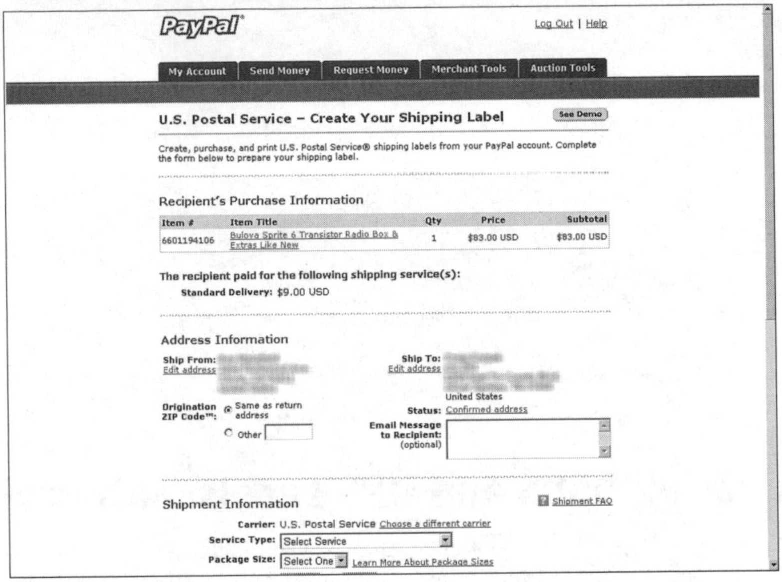

FIGURE 13.8

Part of the PayPal USPS label printing page. (Shipper and recipient addresses are intentionally blurred.)

Package and Address Particulars

Scroll through the page carefully, selecting or confirming the necessary options, because sometimes this feature tends to "forget" earlier settings. For example, the radio button for Origination ZIP Code ("Same as return address") is normally checked, but sometimes it might be unchecked and will need to be clicked again.

Also, the Ship To information should be correctly and automatically filled in for you, but it's good to glance at it just in case.

Scroll down, if necessary, and pick a service type from the drop-down list (Priority, Media Rate, and so on). Figure 13.9 shows Priority Mail as the specified service.

Next, choose the appropriate package size and type from the drop-down list. Flat Rate Box is selected in Figure 13.9.

note For international shipments (covered later in this chapter), get in the habit of entering the exact weight, and remember the exact weight you tell PayPal at this point in the process, because the postal weight and customs form weights must match or things will grind to a halt at the customs form stage.

FIGURE 13.9

Entering package specifics before label printing.

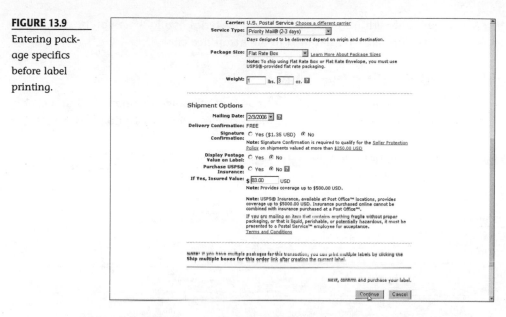

Now enter the box weight. You can either enter exact pounds and ounces, as shown in Figure 13.9, or simply round up to the next-highest pound (which would be 2 pounds in Figure 13.9) because that's what the Post Office will do anyway when charging you.

Signature Confirmation

If you want signature confirmation (required for the Seller Protection program for items costing more than $250), check the appropriate button, which will cost you extra.

Showing/Hiding Postage Amounts (Stealth Printing)

Next you can choose whether to either print the postage amount on the label. Printing labels without the dollar amount showing is also known as *stealth printing*, a technique used by sellers who mark up shipping to make the fact less obvious to buyers. Figure 13.9 shows stealth printing enabled. Postage costs will not print.

USPS Insurance

The radio button below the Display Postage Value on Label button in Figure 13.9 is used to purchase insurance. There are a ton of rules and regulations, as well as exceptions, where insurance is concerned, and you are encouraged to read and perhaps print out the help material available to you by clicking the question mark button next to the insurance choice.

Confirming and Printing the Label

Scroll down until you see the Continue button shown in Figure 13.9 and click it. You should see a page similar to the one in Figure 13.10 titled "U.S. Postal Service – Confirm and Purchase Your Shipping Label." If you have waited too long you might need to log back into PayPal and reenter the information, so it's a good idea to keep things moving once you start the label-printing process.

FIGURE 13.10

Confirming and paying for label printing.

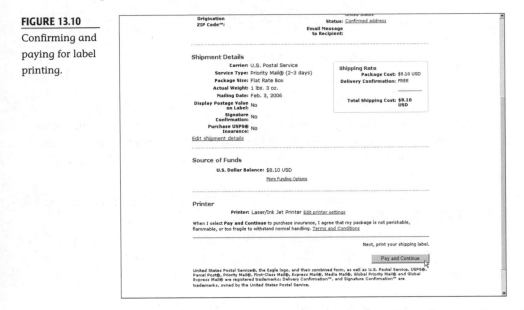

Double-check the facts on this long screen because you are about to spend some money. If all is well, click the Pay and Continue button. You should see a screen like the one shown in Figure 13.11, complete with a sample label.

If you don't see the label window or see the window but there's no label in it, you might see a screen similar to Figure 13.12. Click the "Label did not appear" choice near the bottom of the page. If it still doesn't appear, check your Java version and pop-up blocking options.

FIGURE 13.11

A label preview. (Shipper and recipient addresses are intentionally blurred.)

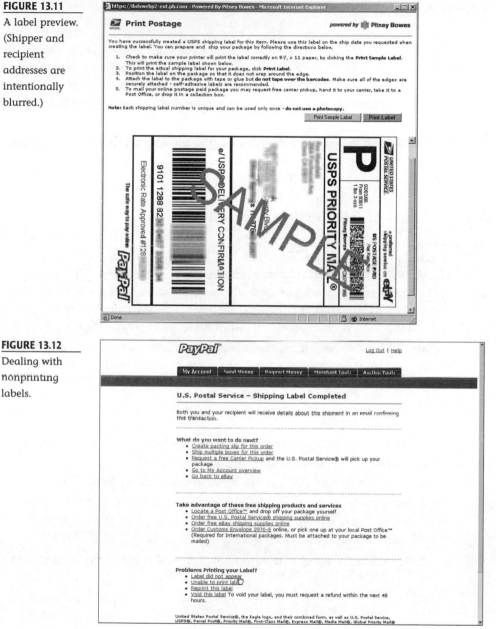

FIGURE 13.12

Dealing with nonprinting labels.

Print a Sample First!

When first setting up your printer to print labels, or if you use more than one printer to print different types of labels, click the Print Sample Label button and check the results before clicking Print Label. Many things can go wrong with label printing, and it's best to get the setup details right before spending money on incorrectly printed labels. It's not impossible to get refunds, but it is time consuming.

Common printing problems include choosing the wrong printer, wrong page (paper) size, incorrect orientation, and so on. You'll be surprised at how many ways there are to screw up postage label printing!

Reprinting a Label or Requesting a Refund

If you visit your PayPal account and see that you have been charged for labels that did not print, it is possible either to attempt to reprint them or request a refund. You must request refunds within 48 hours of the printing problem, and you will not receive an immediate credit, so again, preview label printing when in doubt, and practice on inexpensive shipments. Once you get set up right, this can be a great timesaver, but it takes some effort at first.

Figure 13.13 shows part of the PayPal screen that you can use to request a credit or attempt to reprint the label. Get there by using the Reprint link mentioned earlier if you spot the problem right away, or you can follow these steps:

1. Log into PayPal.

2. Review transactions (Recent Activities), looking for labels you need to reprint or void (see Figure 13.14).

3. Click the relevant Details link in the recent Activity Report.

4. When you see the transaction details and confirm that you have the correct item, scroll down to the bottom of the page. You should see something like the screen back in Figure 13.13.

5. Click Reprint Label to try again or click Void Label to request a refund.

FIGURE 13.13

Reprinting or voiding a label in PayPal. (Shipper and recipient addresses are intentionally blurred.)

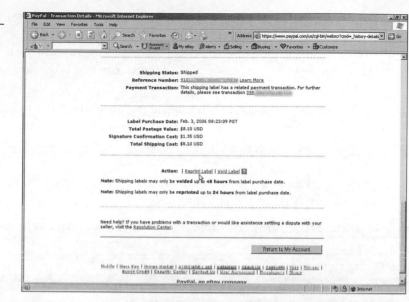

FIGURE 13.14

Review recent PayPal transactions and click the corresponding Details button to start the reprint or refund process. (Shipper and recipient addresses are intentionally blurred.)

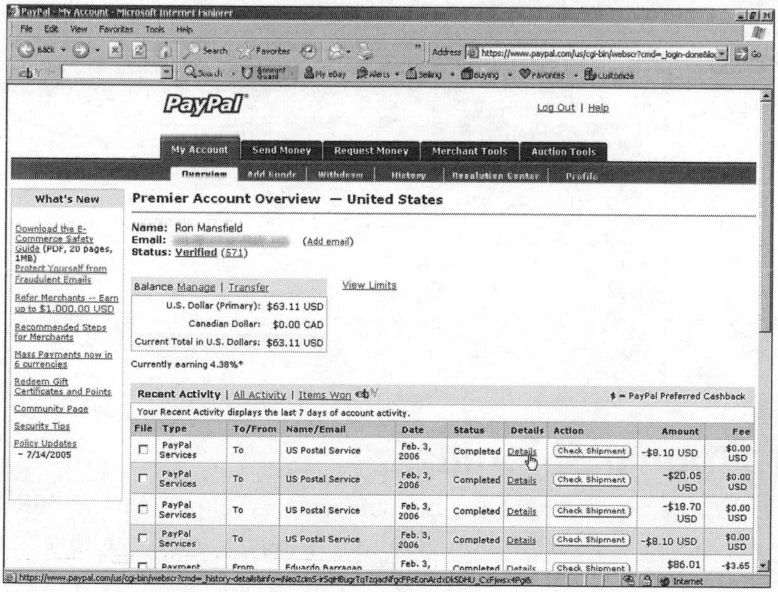

Confirming/Changing Shipped Status

Once PayPal believes a label has been printed, it instructs Selling Manager Pro to mark the item as shipped, inserting the current date, time, and other details.

You can see recently shipped items (or more accurately, items for which PayPal believes labels have been printed) by clicking the Paid & Shipped link in the left navigation area of Selling Manager Pro. You will see a screen similar to Figure 13.15. Notice the little shipped icon (the box) near the right of the item.

If the item has in fact *not* been shipped (because you had a problem printing the label, for example), you can change the status of this item back to "paid" by selecting the item (click the select box at the left of the item) and visiting the Change Status drop-down to choose Paid.

This should move the item back to Awaiting Shipment status, but it will not automatically request a refund for you.

FIGURE 13.15

The Paid & Shipped page in Selling Manager Pro. (Shipper and recipient addresses are intentionally blurred.)

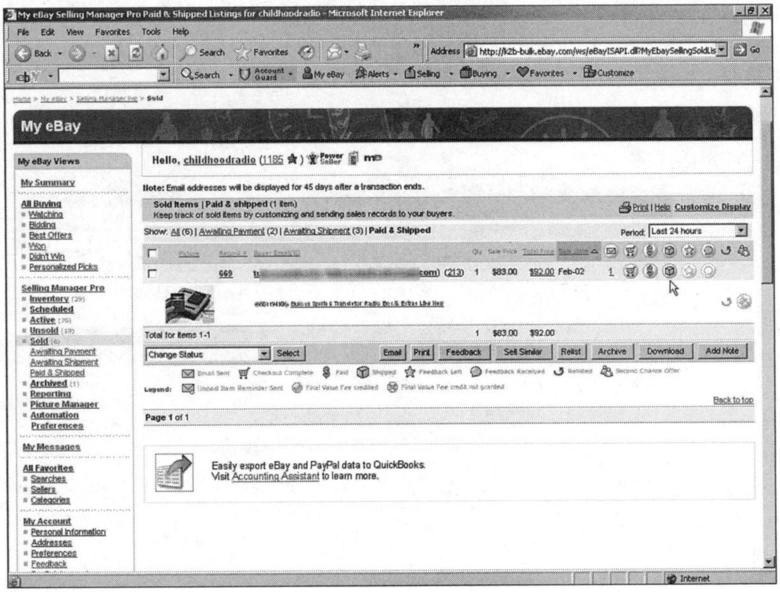

International Shipping

The integrated PayPal shipping features simplify international shipping and customs form printing significantly (again, after you have the printing options set up properly).

When a winner has an international shipping address, the screens change slightly and customs paperwork printing becomes part of the automated process. Things start out looking pretty familiar, as you can see in Figure 13.16.

FIGURE 13.16

Beginning an international shipment.

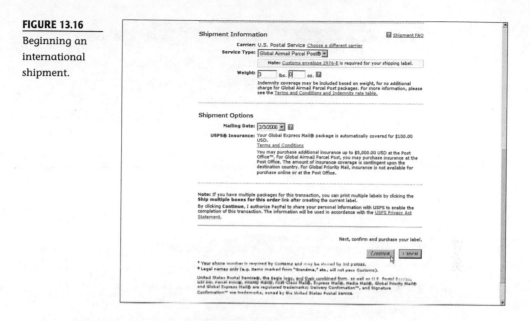

Entering International Shipping Details

Follow these steps for shipping a package internationally via PayPal:

1. Confirm that the item and destination address details look right.

2. You might need to click the Origination ZIP Code ("Same as return address") button. PayPal sometimes forgets.

3. You are asked to enter the recipient's phone number, which you will almost never have at hand. You *must* enter a phone number, and I have found that using your own (American) number keeps the beast happy.

4. Scroll down if necessary and select the correct service type (Global Priority Mail or whatever).

5. Enter the shipping weight and remember what you have entered for later use in the Customs Forms screens.

6. Change the shipping date if you won't be shipping today.

7. Click Continue.

If you have been a good boy or girl, you will see a review screen like the one in Figure 13.17. Otherwise, go back and correct your misdeed. It's probably something simple such as the origin ZIP code or phone number.

FIGURE 13.17
Review, ponder,
and perhaps
agree.

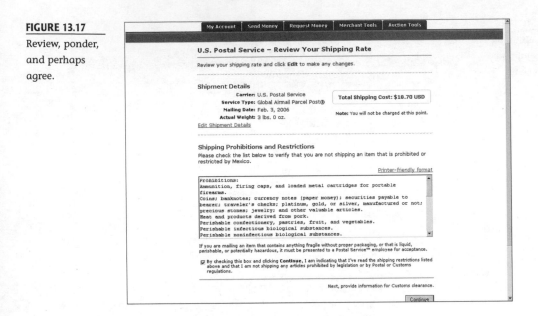

Review the Shipping Rates and Agree (or Don't)

You will see the proposed shipping costs displayed at the top of a long page. If they seem in line, review the Shipping Prohibitions and Restrictions, and if you are in compliance, click the check box to so affirm. Then click Continue. This will take you to the Customs Forms screens. The first one is shown in Figure 13.18.

Creating Customs Documents

Begin by declaring the box contents "Other" using the drop-down and then enter an accurate, reasonably specific description. For example "How-to video" is probably better than simply "DVD" (see Figure 13.18).

You can enter optional details on this screen if you like, such as license and certificate numbers, invoice numbers, and comments, or you can simply bypass them by clicking Continue.

Entering International Customs Package Information

Next you want to enter the description, quantity value, weight, and country of origin information, as illustrated in Figure 13.19.

FIGURE 13.18
Describe the contents fairly specifically.

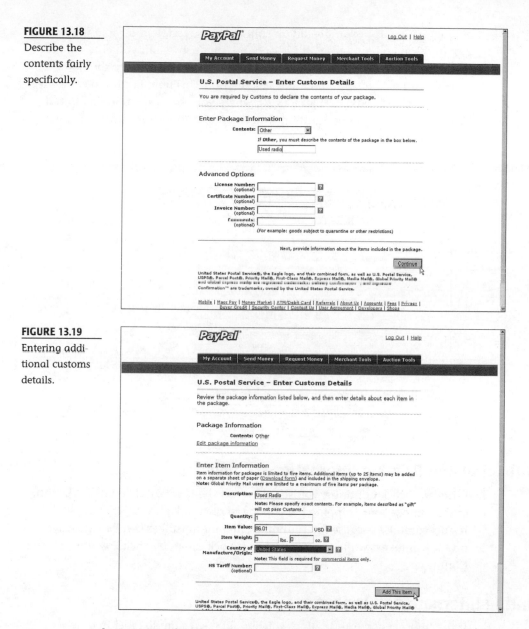

As mentioned earlier, the customs weight and the weight entered back in Figure 13.16 need to agree, so be careful here.

Because it is possible to add multiple items to one customs report, the combined weight of each item entered separately must match the total weight

FIGURE 13.19
Entering additional customs details.

entered earlier. For example, if you ship the same recipient a radio weighing 2 pounds and a battery weighing 1 pound, the first weight you entered, back in Figure 13.16, would be 3 pounds, and the radio weight entry should be 2 pounds and the battery 1 pound. Click the Add This Item button to continue. You will see a screen like Figure 13.20, where you can either add additional items to your customs declaration with the Add More Items button or click Continue if you are ready to ship.

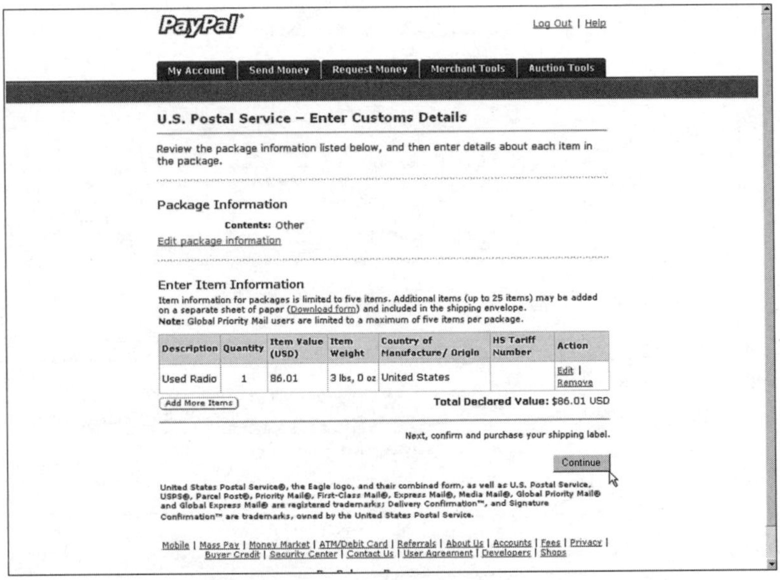

FIGURE 13.20

Add additional customs items or click Continue.

Confirming and Printing International Labels

When you click Continue, you should reach the U.S. Postal Service – Confirm and Purchase Your Shipping Label page, shown in Figure 13.21. Review the results carefully because international shipping mistakes can be expensive, and it will take a while to get your funds back after you click Pay and Continue.

Printing International Postage

If the Internet gods are smiling, you should see a sample label in a newly appearing Print Postage window, similar to the one in Figure 13.22.

Because you will be printing customs forms on 8.5"×11" paper, you will want to be sure you have selected a laser or inkjet printer, not a label printer. Do this with the Select Target Printer button (see Figure 13.22) and print a sample label whenever in doubt.

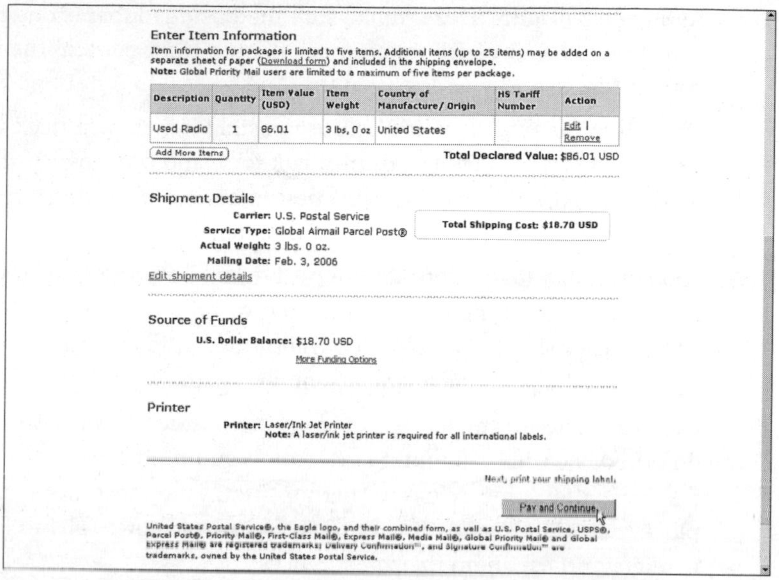

FIGURE 13.21

Review carefully. International printing mistakes can be costly.

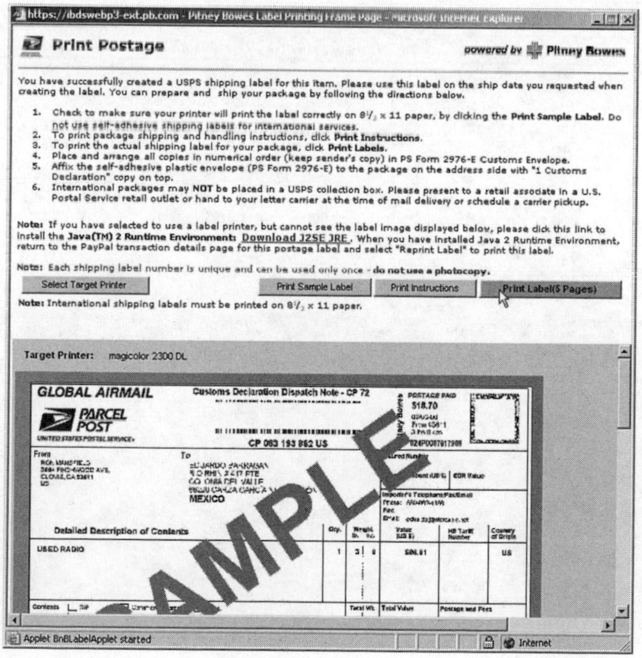

FIGURE 13.22

Clicking "Print Label (5 Pages)" prints postage and customs forms. (Shipper and recipient addresses are intentionally blurred.)

Once the postage label and customs forms print, cut them, sign and date them, and put them in a plastic pouch (USPS Form 2976-E, available for free from the post office).

As shown in Figure 13.23, make sure the postage label is on top. It's the one with the odd "bar code" square near the top-right corner. The last customs copy is yours, and you can keep it.

Don't seal the plastic pouch because postal workers will need to "round date-stamp" the forms. (That's postal-speak for using a rubber stamp that prints today's date in a little circle.) It is best to have a post office employee round-date your copy, but this is not a requirement.

You can either take international packages to a post office or official post office retailer and then hand them to a willing human or give them to your letter carrier. Do not simply drop international items into a mail box. Don't waltz into the post office, drop them on a counter, and then bolt.

Do mail items on the date printed on the postage label and customs forms. To do otherwise will be tempting fate, and you might find the item back on your doorstep after some delay—or perhaps not. The post office is a mysterious place, and things work differently from town to town. Get to know the local workers and ask them their preferences.

FIGURE 13.23

Put the postage page on top. Keep one customs form for yourself.

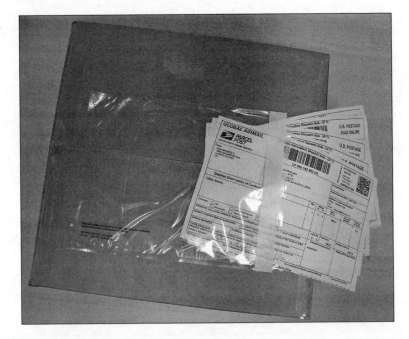

Shipping Via UPS Using PayPal

If you have offered UPS shipping in a listing and a buyer selects it, you can print UPS labels in nearly the same way you print USPS labels. As you can see in Figure 13.24, UPS will be a shipping service choice.

FIGURE 13.24

UPS choices appear if offered.

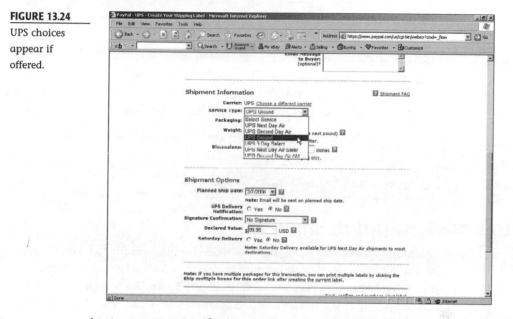

Again, you can specify signature confirmation if you like, and Saturday delivery is an option. You need to enter package type, weight, and usually dimensions. From here on things will remind you of USPS printing.

Third-party Shipping Solutions

There are a number of third-party shipping solutions, all of them with different features and advantages, but none of them as tied into Selling Manager Pro as the PayPal system.

You might want to check out Stamps.com, endicia, and the online systems offered by FedEx, UPS, and other carriers.

If you use third-party services, remember to revisit the item details, mark the items as shipped, and enter the date and actual costs, as shown in Figure 13.25. Don't forget to click Save after entering the information.

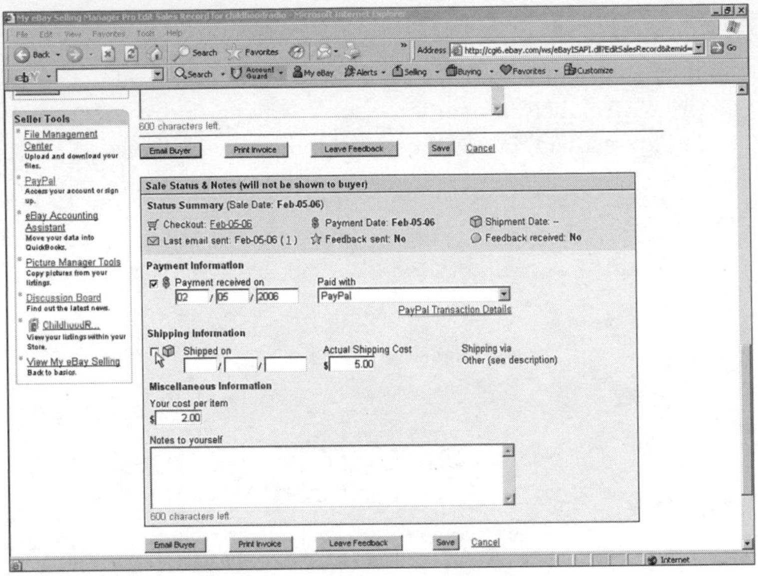

FIGURE 13.25

Manually enter and save Stamps.com and other third-party shipping information.

Automated Shipping Emails

Selling Manager Pro will automatically send shipping emails to buyers if you select the option. Visit the Automation Preferences screen from the navigation area of Selling Manager Pro, as shown in Figure 13.26. Automated shipping emails are probably a good idea unless you want to personalize each one for some reason.

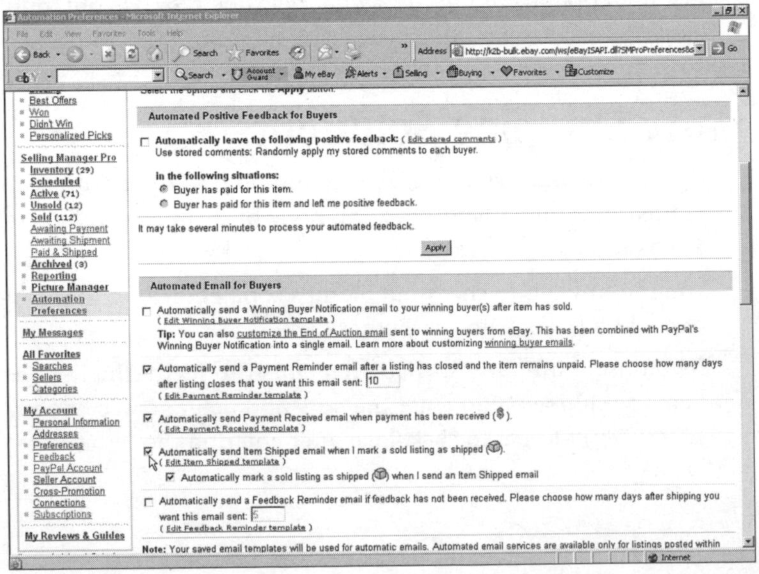

FIGURE 13.26

Selecting automatic shipping notification emails in Automation preferences.

Part III

Promoting Your Store

14

Cross-promoting Your Store on eBay

Cross-promoting yourself and your items on eBay is an important way to get noticed, and to keep shoppers looking at your items rather than your competitors'. This is particularly true for store owners. Visitors browsing auctions need to find your store items.

By the same token, you want people who find your store items from outside of eBay to also spend time looking at your current auctions and non-store Buy It Now items. Fortunately, eBay is providing a growing number of tools to help with driving people to and from your eBay store, auctions, and Buy It Now items.

Promotional Boxes in Active Listings

Figure 14.1 shows an example of a cross-promotional box at the bottom of an auction listing. This box encourages shoppers to look at two other auctions currently running (the radios on either end), an active Buy It Now listing (the signal generator), and a store item (that Heathkit tuner).

FIGURE 14.1

Cross-promotion boxes in listings can keep shoppers looking at your items.

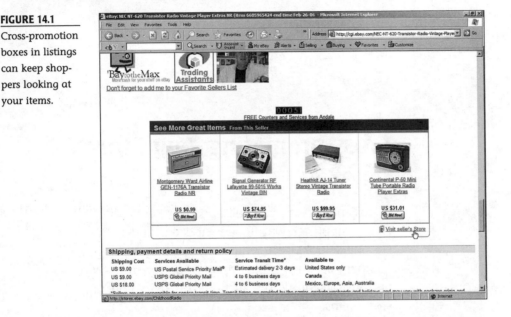

Here are some of the types of cross-promotional links you can create:

- Cross-promotional boxes in listings
- Cross-promotional links in listings
- Promotional boxes on store pages
- Promotional links to and from your About Me page
- "Add me to your favorite sellers" links
- Promotional links for bidders
- Promotional links for winners
- Cross-promotional connections with other seller IDs (yours or others)

These are all items likely to be of interest to vintage electronics hobbyists. If your eBay selling is aimed at a narrow audience such as this, just about any item you are selling will be of interest to people looking at your listings, and eBay can be told to randomly generate the contents of your cross-promotional boxes. For example, the next time I looked at that same listing, the promotional box shown in Figure 14.2 was generated.

FIGURE 14.2

Cross-promotion boxes can deliver random results like these.

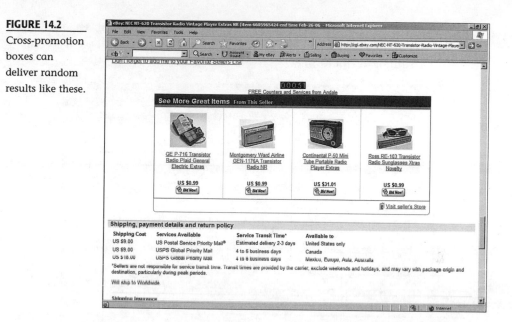

It is also possible to specify exactly which items will be displayed in a promo box when a shopper visits a particular listing. For example, if I had a lot of Heathkit gear for sale, I could specify that the promotional box in the Heathkit Tuner listing should show only Heathkit items. If in my store I sell cables that go with a piece of test equipment, or batteries for a particular radio being auctioned, I can elect to show those related items whenever a shopper lands on a particular listing, or bids on or wins an item that could use them.

This ability to specify what gets promoted is really helpful if you sell diverse merchandise aimed at multiple audiences. For example, it would be much more productive to show men's shoes to shoppers looking at men's shoes, and women's shoes to people looking at listings for women's shoes, than to just randomly cross-promote men's and women's shoes, or shoes and Foreman grills, or whatever.

Creating Cross-promotion Boxes in Listings

Follow these steps to specify cross-promotions in listings:

1. Begin by logging into My eBay.
2. Choose Manage My Store from the left navigation area.
3. Choose the Default Cross-Promotions link near the bottom of the left navigation area.

4. If you have never created any cross-promotions, you will see a screen similar to Figure 14.3. If cross-promotions exist, you will see a screen similar to Figure 14.6.

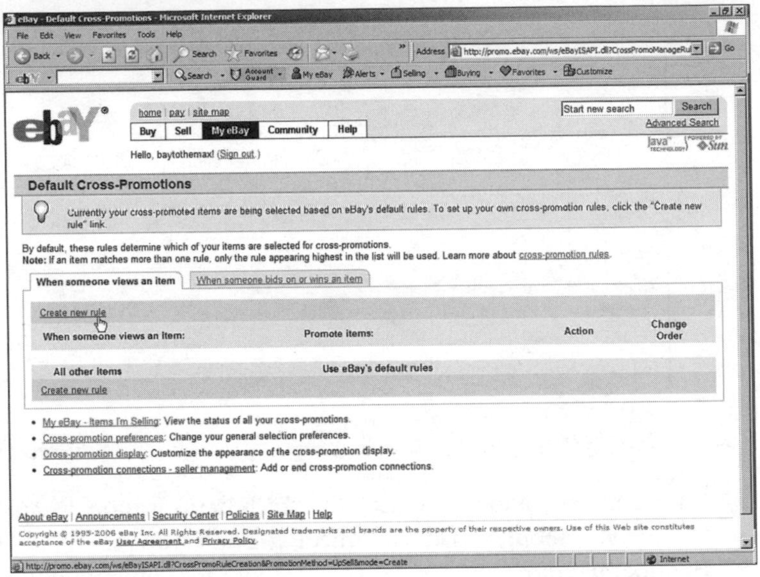

FIGURE 14.3

Setting up new cross-promotion rules.

5. Click the "Create new rule" link and you will see a page similar to Figure 14.4. It contains two drop-down lists. Both drop-downs show the names of store categories you have set up. The top list determines when the rule will be used. For example, if someone views a listing that is in your store's Sports-related category—a tennis racquet, let's say, or running shoes—you can create a rule that engages when the visitor sees listings of items in the Sports-related category. Do this by choosing the desired category from the top list, as shown in Figure 14.4.

tip This works the easiest in a focused store where all the products are obviously of interest to most shoppers. However, if you also sell televisions and answering machines in your store's Consumer Electronics category, people looking for running shoes will see TVs if you set up rules and categories this way.

Sometimes these diversions are a good thing, sometimes not. It's up to you to pick the best marketing strategy for your store. When you shop in local stores, notice how retailers put such things as cartoon DVDs as the end of children's clothing aisles or at checkout counters. Things need not be in the same category to be of interest to a particular shopper. "Mommy! Mommy! SpongeBob SquarePants!"

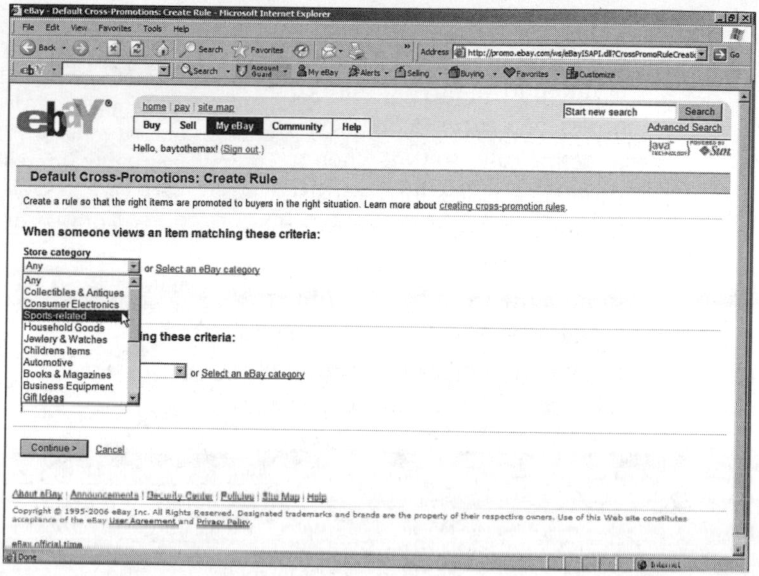

FIGURE 14.4

Specify when you want the rule to be used.

6. You tell eBay what types of items you want to cross-promote when the rule is used. Suppose, for example, you also sell electronic pedometers and MP3 players in a store category you call Consumer Electronics. By choosing that category in the second list, you tell eBay to cross-promote other items of yours from the Consumer Electronics category. Figure 14.5 illustrates this.

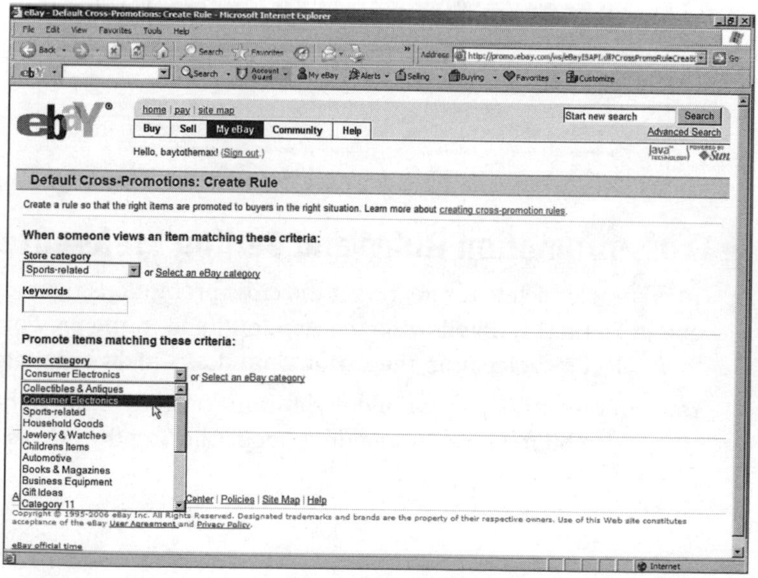

FIGURE 14.5

The second list determines which items shoppers will see in cross-promotion boxes.

7. Continue setting up as many cross-promotional rules as you like. In addition to specifying store categories, you can use title keywords to define rules so that when a shopper searches for "Transistor Radio" in titles, that shopper then can be directed to your items containing the word *battery* in their title, and so on. As you create and save rules, they will appear in a list like the one in Figure 14.6.

> **tip**
> You can have the same or different rules applied when a person views an item and bids or wins, or you can apply different rules for bidders and winners. Click the "When someone bids on or wins an item" link shown in Figure 14.6 to create different rules for bidders and winners.

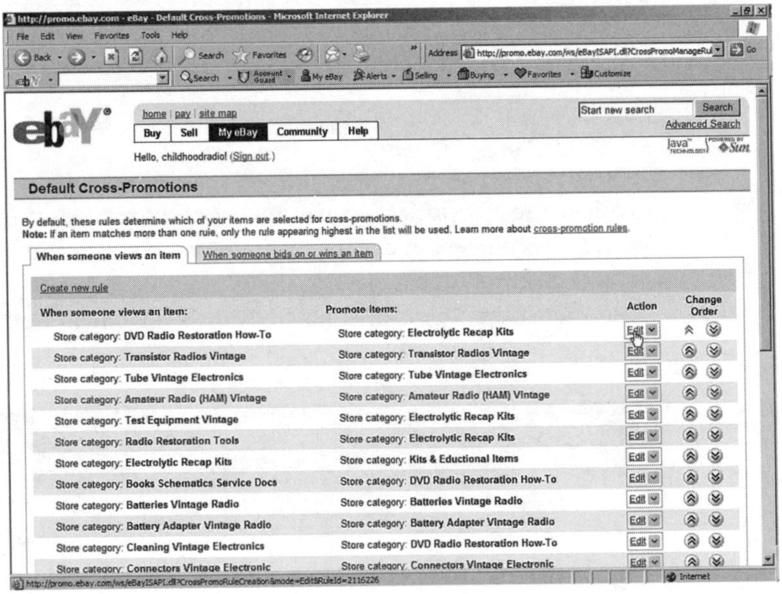

FIGURE 14.6

Saved rules are displayed in a list.

Changing Cross-promotion Rules and Setting Preferences

To change or delete a rule, revisit the cross-promotions page (similar to the one in Figure 14.6), following the steps outlined in the previous section, and then select a choice from the Action drop-down—Edit or Delete.

You can also specify when and if you want to cross-promote by visiting the "Participation in Cross-Promotions" page. Clicking the "Cross-promotion preferences" link at the bottom of the Default Cross-Promotions screen (Figure 14.6) displays a screen similar to Figure 14.7.

From here, you can turn cross-promotions on and off, determine what selling formats are displayed (Store items, BIN, and so on), determine sorting rules, and more.

Manually Specifying Cross-promotions for Items

To manually specify cross-promotion rules for a particular item, open the listing itself and click the "Change your cross-promotion items" link near the top of the listing, as shown in Figure 14.8.

caution If an item matches more than one rule, the rule appearing highest in the list will be used. For example, if the rules in Figure 14.6 were in place and a shopper searched for "Transistor Radio DVD," the first rule, DVD Radio Restoration How-To, would apply. If you'd like to change the order of the rules on your list, use the arrow buttons to move your rules up and down.

Your default cross-promotion rules always apply, unless you've manually selected specific items and changed the rules for them, which is discussed in the next section.

FIGURE 14.7
Changing cross-promotion preferences.

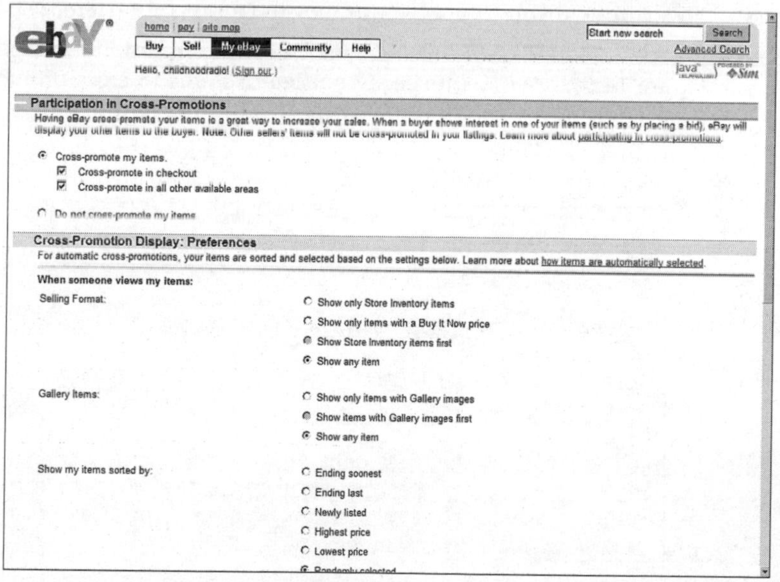

FIGURE 14.8

Changing cross-
promotion
preferences for
specific listings.

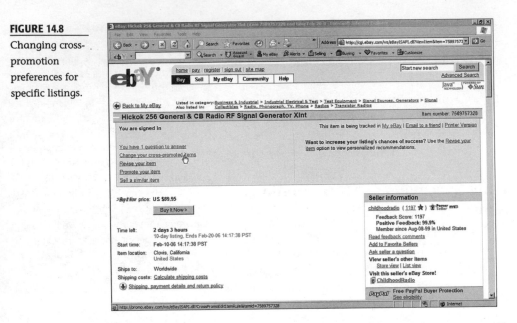

This will lead you to a screen similar to Figure 14.9. Here, you can specify a
different store category by clicking "Change criteria for this item" (shown in
Figure 14.9), or you can specify particular items to cross-promote and specify
their order in the promotion box by clicking the "Change to manual selection" link (see Figure 14.9) to reveal a screen like the one in Figure 14.10.

FIGURE 14.9

Changing the
store category
being cross-
promoted.

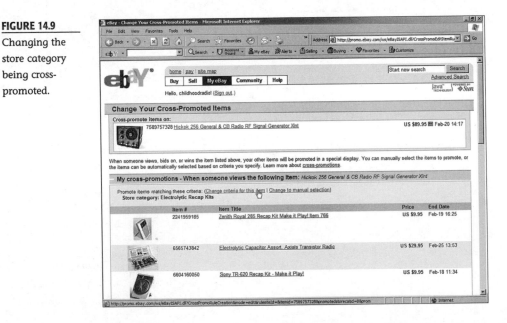

FIGURE 14.10

Choose specific items to promote and arrange their order in the promo box.

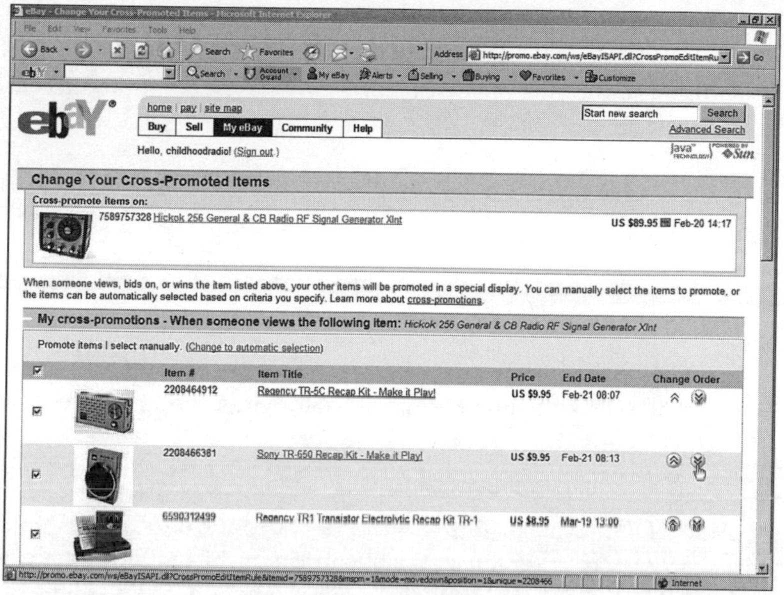

Promotional Boxes in Store Pages

Another important tool is the promotion box feature set that lets you place promotional boxes on *store pages*. Store page boxes come in a variety of shapes and sizes, and can be placed in different locations. They can accomplish a variety of tasks:

- Highlighting important items you want everyone to notice
- Announcing sales, special offers, and so on
- Making it easier for folks to navigate your store
- Keep shoppers looking at your auctions and other live listings

Cross-promotion Appearance Options

There are a number of promotion box options, and they fall into the following broad categories:

- Box location
- Box size
- Box type
- Box name
- Box colors

> **note** These options seem to be evolving over time, so it's a good idea to check back into the cross-promotions setup area occasionally to see if there are new tricks you can play.

Let's set up and modify some promotional boxes. You can use predefined box defaults or roll your own. We'll start out easy. Be sure you have some items listed so that the preview features will have actual products to display.

Quick-and-Dirty Predesigned Store Promotional Box Setup

If ease is your thing, you might want to try eBay's predesigned promotional box. To use it, follow these steps:

1. Visit My eBay.

2. Click the link Manage My Store (not the Cross-Promotion Connections link).

3. Click Promotion Boxes.

4. Click the "guided setup" link, as shown in Figure 14.11. You will see a screen similar to the one in Figure 14.12, with the default settings and their effects displayed. Four promotion boxes will be displayed—two on top and two in the left navigation area. The top-left box (Position 1) will display new arrivals. The top-right box (Position 2) defaults to auctions ending soon. The top box in the left navigation area (Position 3) will show your shipping and payment policies, and the bottom box in the left navigation area (Position 4) you can define or chose not to use. You will learn how to define and alter this and the other boxes in the next section.

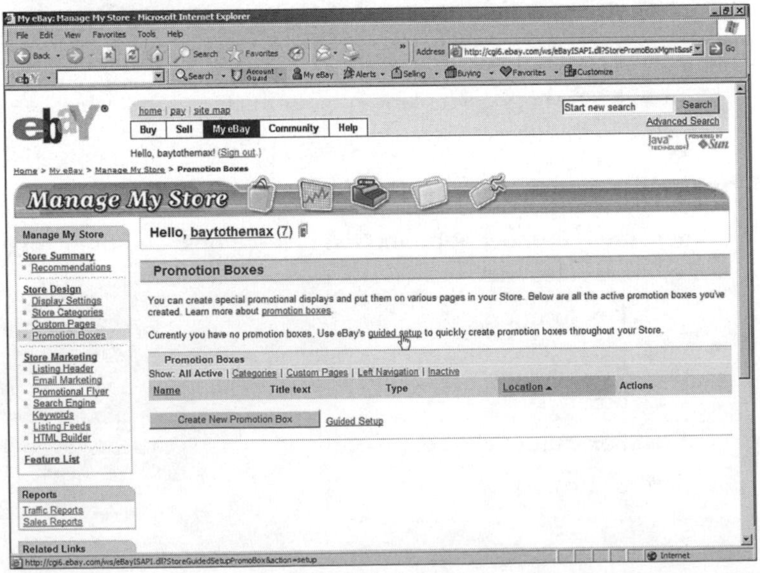

FIGURE 14.11
The "guided setup" link gets you started with default settings you can later change.

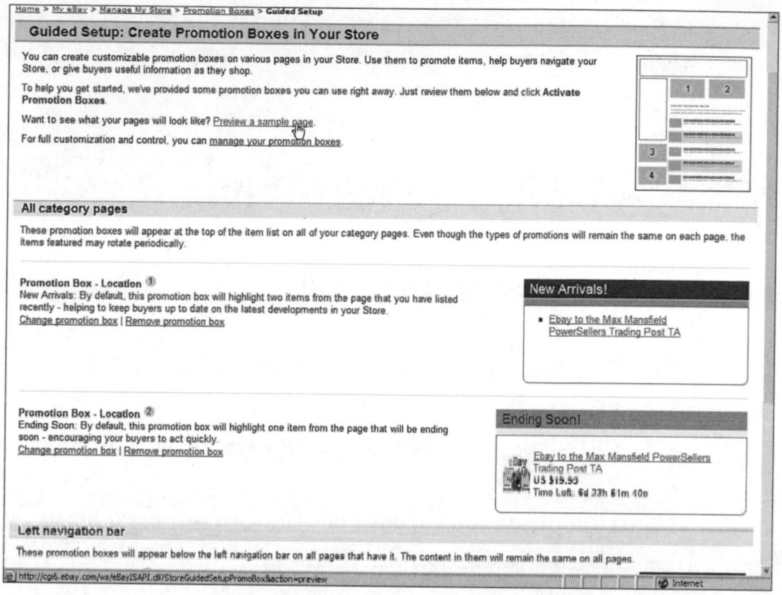

FIGURE 14.12

You can preview and alter promotion box settings from here.

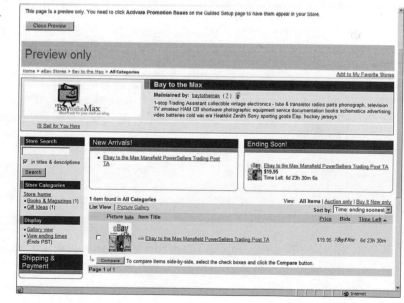

5. To preview the default settings, click the "preview a sample" link. This will open a new window containing a sample listing using your current promotion box settings, as shown in Figure 14.13.

FIGURE 14.13

Previewing your box settings. Don't forget to save them if you like them.

6. If you are happy with what you see in the preview, click the Activate Promotion Boxes button at the bottom of Guided Setup screen shown in Figure 14.12.

Controlling/Modifying Cross-Promotions

Sooner or later you will want to fine-tune your promotion boxes. Begin by revisiting the Manage My Store page.

1. Visit My eBay.

2. Click the link Manage My Store (not the Cross-Promotion Connections link).

3. Click Promotion Boxes. You will see the current box settings, as shown in Figure 14.14.

4. Make and preview your decisions from here (details in a moment).

5. Save your changes.

FIGURE 14.14

Customizing promotion boxes.

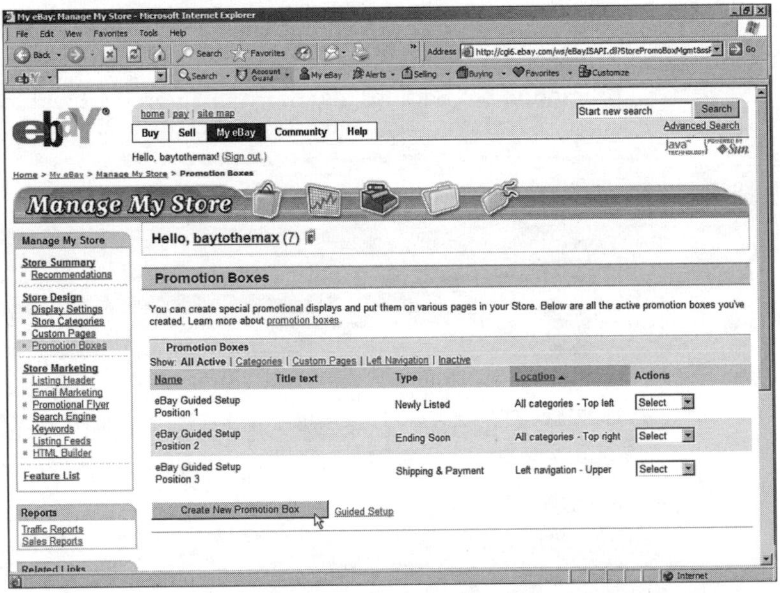

At the top of your listings, you can place two promotion boxes side by side, or you can specify one bigger box. You can also create one or two boxes in the left navigation area.

Promotion Box Sizes

The following sizes are possible:

- **Top left or right areas**—Each can be 275×85 pixels, or 120 characters wide. Dual boxes without borders can be 280×115 pixels, or 140 characters wide.

- **Single box**—If you prefer a single box along the top, it can be 575×85 pixels with a border (or 215 characters wide) or 580×115 pixels with no border (or 300 characters wide).

- **Bordered and borderless left navigation area boxes**—Each can be 170 pixels wide by any height.

Promotion Box Contents

Boxes can have a variety of contents and purposes, including the following:

- **Generic boxes**—Generic boxes show either a listing link with a thumbnail photo or just a box with text-only links to two listings. You can specify the listings manually or have the system select and update them automatically based on criteria you specify.

- **Custom text/HTML**—Custom text/HTML boxes let you include simple text or your own HTML. The recommended size and character limits vary by location.

- **Custom links**—Custom links give buyers alternative ways of finding items in your store. Custom links can point to a store category, a custom page within your store, another on-eBay web page, or a page of custom search results.

- **Graphics**—You can include clickable graphics or pictures that provide access to other pages. Choose from predesigned graphics or provide your own. eBay automatically resizes graphics to fit the boxes. Left navigation bar images should be 170 pixels wide, but can be any length. Dual top box images should be 280×115 pixels each. A single top box image should measure 580×115 pixels.

- **Newly Listed!**—You can display the titles of recent listings according to a time range you define.

- **Ending Soon!**—These boxes can feature a single listing (with a picture and title) that is ending within a specified time range. They provide a great "call to action" and encourage buyers to act now.

- **Shipping and payment information**—You can display information about shipping and payment. By default, the box uses the text from your settings on the Sell Your Item page. Any changes that you make in the promotion box will not change your Sell Your Item settings. It's a good idea to have them match. You don't want to offer combined shipping one place and not in the other, for example.

- **Item showcases**—Item showcases employ a larger picture format from the Item Showcase to highlight as many as four specific listings you define. Otherwise, eBay picks listings according to your rules. This promotion box type cannot be used as the left navigation bar.

- **Store newsletter signup box**—You can promote your email marketing newsletters to buyers. Buyers will be able to click a Sign Up button and subscribe to your newsletters. Newsletters are discussed in Chapter 15, "More Promotional Help from eBay."

Creating a Custom Promotion Box

Choose the area you want to modify by clicking the associated "Show" link. For example, in Figure 14.14, we are looking at the promotion boxes for all active listings. Currently only three are defined. New Arrivals! (a.k.a. Newly Listed!) will show in Position 1 (the top-left box in the listing). The Ending Soon! box will be in the top-right position, and Shipping and Payment shows in Position 3, the uppermost box in the navigation area.

We can edit, duplicate, or remove boxes using the drop-down menus at the right of each existing box, or create up to a total of four boxes using the Create New Promotion Box button shown in Figure 14.14.

Suppose we want a new box. Clicking the Create New Promotion Box button will reveal a screen similar to Figure 14.15.

We can specify an eBay-provided box—Newly Listed, Ending Soon, and so on—or create our own using custom text, HTML, or graphics.

Suppose we want to create a promotion box containing a link that sends people to one of my other stores, childhoodradio, as well as another link to my Trading Assistant Directory page, and a third link to my feedback page. By selecting Custom Links and scrolling down, we will find the specific tools needed to create this type of promotion box (in this case a "links" box). Figure 14.16 illustrates this area of the screen and the associated entries I have made. By refreshing the screen as you work, you can see how the box will look.

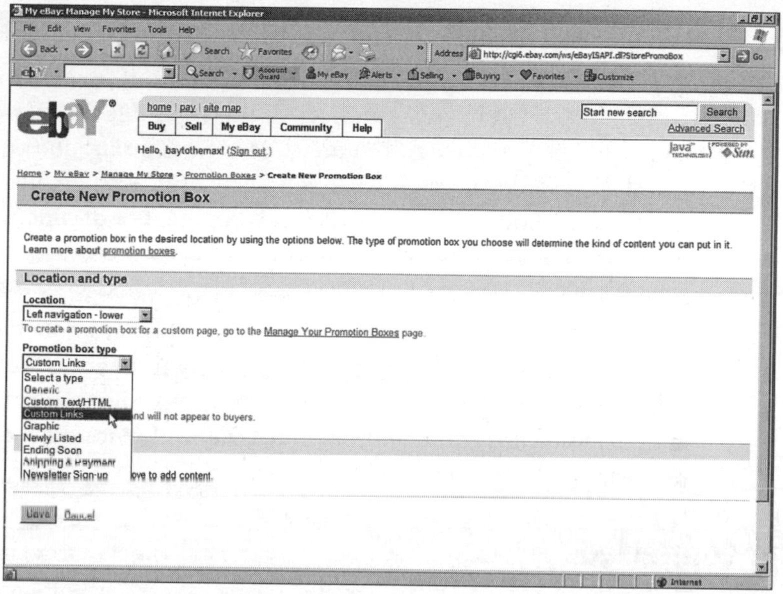

FIGURE 14.15

Specifying the contents of the new box.

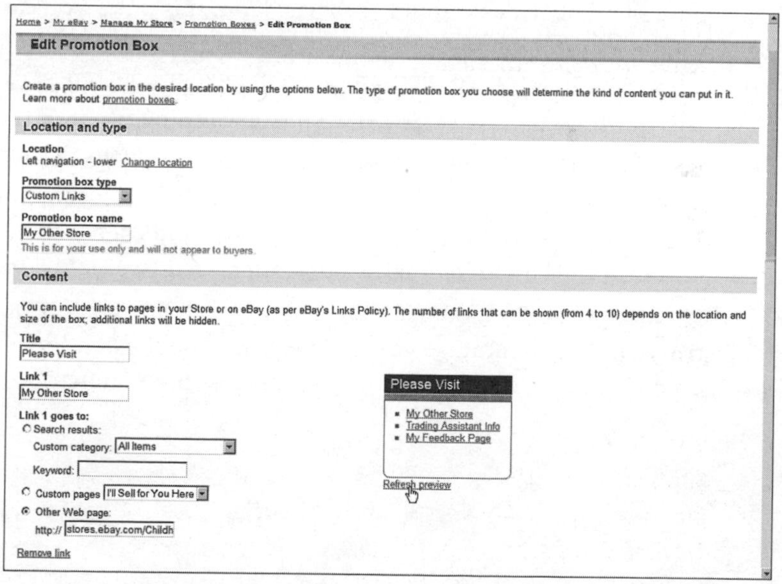

FIGURE 14.16

Creating a "links" promotion box

By using the preview button, it's easy to preview the appearance of any box type before saving it. When you are pleased with your results, be sure to scroll to the bottom of the page and click the Save button. You can also specify sizes and colors of promotion boxes, which is discussed next.

Cross-promoting with Other Stores (Connections)

If you have more than one selling ID or if you want to work together with another eBay seller to cross-promote your compatible businesses, eBay can help. Together, you create what are called "cross-promotion connections." You request a connection with a seller you know and trust. Or, you might receive a request from another seller, which you can accept or decline. If the request is accepted, an active connection is formed.

When a buyer bids on or wins an item belonging to you or the other seller, both your items and the other seller's items will be promoted to the buyer. The other sellers' items will be displayed separately from yours. For example, just under the "See more great items from this Seller" promo box winners see when they purchase an item from you, eBay will place a list of links to some of the other seller's items.

Getting Connected

Use the Cross-Promotion Connections page to perform all your cross-promotion activities with other sellers. From this page, you can request a connection with another seller, accept or decline a request from another seller, end an active connection, or change your preferences.

You can have up to 10 (active and pending) connections at one time. Cancel or decline pending connections if you don't want them to count against your limit.

To start the process, visit your My eBay page and choose the Cross-Promotion link near the bottom of the left navigation area (see Figure 14.17).

From the Cross-Promotions Connections screen (shown in Figure 14.18), you can request and manage your connections. Use the Edit link in the Preferences area of the screen to define the types of cross-promotions you will allow.

FIGURE 14.17
Reach the Cross-Promotions Connection feature from My eBay.

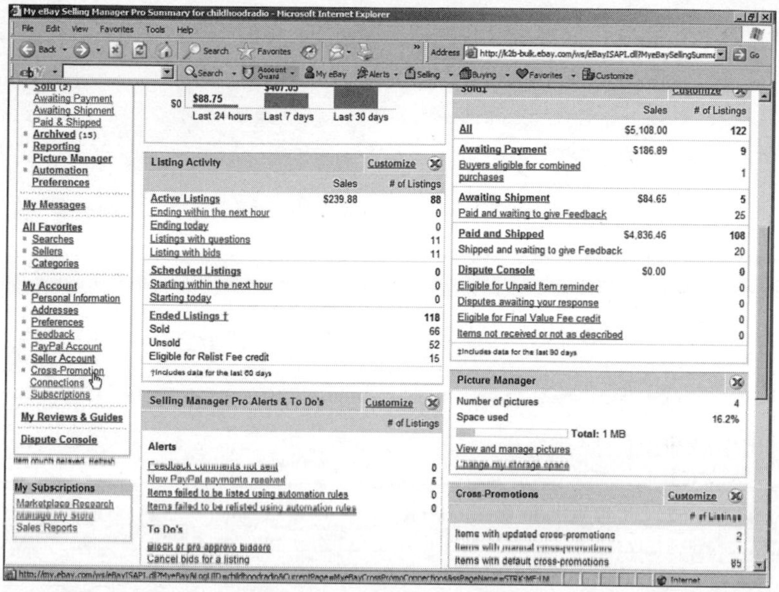

FIGURE 14.18
Manage connections here.

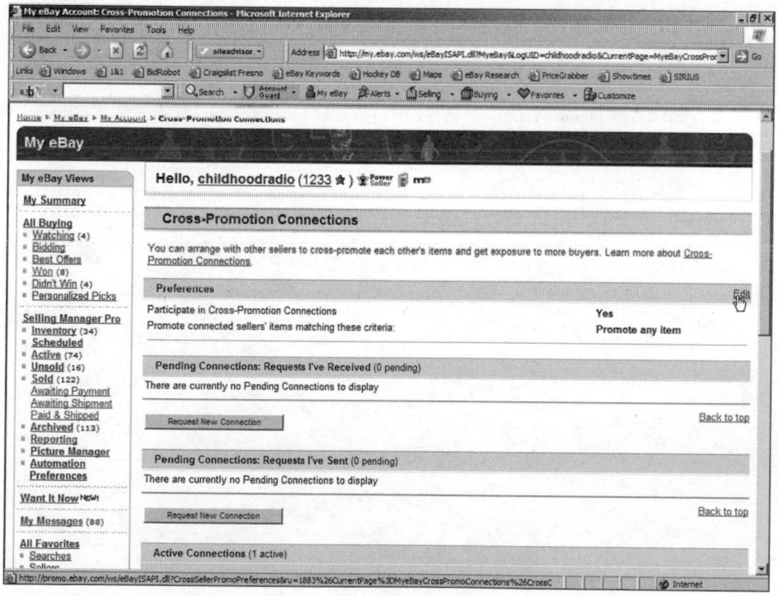

More Promotional Help from eBay

In addition to store cross-promotion tools, eBay has a number of other programs of interest to eBay store owners, including its recently announced eBay Express, (discussed in Chapter 19, "eBay Express and Other Comparison Shopping Sites"), aimed at shoppers in a hurry. Let's start with some of the features that have been in place for a while and save Express for Chapter 19.

eBay Store Directory

Whenever a shopper visits eBay's landing page, he or she is given an opportunity to see an eBay store directory like the one shown in Figure 15.1, offering links to Anchor and Featured stores.

FIGURE 15.1

Part of the eBay store directory.

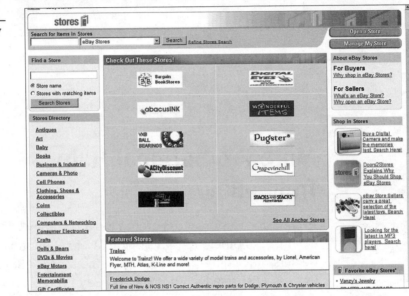

Anchor stores' icons appear in the center of the screen, and rotate in and out of view throughout the day. A link takes shoppers to a list of all Anchor stores, like the one in Figure 15.2.

To have your store appear in the Anchor list, you simply need to pay the Anchor store fee, and you will be in the complete list. Your store will also appear on the front page of the store directory from time to time as it comes up in the Anchor store "rotation."

As you can see back in Figure 15.1, Featured stores get listed beneath the Anchor stores. Here again, only a few of the thousands of Featured stores are displayed for any one visitor, but over time your Featured store will probably appear here.

FIGURE 15.2

Browsing the
Anchor store
directory.

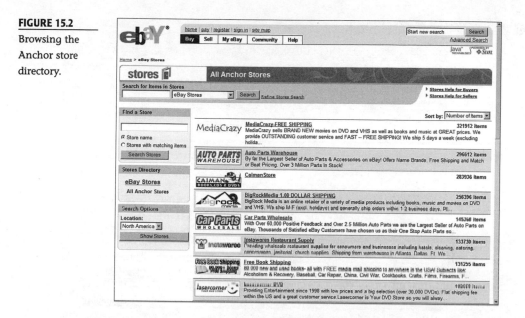

How Shoppers Find Your Store in the Directory

The most likely way store directory browsers will find your store is by searching for it using the two available store search features—store name and stores with matching items—or while browsing by category using the links at the left of the main store directory page.

Unless the shopper knows the name of your store, or at least part of the name, searches will likely turn up many of your competitors as well your own store.

For example, Figure 15.3 shows the results of a search for "transistor radio" using the Search for Items in Stores feature. It's a hodgepodge of items for sale by many, many store owners. The chances of your being on the first screen or two of this list are slim in all but the narrowest categories.

When shoppers use the Store Name search option, you stand a better chance of making the cut, especially if you have put the right keywords in your store header. For example, a search for "transistor radio" in the Find a Store search box with the Stores with Matching Items option checked brings my store to the first page, as illustrated in Figure 15.4.

This time a list of stores appears, and because I have a relatively high number of items with the keywords *transistor radio*, I get pretty high billing.

FIGURE 15.3

The store directory can be searched for items from multiple sellers.

FIGURE 15.4

"Stores with Matching Items" searches produce store name lists rather than lists of items.

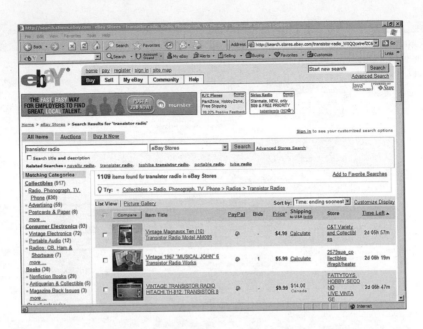

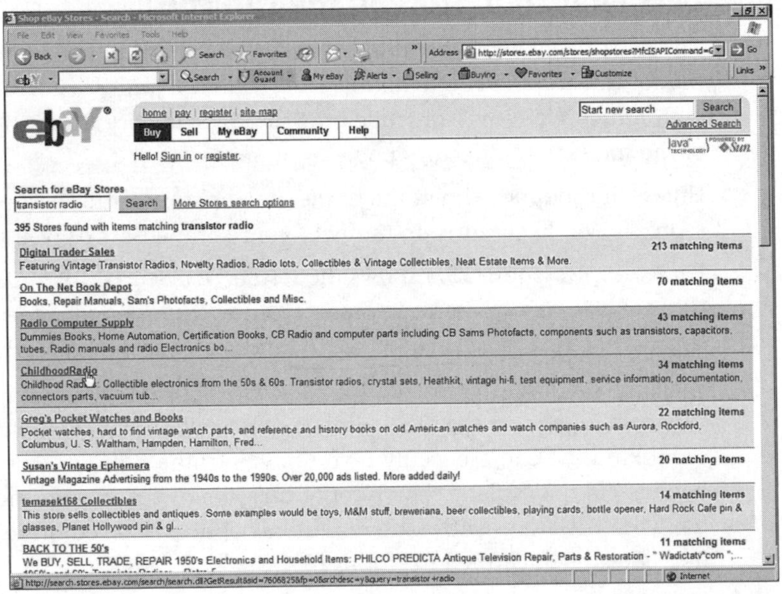

The third way shoppers can find your store is by entering either your whole store name or part of it in the Find a Store search box and choosing the Store Name option. Figure 15.5 shows what happened when I entered "childhood" in the search field.

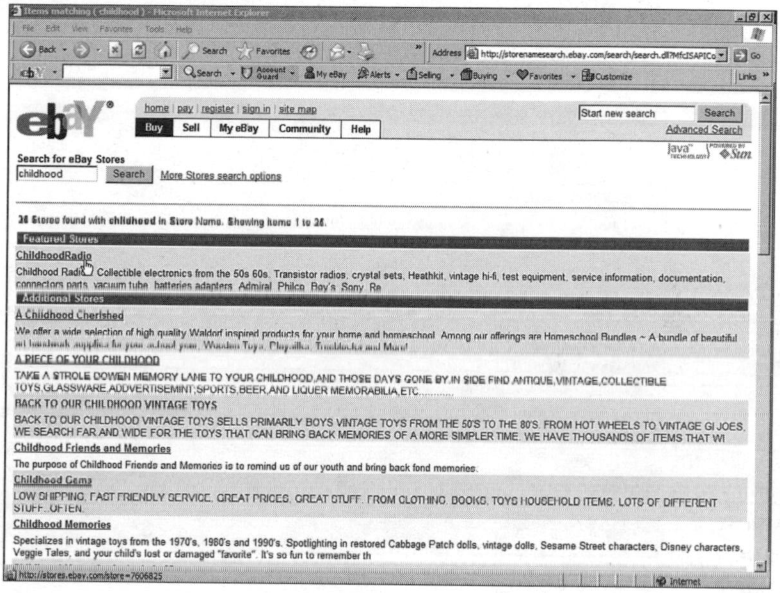

FIGURE 15.5

Partial store names can be used to search the store directory.

Anchor stores, if any, are listed first, followed by Featured stores and then Basic stores.

Your Store Description Should Be Compelling

Once eBayers see your store in a list, they still need to be drawn to it, so be sure the store description they see is inviting, maybe even compelling, if that's possible. The text comes from your store header that you set up in Chapter 6, "Setting Up Your Store." The descriptions in the directory might get truncated. Compare Figures 15.6 and 15.7 to see what I mean.

As you can see, the store directory is a pretty passive marketing tool, and except for paying to become an Anchor store, having a lot of items that match popular search results, and perhaps owning a killer store name, there's not much you can do to influence your ranking in these lists. Fortunately, you can employ more aggressive tools, as described in the coming sections.

FIGURE 15.6

Sometimes, store descriptions are truncated by eBay.

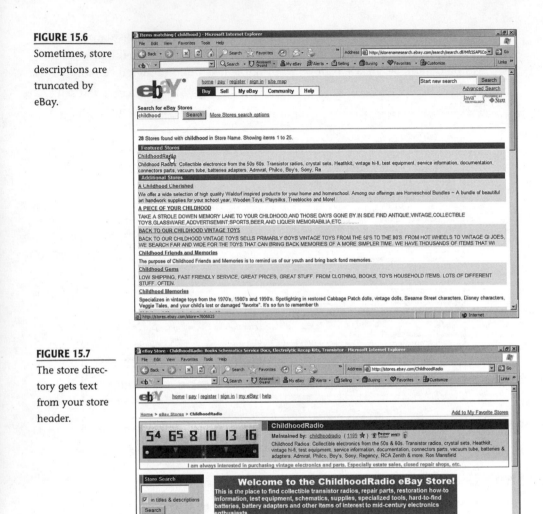

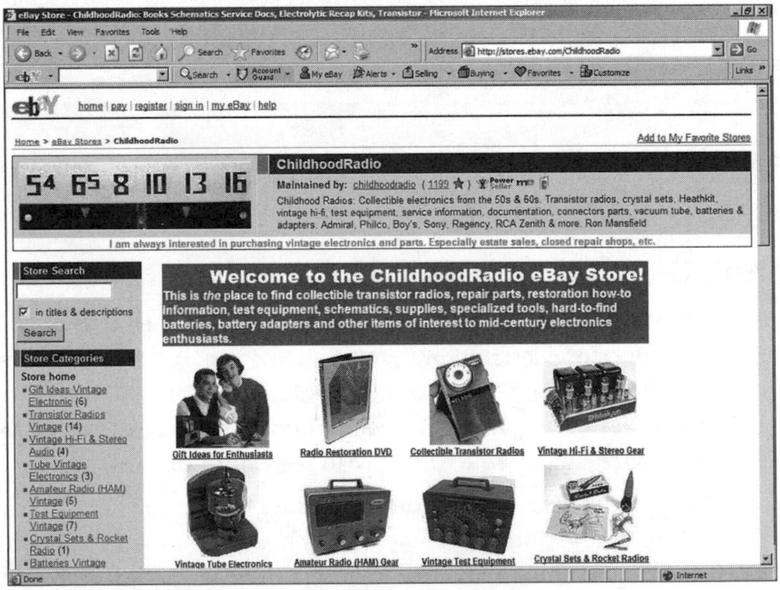

FIGURE 15.7

The store directory gets text from your store header.

Using eBay's Opt-in Email Marketing

If you have done a good job building an attractive store and have a loyal following, you can invite your visitors to join your email newsletter list. You can use the skills you learned in the last chapter to create a promotion box like the one in Figure 15.8, or you can create HTML links that send shoppers to your sign-up page. When buyers add you their Favorite Sellers list, they are offered your newsletters as well.

You can have up to five newsletter lists to narrow your audience. If you sell trading cards, for example, you can have one newsletter for football fans, another for baseball fans, one for hockey fans, and so on.

The number of free emails you can send each month varies by store subscription level, as shown in Table 15.1. Any emails you send over the allocated amount result in an additional charge per recipient.

Table 15.1   Free Email Allocation by Store Type

Subscription Level	Monthly Free Email Allocation	Additional Cost per Recipient (Over Allocation)
Basic store	100 emails	$0.01 per email
Featured store	1,000 emails	$0.01 per email
Anchor store	4,000 emails	$0.01 per email

FIGURE 15.8

You can use promotion boxes to get newsletter subscribers.

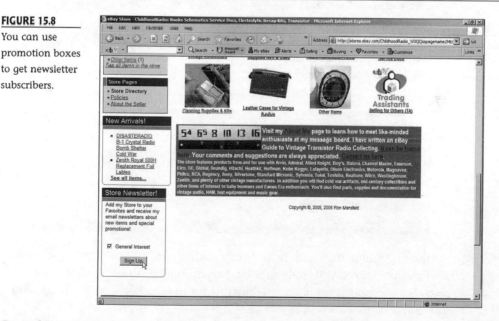

Setting Up Your Newsletter Campaign

In this section, we will look at the necessary steps for setting up a newsletter campaign in detail. First, it's a good idea to get an overview of the general steps:

1. Put store items up for sale.

2. Set up at least one mailing list.

3. Create links inviting people to sign up for your list(s).

4. Design, create, and send emails fitting eBay's guidelines.

5. Monitor the success of your first campaign and sign-up efforts.

6. Refine and continue your email campaign.

Creating a Mailing List

To create a list, visit your My eBay page, choose Manage My Store, and click the Email Marketing link. When you first visit the Email Marketing page in My eBay, it will look something like Figure 15.9.

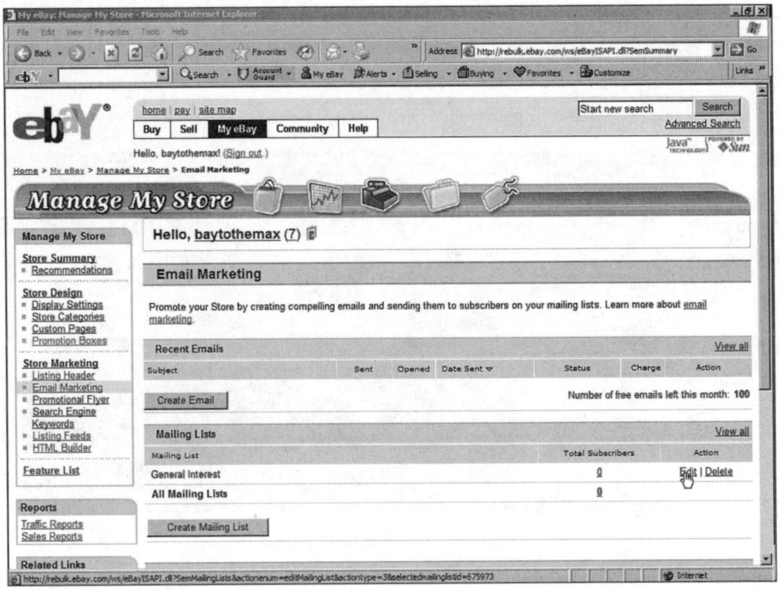

FIGURE 15.9

Start your first email newsletter campaign.

At the beginning, there will be only one mailing list, titled "General Interest." You can use this as your only mailing list, change its name, and/or add other lists. For example, I could change my first list to "Hockey Jerseys" by clicking the Edit link, as shown in Figure 15.9.

Getting Subscribers

As I mentioned earlier, when buyers add you to their Favorite Sellers list, they will be invited to join your newsletter mailing list. But you can be proactive as well. Use the promotion box feature to add a sign-up box to your store pages. You can also create HTML links to your sign-up page that you use in listings and any other suitable electronic arena. Here's one quick way to grab the link info you need:

1. Create the newsletter subscription promotion box.

2. Click the resulting button to get to your subscription page.

3. Copy the URL from your browser.

4. Save the URL someplace handy (in a Word document, Notepad file, or whatever).

5. Insert the URL into your listings and so on.

Creating Emails

Once you have some subscribers, it's time to create your first mailing. You'll need to pick the recipients, create a subject line, header, custom message, and then choose the desired item list and showcase options. You can then preview and send the email or save it in draft form until you are ready to send it. (It's also possible to duplicate and alter prior successful newsletters.)

Begin by visiting the Email Marketing page reached from your My eBay page. Click the Create Email button, and you will see a screen similar to Figure 15.10.

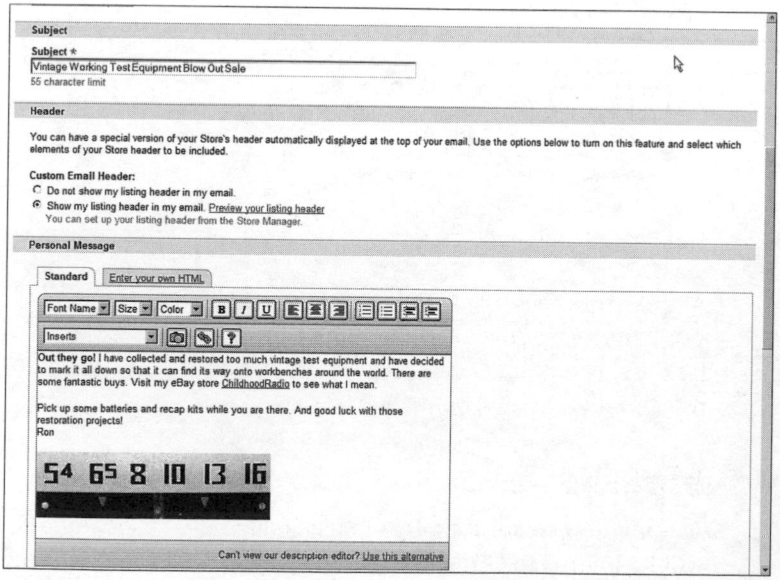

FIGURE 15.10

Create an email.

Begin by creating a subject for the email. It should be compelling and not misleading. You should also consider email spam filters. The title in Figure 15.10 (Vintage Working Test Equipment Blow Out Sale) might get you blocked in a few places because the words *Blow Out* and *Sale* are pretty common in spam titles.

You can enter plain text in the email (good if many of your subscribers are "low tech" or security conscious, and likely not to be able to see HTML in their emails), or you can craft your own HTML code. A third alternate is to use eBay's text-editing and picture-inserting tools to create the HTML, which is what I have done in Figure 15.10.

After typing the text, I used the Bold button for the first sentence, added an HTML link to my store page, and inserted a graphic using the button with the camera icon. If you have your own HTML-creation tools (Dreamweaver, FrontPage, or whatever), you might be better off using them instead, in which case you need to click the Enter Your Own HTML tab first and then paste the code there.

Item Showcases

If you would like to showcase items in your newsletter, you can do this by scrolling down further in the Create Email page to specify what you want to add. You can either include items of eBay's choosing or specify your own specific items, categories, and so on. Figure 15.11 shows where this is accomplished.

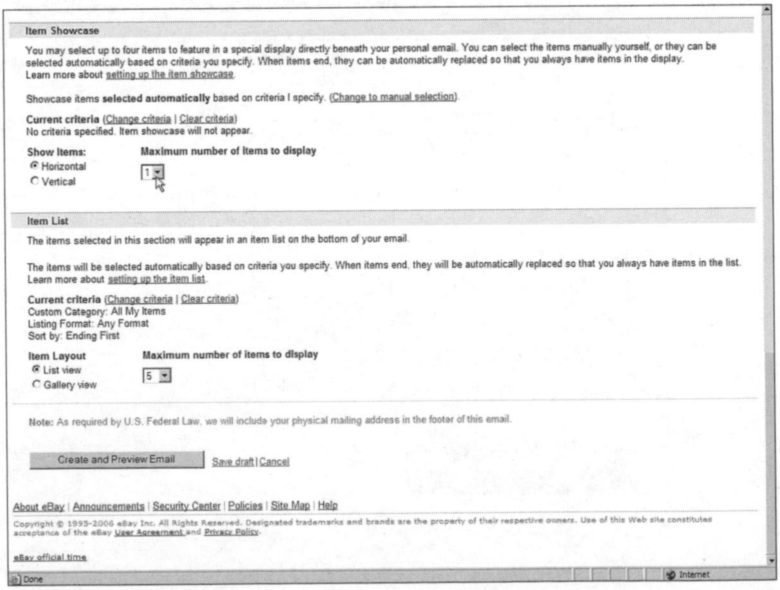

FIGURE 15.11

Adding an item showcase to your email.

Previewing and Launching the Email

Once the email newsletter has been created and attached to an eligible list of
email recipients, you can click the Create
and Preview Email button. Recipients will
get something that looks like Figure 15.12
in their inbox.

FIGURE 15.12

Previewing and
launching your
email.

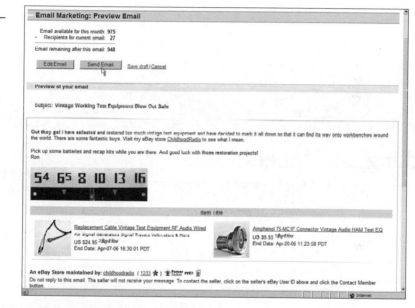

Measuring Newsletter Progress

Once you have sent email newsletters, you can track their progress in the
Email Marketing area of your Mange My Store page. As you can see in Figure
15.13, I just started email marketing for this ID. When I sent the first email in
December, I had eight subscribers, and nobody opened the email. By mid-
February I had 14 subscribers and more than half opened that email. At the
time, I couldn't send the next newsletter (about test equipment) for a while, so
it was saved as a draft.

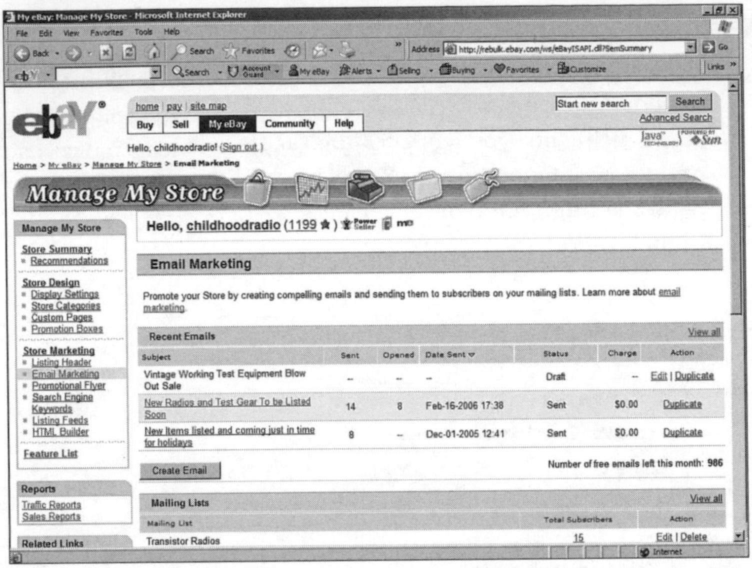

FIGURE 15.13

Track newsletter progress here.

Blocking Subscribers

If you decide to block any subscribers from receiving your email (competitors, for example), you can do so by adding them to your Blocked Bidder and Buyer list. You also can block subscribers in bulk by clicking check boxes on the left subscriber list and then the Block Buyer button at the bottom of the page (see Figure 15.14).

caution By blocking buyers from your mailing lists, you are also preventing them from bidding on or buying any of your items, so use this feature with care.

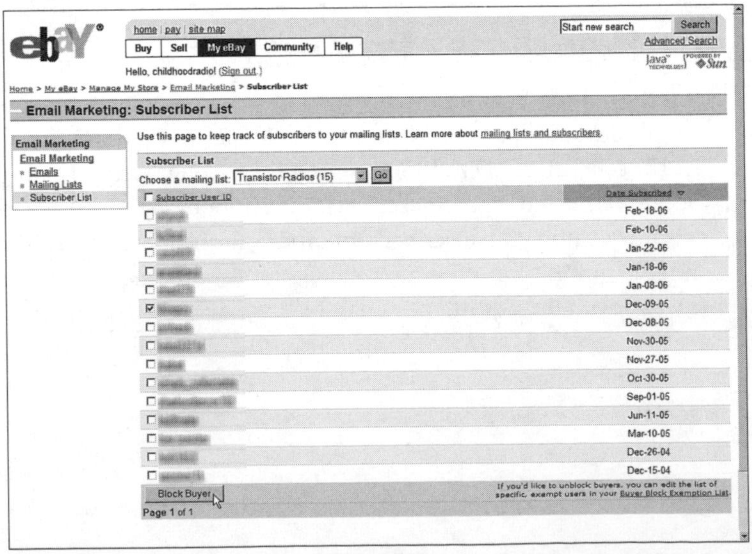

FIGURE 15.14

Blocking subscribers blocks their bids, too. (eBay IDs are intentionally blurred in this figure.)

Printing eBay's Promotional Flyers and Other Inserts

The eBay promotional flyer feature is one of those "almost ready for prime-time" ideas. It is supposed to create a printed promotional piece that you can insert with your shipments. And although you can make it showcase items of interest to your customers, there is quite a bit of handiwork involved to get it to look right.

I think you will be better off crafting your own printed inserts or perhaps even a paper catalog using a better "paper publishing tool" such as Microsoft Word, Microsoft Publisher, or an equivalent. So let's just take a quick look at the way to create a useable handout using this eBay feature.

Begin by choosing the Promotional Flyer link in your Manage My Store page. If you have never created a flier before, you will see something like Figure 15.15. Click the Create Promotional Flyer button.

FIGURE 15.15

Create your first flyer.

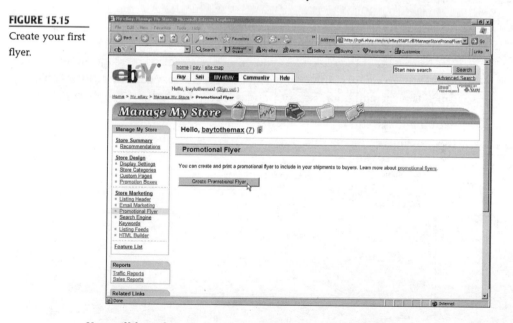

You will be taken to a page similar to the one in Figure 15.16 (which is also where you will land if you have ever created a flyer before).

To keep this simple, let me suggest that you leave checked all the boxes that you see checked in Figure 15.16. Also, make sure the "Use a border with the Store's colors" button is selected.

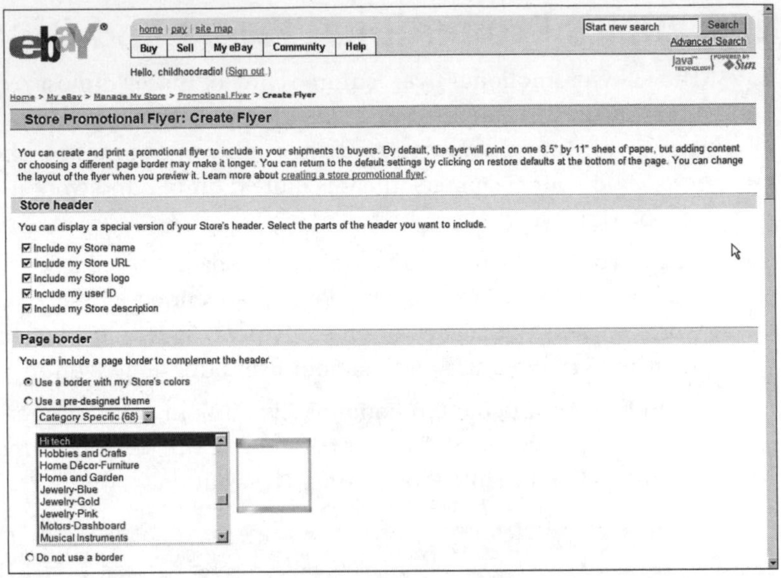

FIGURE 15.16

Specify flyer
features.

The next area of the screen lets you enter a customized message either as text
or HTML. To comply with eBay's regulations, the text cannot include "off-eBay
links, URLs, email addresses, or images." Curiously, phone numbers aren't
mentioned. Figure 15.17 shows this.

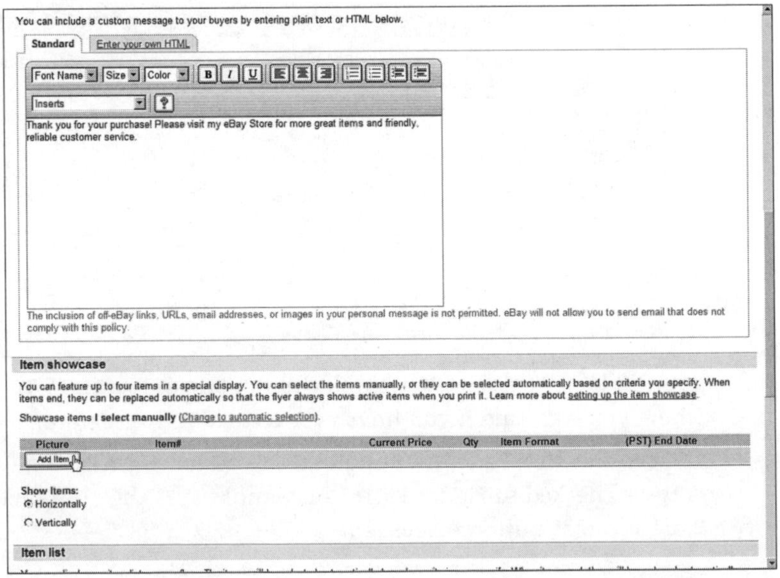

FIGURE 15.17

Add a note, but
don't break any
rules.

Selecting Highlighted Items

Now you want to manually select items to print in your flyer. Begin by clicking the Add Item button under the Picture heading.

You will see a screen similar to Figure 15.18, showing all your active items.

You will want to force the feature to use store items, because there is a very good chance that auction or Buy It Now items will end before the package containing your flyer arrives on your customers' doorsteps. Therefore, pick store items as I have done in Figure 15.19. At the time this was written, at least, only photos that eBay hosts seem to be available for use in flyers. (Did I mention this would be a painful process?)

Each time you select an item, you get taken back to the screen shown in Figure 15.16, so scroll down and pick again. You can choose up to four items to highlight this way.

When you have selected the items to highlight, you can then specify how many of which (if any) other items you want to add to your flyer. In other words, you could highlight four items and show a total of 10. Again, picture hosting is an issue, and here, too, you will want to use only items that will be available when customers have the flyer in hand. You can also add promotion boxes, but of course they won't be clickable because they are on paper.

When you are done, preview and print the flyer to see what you think.

FIGURE 15.19

These items will
be highlighted.

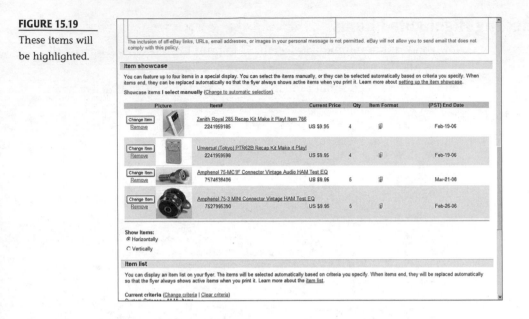

Buying eBay Keywords

At the opposite end of the effective tools spectrum might be eBay Keywords. These can be powerful traffic builders, especially if you are a niche seller. They work in crowded categories, too, of course, but because the price of keywords is set by an "auction" of sorts, popular keywords cost quite a lot more than quirky ones. It is also possible to have ads placed at the top of category search results pages, which is a somewhat riskier scheme in broad categories.

In any case, what you are buying is space along the top of search pages. For example, a moment ago when I searched eBay for "sony mp3," I got the search results page you see in Figure 15.20. Notice the three ads along the top of the page (one long one and two short ones). Two are for a 7-color backlit radio (offered by the same seller), and one is for Glow Gear, to be used at raves.

Notice that not one of these ads has anything to do with Sony MP3 items. The people advertising that other stuff (the rave gear and such) found their way to the top of my screen by purchasing keywords in the hopes that they can distract me from what I was really doing, which was looking for Sony MP3 items.

At this point, it has cost them nothing to have their ads up there. If I click on one of the ads, it does cost them money, and I will be taken to the eBay page they specify (a specific item of theirs, a store page, all the items they have listed, and so on).

FIGURE 15.20

Paid keyword ads populate the top of search pages.

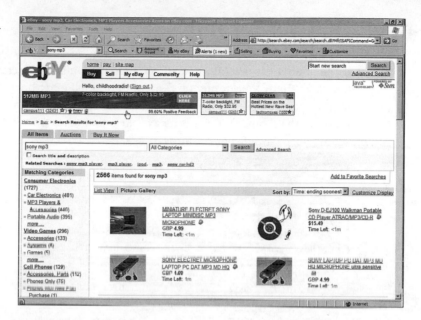

The keyword or phrase that searchers use determines how much a seller pays per click. For example, as I write this, if I search for "sony" and click a resulting ad, that ad's seller will pay eBay $2.39 for my click, even if I don't buy anything from the seller. Ouch.

It can get worse. If I search for "sony projector" and click an ad, the seller will pay $4.00. Searching for "sony remote" will potentially cost only a dime, because not too many sellers have specified that phrase as something they are willing to pay for.

There are filters (called *frequency caps*) in place to keep competitors from emptying each other's advertising coffers by clicking away on each other's ads all day, and as a seller you can set limits of course, but as you can see, some people are willing to pay quite a bit for a click.

That's it in a nutshell. As a seller, you pay eBay when shoppers click your ads that are plastered on the tops of search pages. How much you pay depends on search words or phrases shoppers use, and how much other sellers are willing to pay for those same words and phrases.

Occasionally, eBay offers promotions for this feature, where they will match your investment dollar for dollar. They happen to be doing that as I write this, so you will also see how you can get twice the exposure for your money, at least in theory.

Creating a Keywords Campaign

Begin your eBay Keywords campaign by clicking the Buy eBay Keywords link near the bottom of your Manage My Store page. You'll see a screen similar to Figure 15.21. Here, you name the campaign and tell eBay how much you are willing to spend before being asked to refill the coffers. Because a promotion is going on at the moment, there is also a place to enter a promotion code matching your PowerSeller or store level.

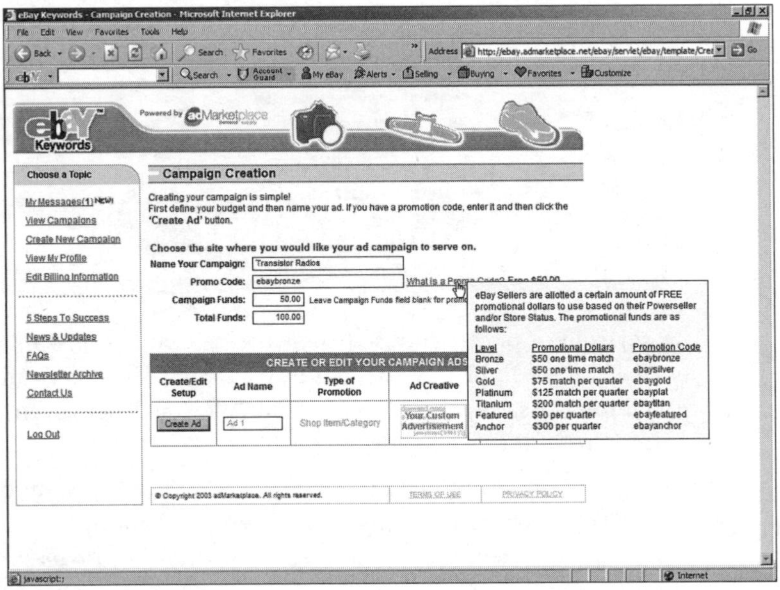

FIGURE 15.21

Setting up an eBay Keywords campaign.

You can have multiple campaigns and turn them on or off. Let's set one up called "transistor radios." Once you have decided how much to spend on your campaign, it's time to create an ad by clicking the Create Ad button, taking you to a screen like the one in Figure 15.22.

Here, you specify a landing page, which could be your store, a list of all the items you are selling, a specific item, and so on. I want to send traffic to my store, so that's my choice in Figure 15.22.

Scrolling down that same page brings you to the place where you create the ads you want shoppers to see. They appear in three different formats, as you can see in Figure 15.23. You can enter a maximum of 13 characters for the box title and no more than 45 characters for the text in the box. I've chosen "Make it Play!" for the title and "RESTORATION SUPERSTORE HERE" for the text.

FIGURE 15.22

Choose a landing page.

FIGURE 15.23

Design the ads.

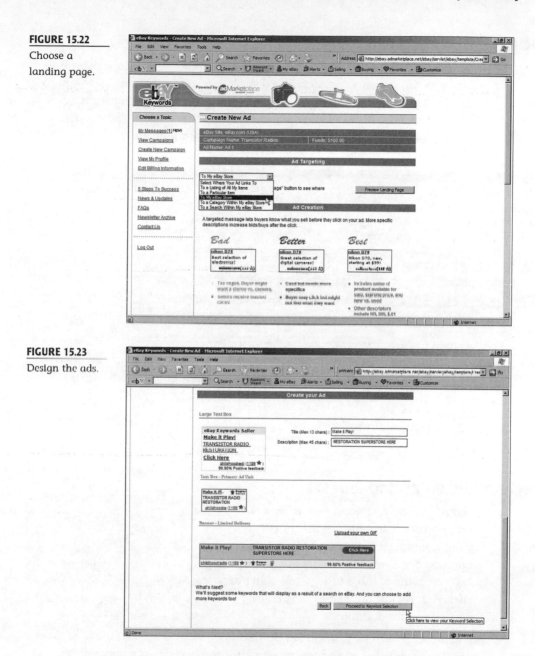

You will see previews of the ads as you work. It is possible to design graphics for the large ad elsewhere (in PhotoShop or whatever) and upload them here. Because these are GIF files, they can contain animation if you like. When you are happy with the appearance of all three ad formats, click the Proceed to Keyword Selection button.

Specifying Maximum Click Costs

Figure 15.24 illustrates a crucial step. You are asked to specify a maximum you are willing to pay per click. The default is $5.01, and you might want to change it to something smaller, especially if you are just getting started. I've decided to specify $0.25 as the maximum for the time being. You are able to change this, and you will see how and when to in a moment.

FIGURE 15.24

Consider lowering the maximum you'll pay per click.

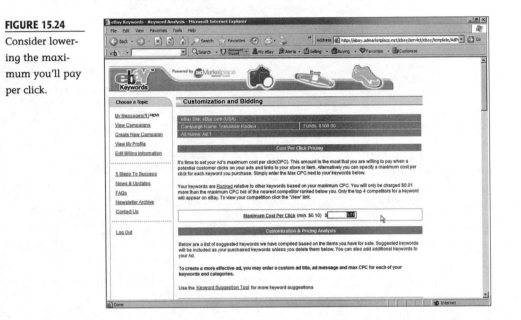

Selecting Keywords and Phrases

Not surprisingly, choosing great keywords and phrases is the meat of the matter. You want the right shoppers to see your ads, and you don't want too many false hits, because some of those turkeys are going to click your ad just out of curiosity, costing you money for nothing.

tip
If you want to explore keywords not suggested by your current listings, you can use an eBay feature called the Keyword Suggestion tool. You can reach it by clicking the link shown at the bottom of Figure 15.24.

As you scroll further, you will see that eBay has suggested some keywords and phrases, as well as some possible search categories, all based on your current listings. All the suggested keywords and phrases will be used unless you delete them by putting check marks in the left boxes and clicking the Delete button (see Figure 15.25).

FIGURE 15.25

Study the proposed keywords and their costs. Delete ones you don't want.

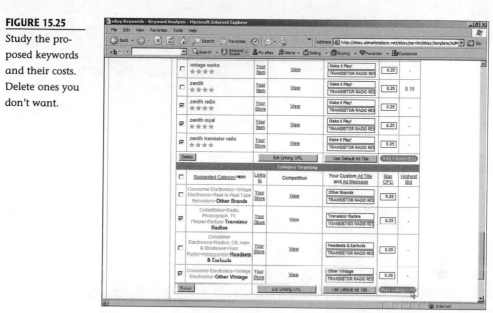

Generally, specific phrases are more efficient (exacting) then general ones. I sell things for collectors of vintage Sony radios with model numbers such as TR-610, so whereas paying more than $2 for "Sony" clicks makes no sense, I can purchase "Sony TR-610" clicks for a dime. Therefore, I don't buy the word *Sony* alone, but I do buy the phrases *Sony TR-610*, *Sony TR-650*, and so on.

In the Category Targeting section, you can pick category searches that will result in ad placements, too. These can get pretty costly and provide poor results if they are too broad. For example, I might want to delete all but the Transistor Radios category from my list shown in Figure 15.25.

Adding Long, Specific Lists of Keywords

It is also possible to type comma-separated strings of desired keywords, or even import .csv files containing desired words and phrases, as shown in Figure 15.26.

Determining Click Costs

Click costs are constantly in flux, and vary as competitors pick up and drop keywords, phrases, and categories. You can see what the going rate is for keywords you are considering by looking at the rightmost column shown in Figure 15.25. If the cell is empty you are the only seller currently interested and the cost per click will be the minimum eBay charges, ($0.10 as this book is being written).

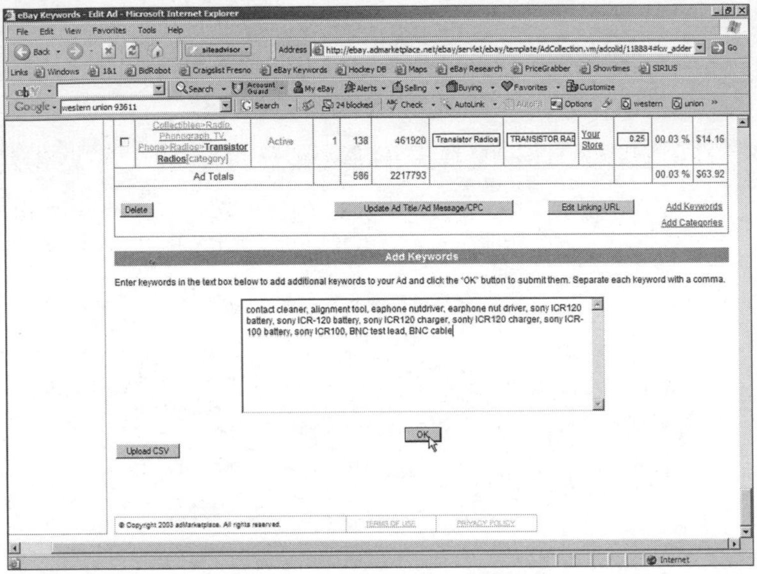

FIGURE 15.26

Entering comma-separated keywords and phrases.

If others are interested in a particular word or phrase, it will cost you more. For example, in Figure 15.25, someone is willing to pay $0.15 for the word *Zenith*.

When you are done reviewing, adding, and deleting keywords, phrases, and categories, scroll down to review the campaign, as shown in Figure 15.27. You will see the campaign name, total funds available, and copies of your ads. If you want to create additional campaigns, click the Create New Campaign button; otherwise, click Transfer Funds.

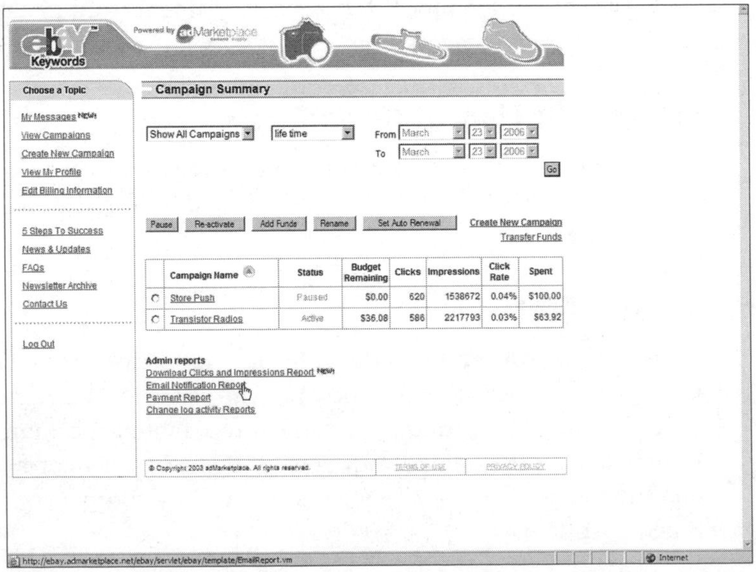

FIGURE 15.27

Review and get ready to pay.

You will be asked to provide credit card information, including those pesky card-verification numbers, so have the plastic handy.

Managing and Monitoring Keyword Campaigns

It takes awhile for eBay to approve your campaign (sometimes 24 hours or more). You can tell when your campaign has been activated by revisiting the Campaign Summary reached via the Buy eBay Keywords link on the Manage My Store page.

From here, you can pause campaigns, refinance them, revise them, and so on. Figure 15.27 shows an example of two campaigns—one I have paused, and the new one waiting for eBay's approval.

It is also possible to download clicks and impressions reports from this page. You will get emails from eBay at various milestones in your campaign—funded, out of funds, and so on. You can read a summary of these emails by clicking the Email Notification Report link shown in Figure 15.27.

Writing eBay Guides and Reviews

Recently eBay has added a feature that lets sellers pontificate on subjects they know. This is a way to draw newcomers into your store, or perhaps get folks interested in a hobby. You can also use these guides to help readers gain confidence in you as a seller. Guides showcase your items for sale. They also showcase other sellers' items beneath yours. Figure 15.28 shows part of a typical guide.

FIGURE 15.28
Part of a review guide.

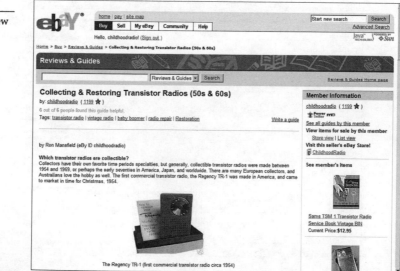

The quickest way to start writing a guide or review is to visit http://reviews. ebay.com/, as shown in Figure 15.29, and click the "Write a guide" link in the Guides panel. Start a review with the "Write a review" link on the Reviews side.

FIGURE 15.29

Write a review or guide.

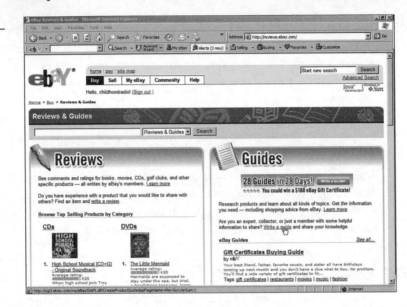

Your work should be original and on topic. You can add up to 10 photos or other graphics. Only the first 200 characters are used when people search for topics, so pack some keywords in there, and enter searchable "tags" at the bottom of the screen. Follow the rules. They are displayed for you, as you can see in Figure 15.30.

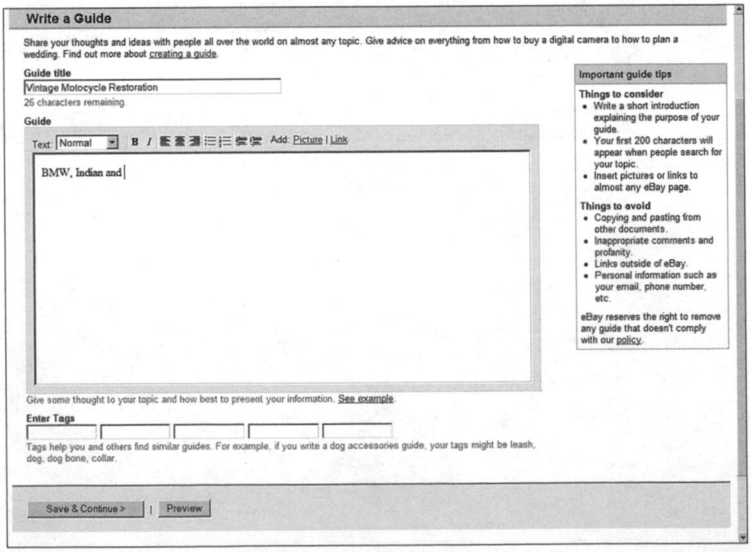

FIGURE 15.30

Start a guide.

Promoting Your Store Outside of eBay

It's no longer enough to simply hope that folks will find your stuff while rummaging around on eBay. Successful sellers drive traffic to their listings, or in the case of eBay store owners, drive visitors to their eBay stores. This chapter and the four that follow it show you different ways to accomplish this.

Your Own Website(s)

Many sellers have their own websites designed to attract visitors from any number of places. For example, I have a personal website (www.RonMansfield.com) used to promote my books, consulting, and other services. The landing page is shown in Figure 16.1.

FIGURE 16.1

Promote your store on your other website(s).

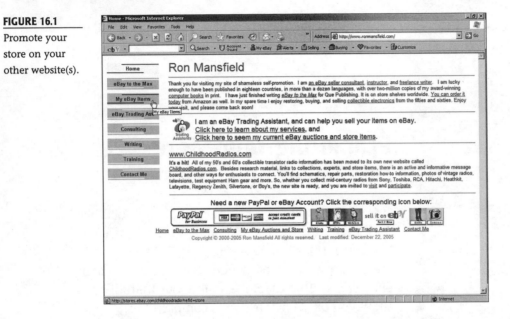

As you can see, I have several links, buttons, and so on leading to my eBay listings. They all point to my eBay store landing page, and people who buy items as a direct result of coming from these "off-eBay" links save me money because eBay reduces the final value fee in these instances. You will learn more about this in Chapter 17, "Store Referral Credits (eBay Fee Discounts)."

Blogs and Enthusiasts Sites

Another way to promote your eBay store is to find ways to get links placed on websites attractive to people interested in items like the ones you sell. These can be your own websites or third-party sites.

For example, I run a second website for vintage electronics enthusiasts (www.childhoodradios.com). It has lots of research materials, links to other collectors' sites, and perhaps most important of all, an active message board. Figure 16.2 shows the top level of the message board. Notice the buttons on the left. One of them leads directly to my eBay store.

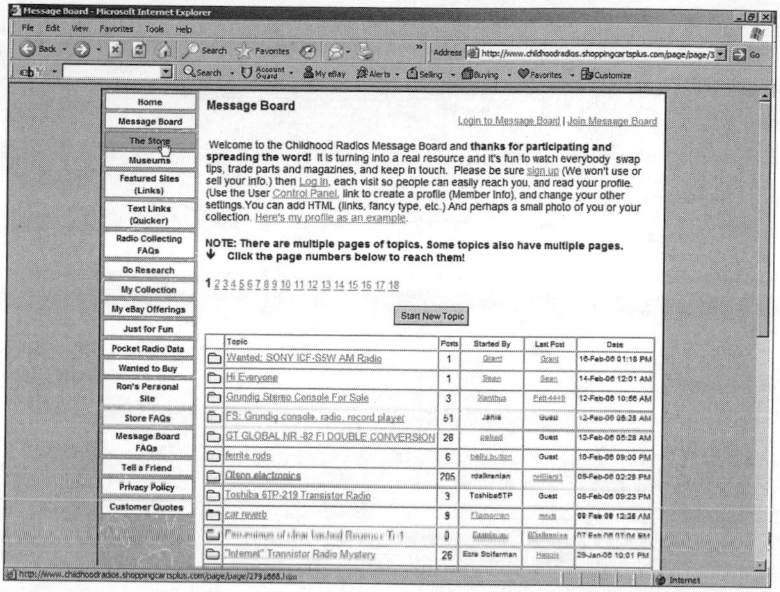

FIGURE 16.2

Help build a community.

Specialized websites such as my "off-eBay site" and blogs are great ways to build a community and establish yourself as an important resource in it.

In a Karma-like way, the time, expense, and energy spent building and maintaining these virtual places should come right back to you. Every now and then, for example, someone will visit my forum and write "I need this battery or connector and can't find it anywhere." Before I can even jump in, some other message board visitor will reply, "Hey, I think Ron sells those in the store."

Which is all good, but for me at least, the best part is watching the community take shape, help itself, and grow.

Build External Links with eBay's HTML Builder

To link from any other site (or blog or email), you simply need to use your store's URL, which is in the form http://stores.ebay.com/YourStoreName. So, my ChildhoodRadio store's URL is http://stores.ebay.com/ChildhoodRadio. You can plunk your URL into just about anyplace that allows links.

But you can make much fancier links by either handcrafting them in HTML yourself or by using one of the many HTML-creation tools available to us all today. There's even one built into eBay's Store Toolkit. It's called HTML Builder, and you reach it from a link in the left navigation area of your Manage My Store page. Figure 16.3 shows the main page of HTML Builder.

FIGURE 16.3

HTML Builder is found in the eBay Manage My Store page.

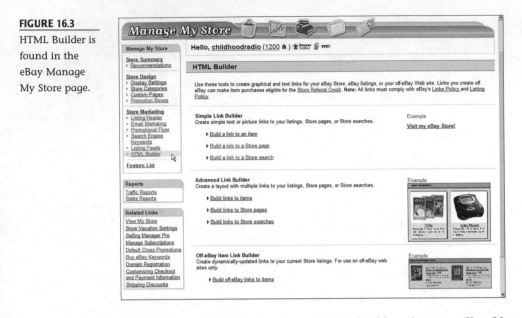

There are three main subcategories of HTML-building features offered by this tool:

- Simple links
- Advanced links
- Off-eBay links

Creating Simple Links

The simple links feature lets you easily construct text links to a particular item, store page, or store search. For example, to build a link to a specific item, you would begin by clicking "Build a link to an item." You will see something like Figure 16.4. You must refer to an active item, ideally one in your store, or something that won't expire before people will stop clicking the link. For example, these links are best for store items that you always keep in stock.

Text Links to an Item

In this example, I want to build the code for a simple text link with a small photo to promote a battery that is used by a particular radio. I've entered the item number of the battery, the text I want to appear as the link, and because this store item has a gallery photo, I'll use it as the image.

FIGURE 16.4

Building a text link.

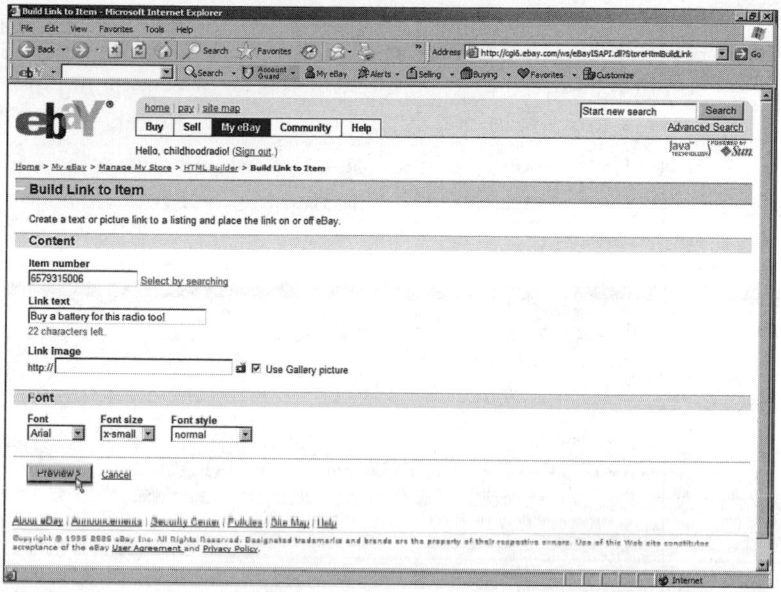

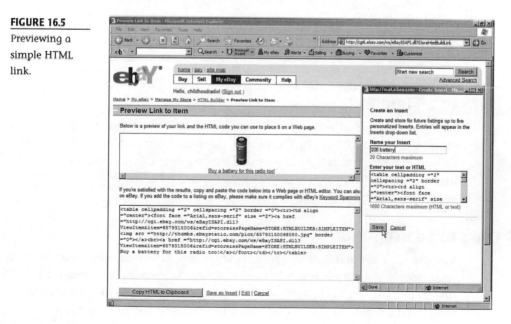

I could have specified a different photo-hosting location, or chosen not to show a photo at all. When done, I click the Preview button. Figure 16.5 shows the results.

FIGURE 16.5

Previewing a simple HTML link.

Bam! A nice little link with a photo and the code to create it. This can be copied and pasted into any off-eBay website or into an eBay listing. The code can also be saved for later use, which is what I am doing in Figure 16.5. If the preview proved disappointing, I could always modify it.

Saved HTML shows up in a drop-down list when you create new listing descriptions containing HTML during the "Sell Your Item" process. Figure 16.6 shows this.

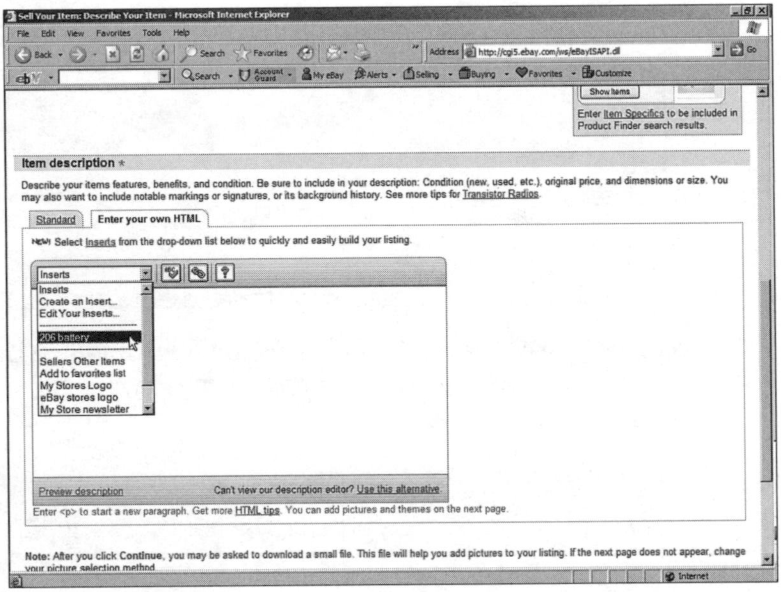

FIGURE 16.6
Saved HTML is available when you create new listings.

Text Links to a Store Page

Linking to a store page is similar to linking to an item, except you are provided a list of your store pages and store categories from which to choose. By default, the link text is the same as the store page or category name you specify, but you can change this, as shown in Figure 16.7. Preview, copy, paste, and/or save this HTML code as before.

Text Links to Search Results

You can also create links that provide shoppers with search results from within your store. For example, I sell Toshiba radios, parts, service documentation, and so on. This stuff is in many different store categories, but I can create the code to do an in-store search and round the items up for Toshiba enthusiasts.

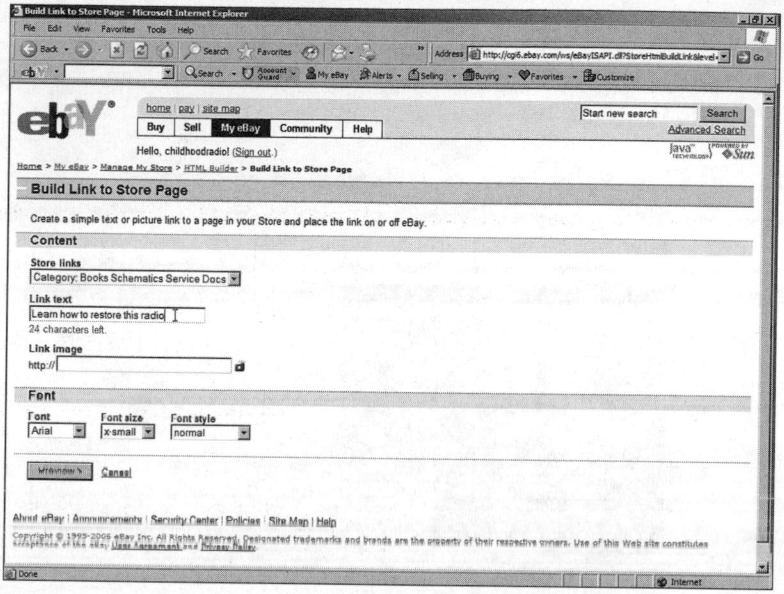

FIGURE 16.7
Choose from
store categories
for category
links.

Figure 16.8 shows the technique. As you can see, it's possible to filter results and only show auctions or store items and so on.

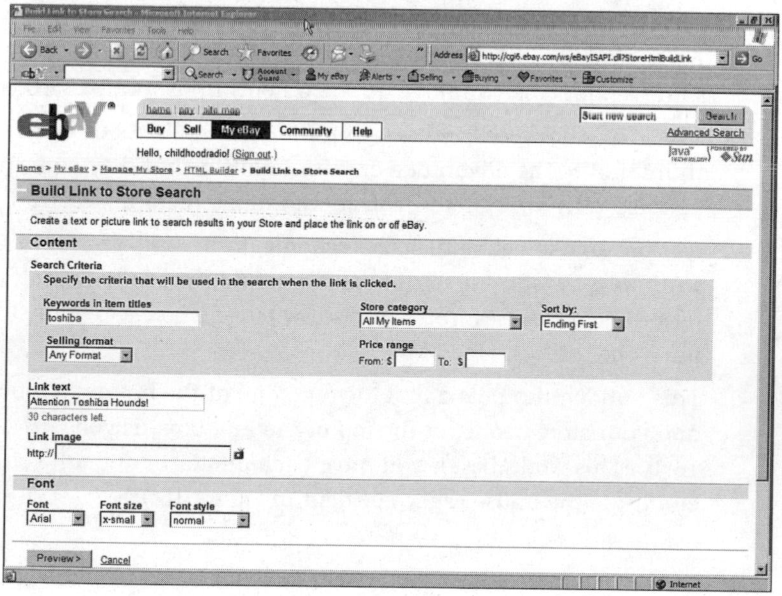

FIGURE 16.8
Creating links
that search.

Making Advanced Links

Advanced links create fancy boxes with multiple items, photos, and descriptions. Figure 16.9 shows an example.

FIGURE 16.9

An advanced link code creation.

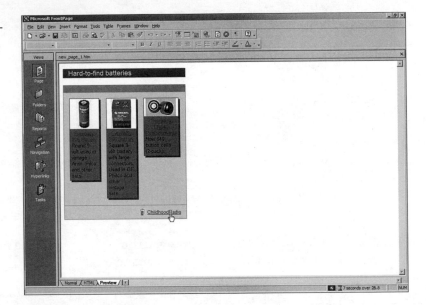

As you can see, it's a good idea to make the descriptions short, and about the same length. You can have up to 20 items in as many as 10 columns.

You can either specify your own photo-hosting URLs or use the listings' thumbnails. The advantage of thumbnails is that they come "pre-sized." If you use your own photos, you should make them all about the same size.

It is possible to define the color scheme, fonts, text sizes, and so on. You might want to play with these because the defaults make it difficult to read the lettering in some cases. You can also switch the boxes to your store colors, which might be the best idea of all.

This builder also puts a link to your store at the bottom. Optionally, you can add your store header at the top of the link box, as you can see in Figure 16.10. This works best if you have wide photos or enough columns (items) to eliminate the unused space evident in Figure 16.10.

FIGURE 16.10

You can add your store header to advanced link HTML code.

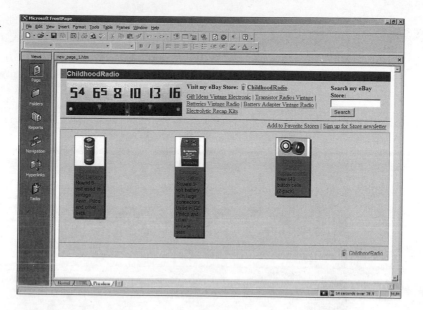

Building Off-eBay Links

All the techniques you have seen so far can be used on or off of eBay, but eBay has provided additional HTML-building tools for offsite work. These can be "dynamically linked" so that they update with your listing. Figure 16.11 shows an example.

FIGURE 16.11

Advanced off-eBay links can show current, constantly updated listings.

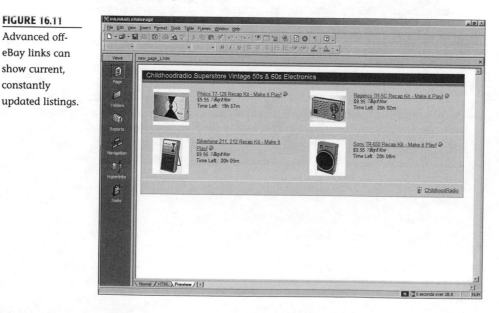

Here, too, you can fiddle with text appearance, colors, and so on. You can display up to 50 listings this way in either List or Gallery view. Both include thumbnails, but List view makes an odd, wide page with nothing in the middle, so you will probably prefer Gallery view. You can opt to show your store header as well. Figure 16.12 shows part of a page with the store header. I've also made the background white to remove the appearance of uneven "framing" around the photos.

FIGURE 16.12
You can display the store header here, too.

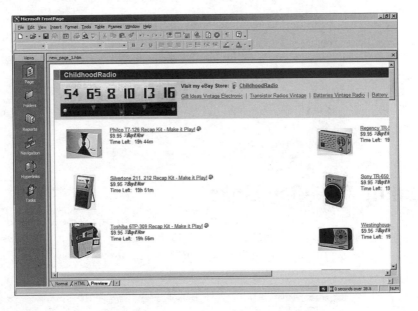

Use HTML in Your Emails

Now that you can quickly contrive HTML promotional boxes, try inserting them into emails as well. Figure 16.13 shows an example.

tip Remember, you can use this HTML just about anywhere—emails, blogs, message boards, in your listings, and on your websites. Be creative.

FIGURE 16.13
Use the HTML
you create in
emails, too.

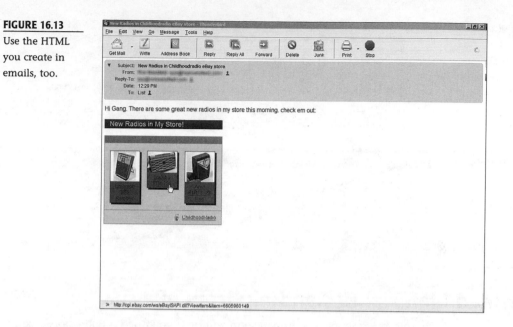

Promoting Your Store in Printed Materials and Elsewhere

We have already touched on one type of print advertising—those inserts you can make using the Promotional Flyer featured discussed in Chapter 15, "More Promotional Help from eBay." But there are many other things to try.

I print a catalog of my store items, like the one shown in Figure 16.14, and include it with the items I ship. I also make it available in PDF form on my websites. People love to curl up with catalogs. Consider adding a coupon or some other call to action.

Alternatively, instead of a full-fledged catalog, you might want to try a lighter, smaller, less expensive tri-fold brochure, again perhaps with a coupon, sale notification, or some other compelling reason to visit your eBay store.

Put Your Store URL on Everything!

By now you should know your eBay store's URL and be using it on everything. Put it in your email signature. Put it on your letterhead. Include it on your business cards. Make T-shirts and wear them to events you attend.

FIGURE 16.14

Consider including catalogs or brochures with your shipments.

Printed Material Design Help from eBay

If you are a PowerSeller (and you soon will be if you open a good store), you can put your PowerSeller logo in your print items, and even take advantage of free templates eBay provides to help you make business cards, letterhead, thank-you notes, envelopes, and more. Figure 16.15 shows a couple of examples.

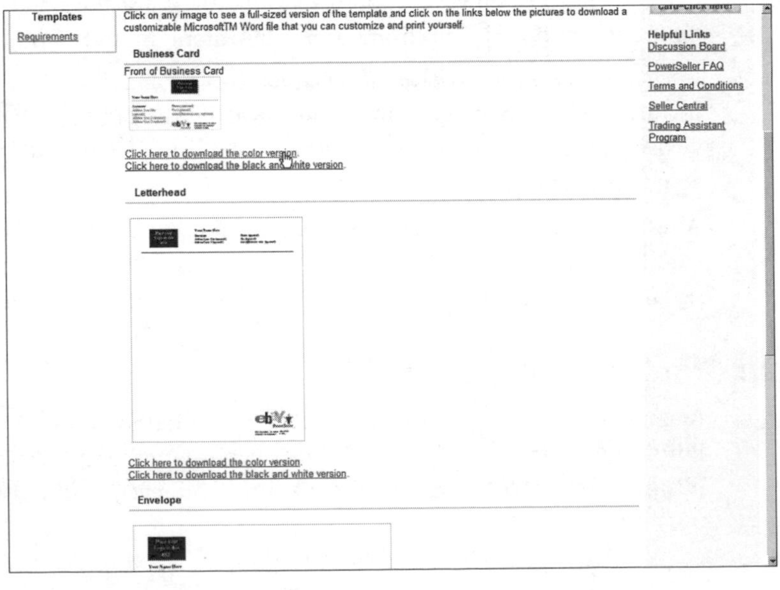

FIGURE 16.15

PowerSellers can download templates including the PowerSeller logo.

Reach these templates by visiting the PowerSeller portal; then visit the resources link and select Logo and Icon Resources. The templates work with Microsoft Word and compatible applications.

Swag

Everybody loves swag—coasters, baseball caps, logowear of all sorts—and you can create some of these inexpensive giveaways to help your shoppers keep you in mind. The best are everyday items people will use by their computers—pens, notepads, coffee mugs, and so on. And because you will be shipping them, lighter items are probably better.

You can buy them locally, or design and order them online. For example, Figure 16.16 shows me designing a new pen online at customink.com.

FIGURE 16.16

Design and order your swag online.

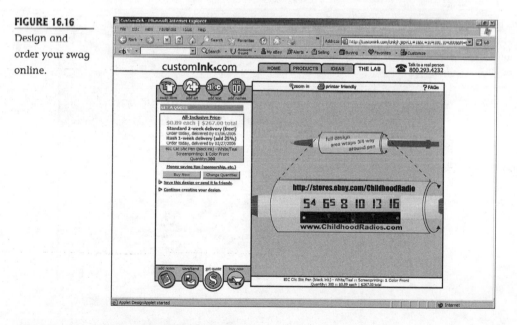

eBay Co-op Advertising

If you are a PowerSeller, you can get matching funds from eBay for certain print advertising expenses as long as they meet eBay's stringent (and mercurial) requirements. The ads need to appear in eBay-approved publications. You need to

- Be a PowerSeller in good standing.
- Fill out a registration form.

■ Agree to eBay's Terms and Conditions.

■ Design your ad(s).

■ Submit them for preapproval.

■ Run and pay for the ads.

■ Submit a reimbursement request form along with tear sheets for the ad(s), an invoice, and a rate card including circulation numbers.

While all this sounds like time-consuming, hard work (which it is), the rewards can be worthwhile. This program is actually not run by eBay directly; it's administered by a third party. To learn more about co-op ad funds, visit http://www.ebaycoopads.com.

There you will find the necessary forms, guidelines, approved publications lists, and more. Figure 16.17 gives you a sense of this.

FIGURE 16.17

Some of the publications eligible for eBay co-op advertising funds.

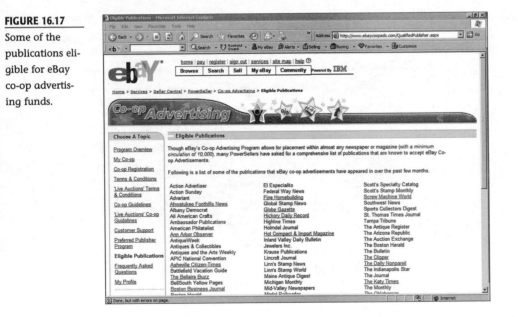

Store Referral Credits (eBay Fee Discounts)

Throughout this book, I have suggested that you put some effort into pushing people from "off of eBay" to your eBay store using private websites, blogs, email newsletters, forums, shopping search engines, and other Internet marketing techniques. I have also recommended that you include your eBay's store URL on business cards, letterheads, advertising, and so on.

If you have taken that advice to heart, here's where you get the payoff, or at least one of the mighty big ones. The official name for this feature is "Store Referral Credits," but I like to think of it as the "Final Value Fee Reduction" feature.

Shoppers who visit your store from outside of eBay and then buy things from your store reduce your eBay final value (FV) fees for the items they purchase by a whopping 75%. So if the eBay final value would have been $10.00, for example, it will now be $2.50 instead. This is potentially one of the longest pry bars in your toolbox, and you should use it every chance you get.

What's "Outside of eBay"?

Any site that does not contain "ebay.com" in its URL is considered to be "outside of eBay." So, a shopper using eBay's search tools at www.ebay.com or www.motors.ebay.com to find your store items would *not* qualify you for the discount, but someone using Froogle does meet the outside-of-eBay criteria. People

note Shoppers must have cookies enabled in their browsers for you to get referral credits, and they must purchase during the same browser "session." (Read more about this in a moment.)

who click to your store from a link found on your personal website qualify. People clicking your store URL (http://stores.ebay.com/ChildhoodRadio, or whatever), would qualify you for the discount. If you place your store URL in marketing emails, blogs, and anyplace else that can hold a hyperlink, you can earn the referral credit.

Where Should You Send Shoppers

You can get the fee reduction by sending shoppers from outside of eBay to any of the following landing spots. As you will see momentarily, for many sellers some of these are better choices than others. You can get referral credit when shoppers are pointed to one of the following:

- Your store's landing or home page
- The listing page for a store inventory item
- A custom category or subcategory in your store
- Your About Me (a.k.a. About the Seller) page
- Custom store item searches you create for shoppers

The Importance of Adding "refid=store" to Links

There is one slightly confusing requirement when creating links that qualify for discounts, and we might as well get it out of the way up front. When building referral links, you need to add "referral ID codes." Which is to say, you must sometimes, but not always add "refid=store" to your links when building them. In "refid," the "ref" part stands for "referring," and "id" stands for "eBay ID." So what we are saying to eBay when we build these links and people click them? We're saying, "Hey, here comes somebody from off of eBay *referred* to eBay by me, eBay seller *so-and-so*."

Just to make it interesting, at times you need to preface "refid=store" with either a question mark or an ampersand ("?refid=store" or "&refid=store").

Which part of the store you refer to dictates whether you use an ampersand or question mark. Stick with me on this. It will begin to make sense in a moment.

Sometimes eBay can determine that you are due the fee reduction without the referral code appendage, sometimes not, so it's probably a good idea to always include it, except in print, on business cards, and so on. Let's look at the various types of links, when to use them where, and how they should look.

Store Landing or Home Page Links

The safest, and perhaps simplest way to earn referral discounts is to simply point shoppers from outside of your store directly to your store's landing page (http://stores.ebay.com/ChildhoodRadio, or whatever). This will take them to your store's home page, and eBay will figure out automatically that the shopper came from outside, even without the referral ID added to the end of the URL. (Nonetheless, it's safest to add the ID code, so http://stores.ebay.com/ChildhoodRadio?refid=Store is safer than the unembellished store URL http://stores.ebay.com/ChildhoodRadio.)

The great thing about bringing shoppers to your store's landing or home page is that if it's a good page, it will give shoppers an overview of everything you have to offer and get them intrigued.

The downside is that if a shopper is in a hurry or is looking for something specific, and you have a large and varied selection, he or she might go elsewhere after being put off by the size and scope of your store. So there are times when you will want to build links to specific items or store categories. You might even want to do specific searches within your store ,for them.

Store Item Listings Links

If you build links to store items, be sure the items are store inventory items, not auctions or BINs, and will be around for a while. This is particularly important if the links you build will be visible on the Internet for a long period of time.

Link only to items with plenty of inventory. Keep the shelves stocked and the listing live at all times if possible. You don't want to get negative feedback or a bad reputation for doing a great job of promoting items you can't deliver.

If you must "take down" a store inventory listing and relaunch it, the links to the old item will be dead. For example, suppose you list 12 of the same batteries in your store, and eBay assigns the listing number 6590306837. If you build links to that listing (6590306837), once the 12 batteries

caution Only point shoppers to store inventory items. Pointing them to auction items or traditional Buy It Now listings will not earn you the credit!

sell, the links will point to items no longer available. It would be better instead to point to the store category or subcategory where you showcase all your batteries. If this is even remotely likely to happen, consider linking to the store category containing the item(s) instead.

To create a link to a specific store item, simply visit the item's listing with your browser, copy and paste the URL from your browser (see Figure 17.1), and then add "?refid-store" at the end. Figure 17.2 shows me creating a link like this in a Thunderbird email.

Custom Category or Subcategory Links

Pointing people to categories can be a good idea if you offer a diversity of goods or if you want to split shoppers off into subclassifications. For example, if you have a shoe store you might have categories and subcategories for men's shoes, boy's shoes, and so on.

FIGURE 17.1

Copy the URL from your browser.

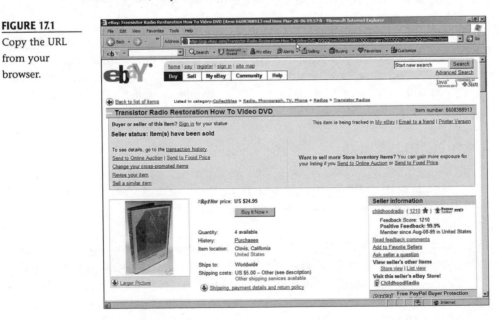

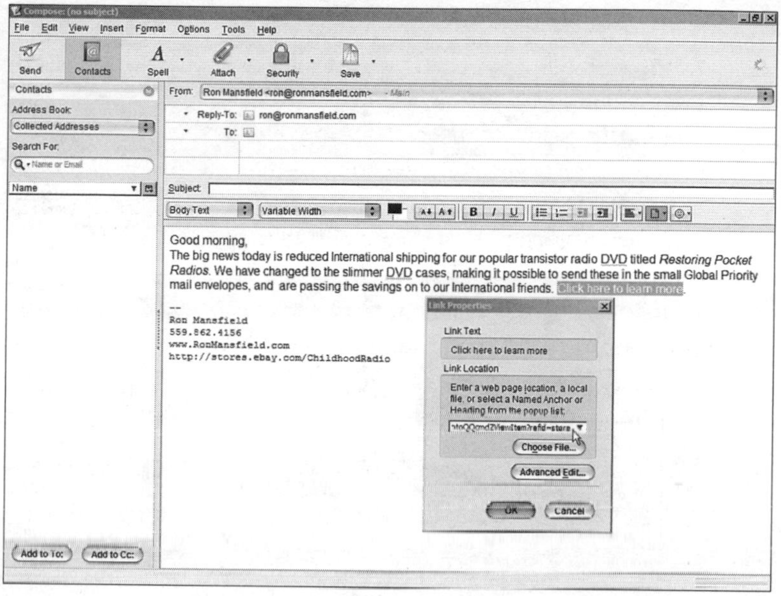

FIGURE 17.2

Add "?refid=store" when linking to specific store items.

You can drive people from outside to these custom store categories by using the same search techniques you learned for creating custom pages back in Chapter 8, "Custom Store Pages." The difference is, here you need to append the links with the referral ID to get the fee discount. Refer to Figures 17.3 and 17.4 while digesting the steps.

1. Visit your store and click a category link (Batteries, for example).

2. Copy the resulting link from your browser to use as the beginning of the new referral link you are creating.

3. Paste the link in its destination web page, email, or whatever.

4. Add "?refid=store" to the end of the new link.

About Me Links

It is possible to link from the outside world to your About Me page (which eBay also calls the "About the Seller" page on some parts of the site). Visitors who land there and subsequently purchase from your store can qualify you for credits.

I think driving people to your About Me page rather than to something specific to buy is a risky thing to do. You run the risk of people saying, "Oh, he collects radios...whatever," and then moving on to another seller's merchandise. I would personally rather have people see my storefront, one of my store categories of interest to them, or a specific item instead.

FIGURE 17.3

Select the browser link for the desired category.

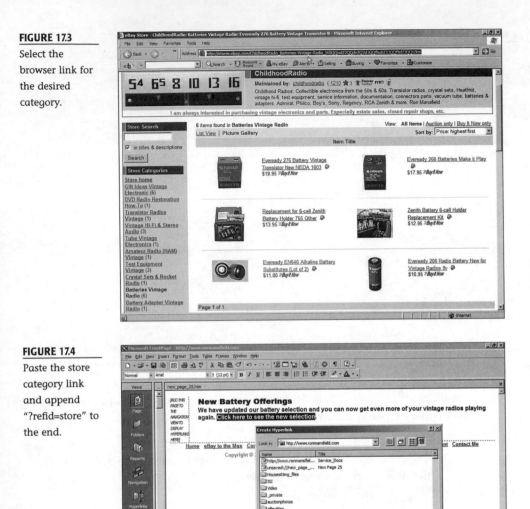

FIGURE 17.4

Paste the store category link and append "?refid=store" to the end.

But if you have a killer About Me page and want to send people to it, here's how to do that:

1. Navigate to your About Me page with your browser.

2. Copy the link from your browser to use as the beginning of the link.

3. Paste the link in its destination web page, email, or whatever.

4. Add "&refid=store" to the end of the link.

Custom Searches You Create

You have already seen the power of custom in-store searches you create for shoppers back in Chapter 8. These searches round up and present just the items in your store that meet the search criteria. For example, I could search my entire store for things of interest to a Sony transistor radio collector and present a search results page showing just those items.

Once you have generated the search results, copy and paste the resulting browser link, as you have seen several times before in this chapter, and then add "&refid=store" to complete the link. Notice that you need to use an ampersand (&) here rather than a question mark. Whenever a URL already contains a question mark (?), use the ampersand before "refid=store". Otherwise, use the question mark before "refid=store".

Confirming Referral Credits

You can see the results of your off-eBay referrals by checking your eBay bill following the addition of the referral links. You should see the full final value fee followed by the discount when you have earned it. Figure 17.5 shows an example of this.

You will get an email each month from eBay when your invoice is ready. You need to check the invoice details to see discounts. You can use the details link in the email or you do the following:

1. Visit your My eBay page.

2. Click the Seller Account link.

3. Click the View Invoices link.

4. Pick the desired month from the drop-down list.

5. Scroll through the details.

6. Review the Payments and Credits section (see Figure 17.5).

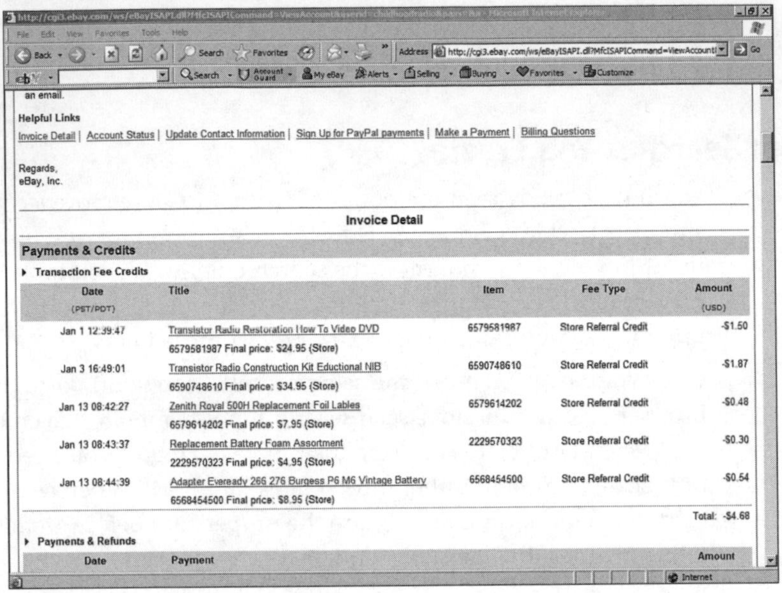

FIGURE 17.5

Be sure to confirm your discounts by checking your eBay bills.

When Won't You Get Credit?

There are a number of reasons why you will *not* get credit when you think you should. Here are the main ones:

- The shopper's browser won't accept cookies.
- The buyer visits your store from within eBay, (clicks a store link in one of your auctions, finds you in the store directory, and so on)
- The shopper closes the web browser window used to navigate from outside of eBay to your store, store category, or store inventory item.
- The shopper wins an auction or Buy It Now item viewed in your store (credits are only given for store *inventory* items).
- The shopper visits someone else's store after visiting yours (neither store gets credit).

Getting Noticed by Search Engines

The folks at eBay do a pretty good job of helping promote our store items on the Internet without our intervention. But there are things we can do to improve our chances. RSS feeds and the exporting of store listings are covered in Chapter 20, "Really Simple Syndication (RSS)," so we'll ignore those topics for the moment and concentrate here on keywords used by search engines.

Let's start with a look at the keywords eBay automatically publishes for your store pages. We'll look at the generic way first. We'll also discuss a slick tool eBay provides that can help you see and change your keywords more easily.

About Page Titles and Meta Tags

Most search engines look at, among other things, the page titles and meta tags associated with your store pages. These are sometimes also called *meta descriptions* and *meta keywords*. They are created automatically for you by eBay, but you can change them.

Using the "Source" view in your browser, you can find your eBay store page's title and meta tags in the page's HTML source code, as follows:

```
<HTML>
<HEAD>
<TITLE>Title Tag Goes Here<TITLE>
<META name="description" content="Meta Description Tag Goes Here">
<META name="keywords" content="Meta Keywords Tag Goes Here">
<HEAD>
<BODY>
Other code here
<BODY>
<HTML>
```

You can see your store page's title on the top blue bar of your browser window.

An easier way to see the meta tags associated with your listings is to use the Keywords link in the navigation area of your Manage My Store page. You'll see a page something similar to Figure 18.1 that contains your keywords.

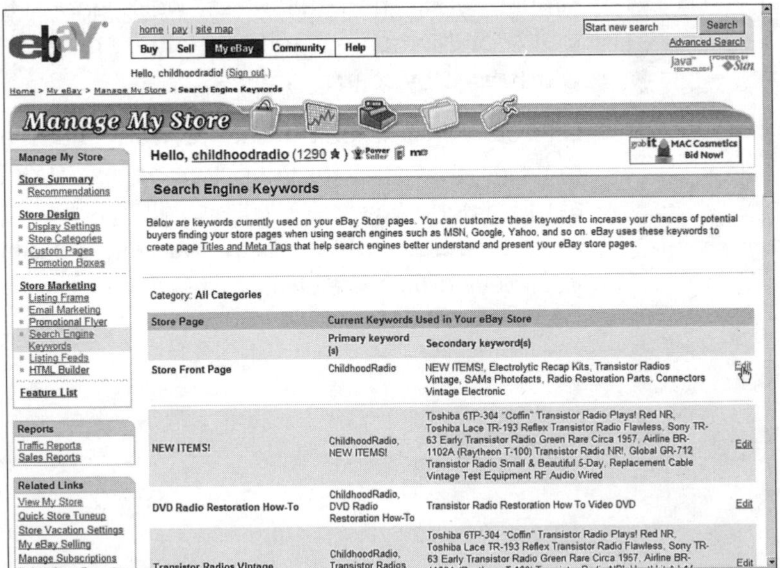

FIGURE 18.1

Typical eBay-generated search engine keywords.

Here you can see (and edit) the keywords for each page. To edit, click the Edit link at the right edge of each page listing (see Figure 18.1). You will be presented with a screen that looks similar to Figure 18.2, where you can make changes. But don't just yet.

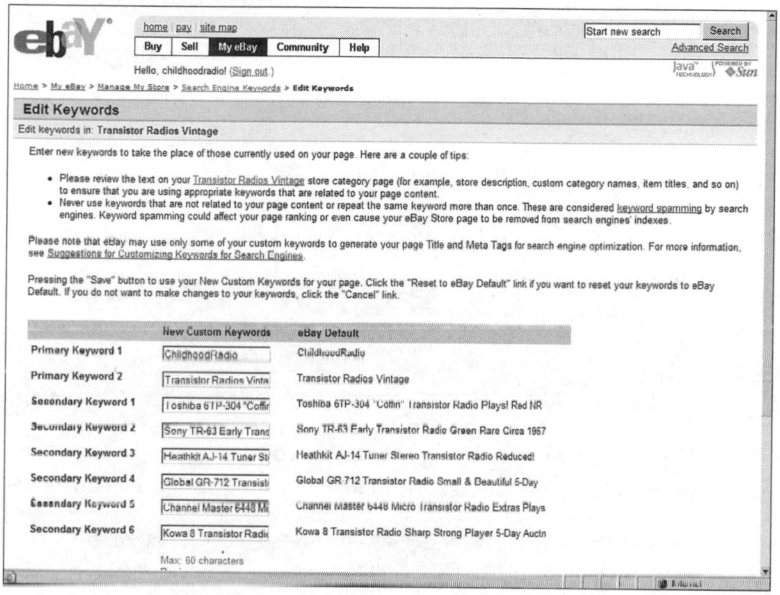

FIGURE 18.2

This is where you edit keywords.

Many of the keywords change automatically over time as you list and sell items. You might be wise to leave these alone if they are working for you—and they often work for me, especially because I use many Good 'Til Sold and long auctions. If you do decide to change these keywords, give some thought to the new ones. The following sections provide some tips.

How Are Shoppers Searching Your Store?

It seems obvious, but one way to drive more traffic to your store from both inside and outside of eBay is to make sure your store pages contain keywords and titles that people are actually searching for. You can and should subscribe to Traffic Reports, which show you what search words people are using when they visit your store. Reports are covered in more detail in Part IV, "Reports," but let's take a quick look at the Finding Methods Reports here. Figure 18.3 shows the starting point for keyword reports, available once you subscribe to traffic reports, as discussed in Chapter 23, "Using eBay Store Traffic Reports."

FIGURE 18.3

Launch optional keyword reports.

FIGURE 18.3

Launch optional keyword reports.

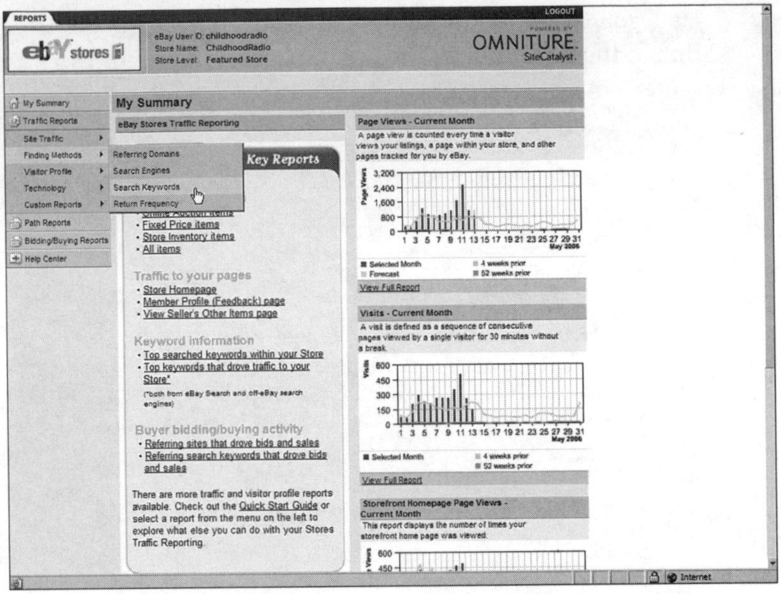

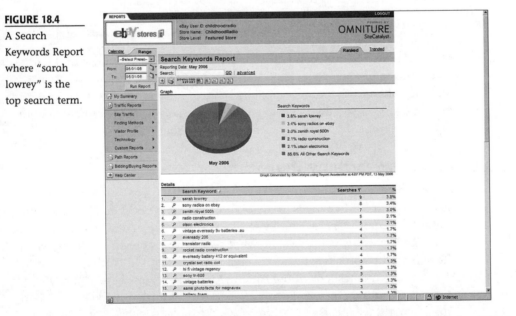

The Search Keywords Report shows you how people search your store over the time period you specify. You can see an example in Figure 18.4.

FIGURE 18.4

A Search Keywords Report where "sarah lowrey" is the top search term.

At the time I was writing this book, I acquired one of the world's largest and most well-known collections of transistor radios, previously owned by Sarah Lowrey. Word got around that I was selling the collection, and within two weeks people were searching my store for "sarah lowrey," making that a very popular search term. If it's not in my list of keywords, it had better be, huh?

The report in Figure 18.4 covered the month of May (the first two weeks in May, actually). You can also look at longer time periods (up to 12 months' worth), which can be useful, and will probably give you different results than shorter time periods.

Changing Keywords

Once you know some keywords you want to change, simply go back to the Keywords link in Manage My Store and make the changes. Figure 18.5 shows me adding "sarah lowrey." It can take 30 minutes for your store search keywords to update on eBay, and it might be as long as 30 days for the search engines to catch up, but this is usually not the case.

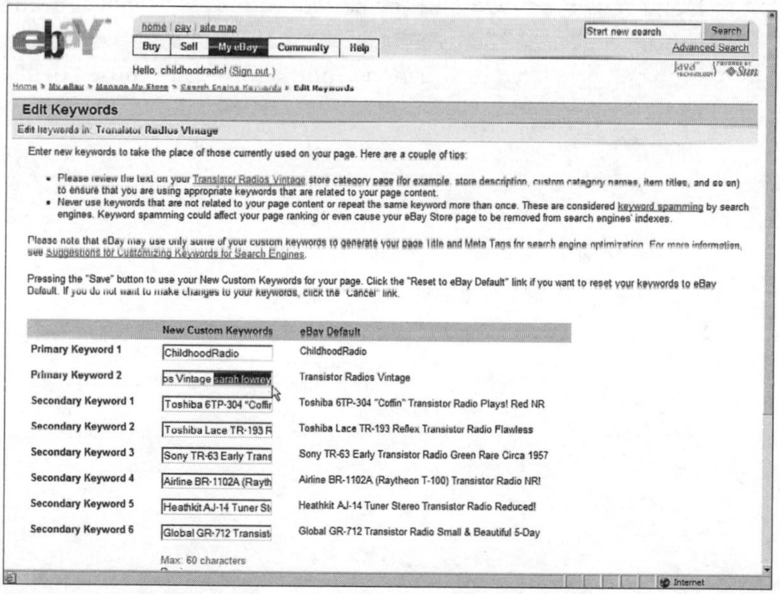

FIGURE 18.5

Edit keywords.

Keyword Tips and Cautions

Avoid keyword spamming. You can incur eBay's wrath, and even be ignored by search engines, by using words not associated with stuff you actually sell (for example, Rolex when you actually sell Timex watches). If eBay automatically assigns item titles as keywords and you are in the habit of repeating popular search terms in your titles (which is often a good idea), when you go to update your store's meta tags, eBay will scold you for using the same repetitive terms they've plucked from your titles and placed in the Tags list for you automatically. For example, I always try to use "transistor radio" in my listing titles, and eBay often inserts those titles in the secondary search terms. However, if I try to alter the store's meta tags, I'll be required to remove the fourth and subsequent occurrences of "transistor radio." Hey, if it was easy, everybody would be a PowerSeller.

Use keywords your potential buyers are likely to search for (for example, "watch" or "clock" instead of "timekeeping devices").

Choose keywords that are consistent with the content on your pages. For example, use store category names and listing titles as keywords. This is what eBay does automatically for you, by the way. This is also a reason to pick powerful store page names and item titles.

Use keywords that are synonyms. For instance, "clock" and "watch" and even "wristwatch" are related.

Don't repeat any word in the keyword phrases more than three times. For instance, you should avoid using "dvd," "dvd player," "dvd burner," "dvd blanks," and "dvd recorder" as your keywords because "dvd" is repeated more than three times. A better set of keywords would be "dvd player burner blanks recorder."

eBay Express and Other Comparison Shopping Sites

Shopping comparison sites is one way to round up items for sale by multiple merchants and let shoppers find the best deal. Many comparison sites also offer the opportunity for customers to rate their shipping experiences with the various merchants.

Now eBay has added eBay Express to the mix, a comparison shopping site composed of only eBay sellers, at least for the moment.

By having an eBay store, creating RSS feeds, and opting to export your store listings to search engines and comparison sites, you can drive shoppers to your eBay store from the likes of Froogle, Yahoo! Shopping, Shopping.com, and others. To do this, follow these steps and refer to Figure 19.1.

1. Visit Manage My Store.

2. Click the Listing Feeds link in the left-side navigator.

3. Click the Distribute Your listings via RSS radio button.

4. Click the radio button labeled "Make a file of your Store inventory listings available."

5. Click Apply.

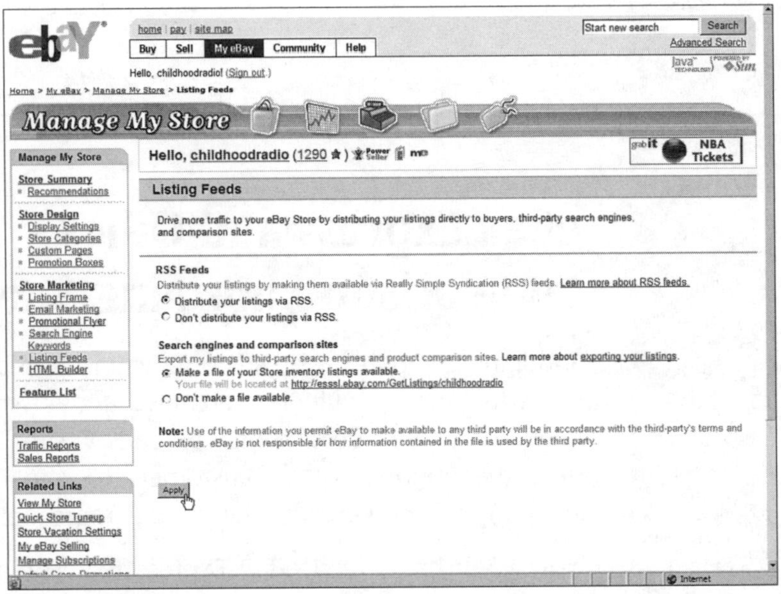

FIGURE 19.1

Enable RSS feeds and export store listings to third parties.

The world of comparison shopping is constantly changing, and it seems like new sites are appearing every week. Others fail and disappear. Some charge for their services, but many are free, at least for basic exposure. Let's see at how a search for those recap kits I sell looks on some of the more-trafficked comparison sites. In each case, I have simply searched for "recap kits."

Froogle and Google

As you can see in Figure 19.2, Froogle (www.froogle.com) does a wonderful job of showcasing my eBay store items. Even my gallery thumbnails are displayed. It's almost too easy.

A Google (www.google.com) search turns up the kits as well, but in a less dramatic way, as you can see in Figure 19.3.

FIGURE 19.2

Froogle does an excellent job of showcasing eBay store items.

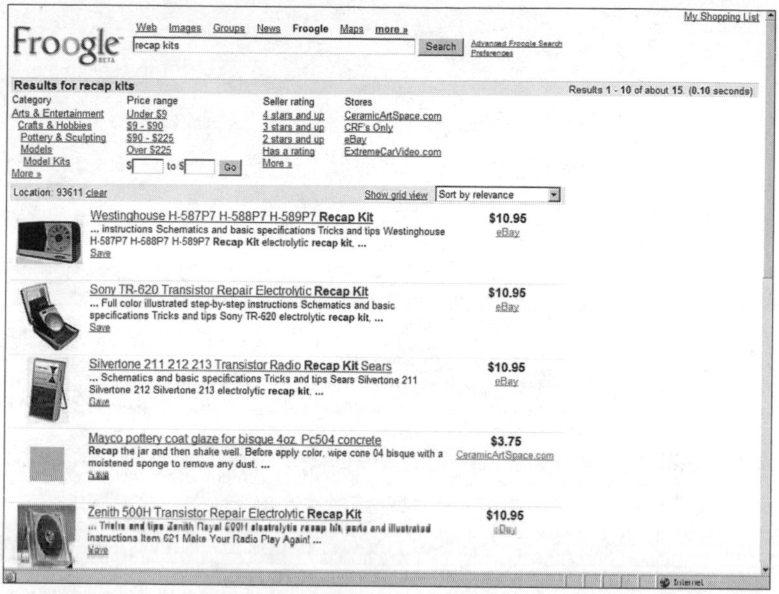

FIGURE 19.3

Store inventory feeds make it to Google too, but less graphically.

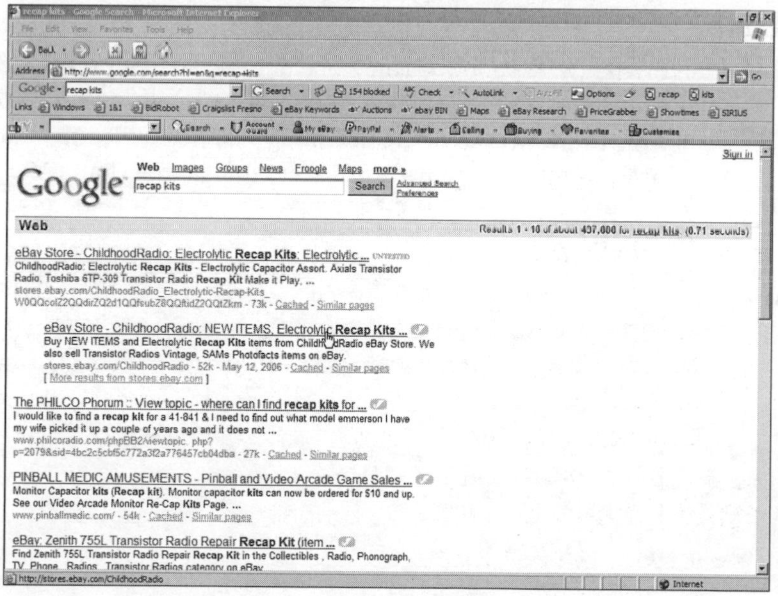

Yahoo! Shopping

Yahoo! Shopping searches reveal the store items, but here again they have the text-based appearance of a Google search, as you can see in Figure 19.4.

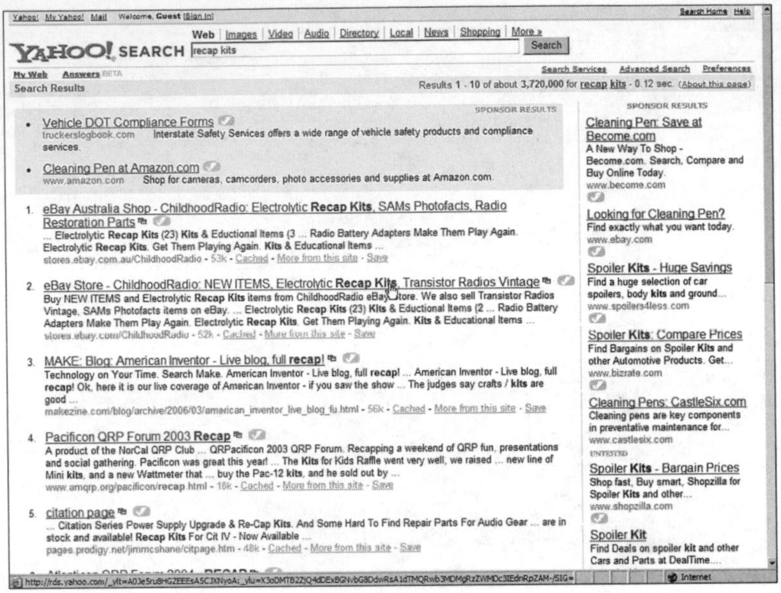

FIGURE 19.4

Yahoo!
Shopping search
results are text-
based links.

FIGURE 19.4
Yahoo! Shopping search results are text-based links.

ShopWiki

ShopWiki (www.shopwiki.com), one of the new kids on the block, does a really nice job of showcasing my eBay store items, again with next to no extra effort on my part. However, notice that ShopWiki has pulled the main photo from my listings rather than use the Gallery image (see Figure 19.5).

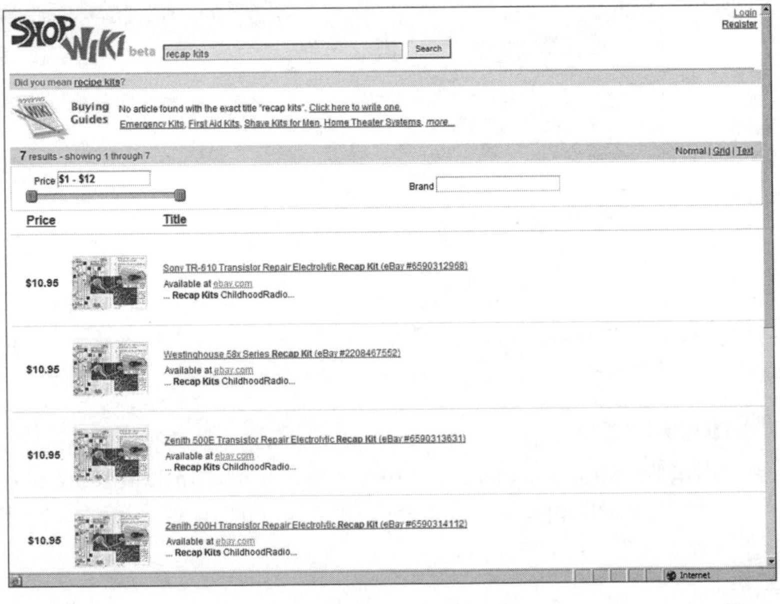

FIGURE 19.5

ShopWiki is
new, and cool.

FIGURE 19.5
ShopWiki is new, and cool.

Clicking a link takes you to a summary that has been automatically culled from my listing description. There's a link to the actual listing, and a chance to rate the product. Shoppers can also elect to add price alerts, create wish lists, or email found items to friends. It's excellent, and free.

Shopping.com

You would think that now that eBay owns Shopping.com, our stuff would get special treatment there, huh? But instead, shoppers need to scroll down quite a ways to click a special eBay search link that opens the listing, as you can see in Figure 19.6. Items do appear at Shopping.com, and again the service is free. Chances are eBay item visibility will improve over time.

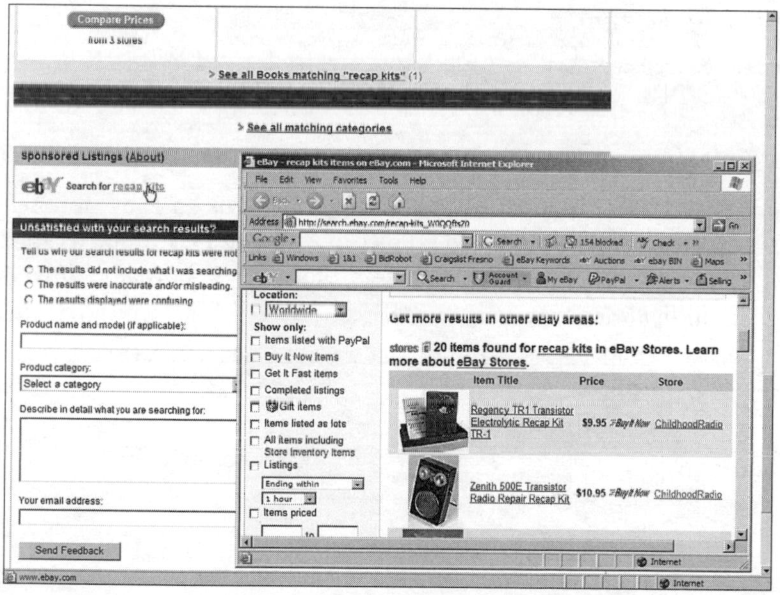

FIGURE 19.6
Shopping.com is disappointing, at least at the moment.

eBay Express

The big news, of course, is eBay Express (www.ebayexpress.com), shown in Figure 19.7. It's a new, separate site set up by eBay giving shoppers an opportunity to compare items from diverse eBay sellers, and dump them into a shopping cart where they can check out and pay for their multiple items from multiple sellers with one click. Well, okay, with a lot of clicks, but they can treat the whole shopping experience as a single transaction.

FIGURE 19.7

eBay Express is here. But is it right for you?

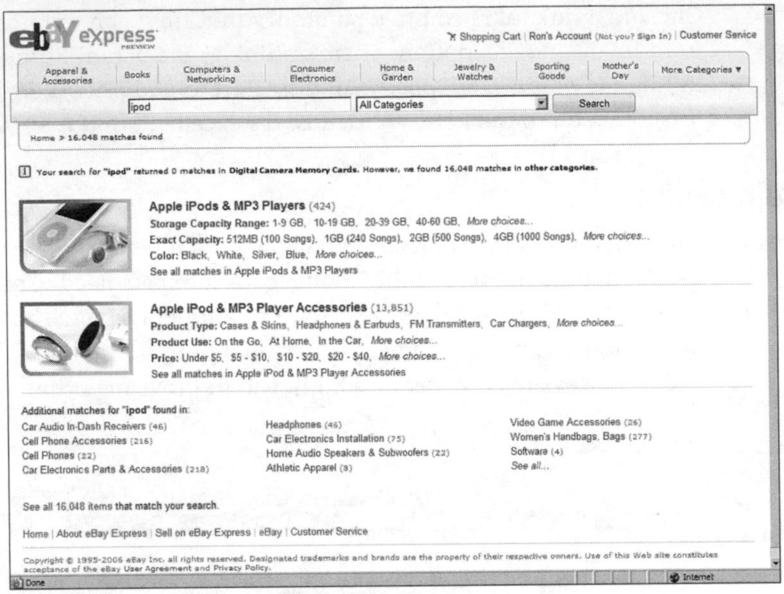

Express can be an effective outlet for you as an eBay store seller, but there are some considerations to ponder first. Figure 19.8 shows a typical Express representation of an eBay store item. Figure 19.9 shows the same listing on eBay proper.

FIGURE 19.8

An eBay Express listing.

FIGURE 19.9

An eBay store listing.

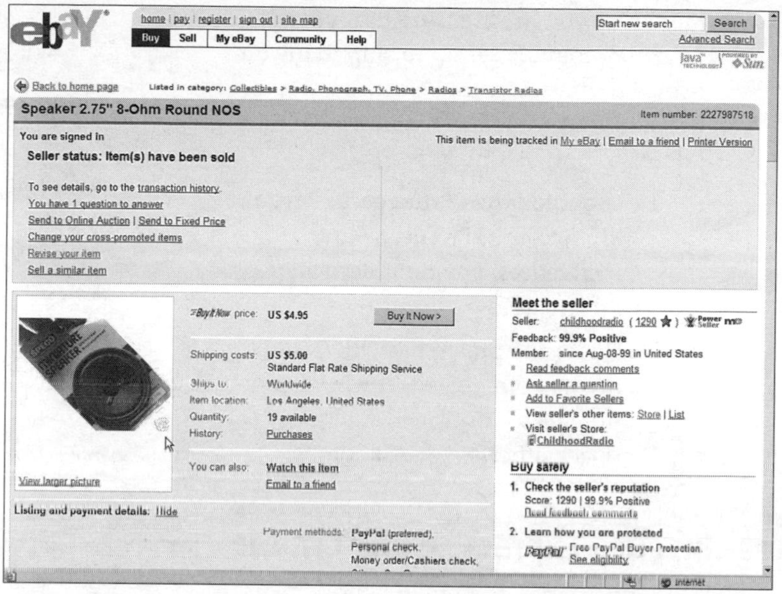

Besides the different appearance of your listings in Express, buyers are required to pay with PayPal and you cannot accept money orders, checks, and so on. This can be confusing to shoppers. Therefore, if you enable Express, you might need to change the boilerplate payment information in your store listings or change your store policy to match the Express restrictions. You can sell used items in your store, but there are restrictions preventing the sale of many but not all used items via Express. Also, items purchased through Express do not qualify for the "final value" discounts earned when buyers find your items from "off-eBay" sites.

Experience and Feedback Requirements for eBay Express

You need to be set up as a U.S. registered seller, or Canadian registered seller shipping from the U.S. You must maintain a feedback score of 100 or more, 98% positive or better, and make your feedback public. In my opinion, anyone with a store should have 100 or more sales under their belts or be on their way there, and have public feedback, so that's no problem.

PayPal Requirements for eBay Express

You will also need a PayPal Premier or PayPal Business account—again, probably an excellent idea for any store seller. What you must realize, however, is that shoppers cannot pay for their purchases other than via PayPal, so the terms and conditions in your listings should reflect this dilemma.

Moreover, you must ensure that your PayPal account is set up to ship to unconfirmed addresses or make sale-by-sale decisions ("Ask me for unconfirmed addresses"). Here's how:

1. Log into PayPal and go to PayPal, My Account, Profile, Selling Preferences, Payment Receiving Preferences.

2. Under the preference "Block payments from U.S. users who do not provide a Confirmed Address," select either No or Ask Me.

note If shoppers buy from your store and want to pay by check or money order, and you approve, they can do it. If they buy the same item via Express, they cannot pay by check or money order, and this is sure to cause them some confusion.

note Shipping to unconfirmed addresses does put you at some risk where PayPal seller protection is concerned, and you should give this some serious consideration before selling via Express.

Meeting the eBay Express Listing Criteria

Only fixed-price or store inventory items can be sold via Express, and you must indicate each item's condition (that is, new, used, or refurbished) in a new field. There are some category-specific exemptions to this, and the rules seem to change. Other conditions include the following:

- You need to use prefilled item information for listings within Books, DVDs & Movies, Music, and Video Games.

- Individual items must not exceed $10,000.

- You must include shipping costs (flat, calculated, or free) in the shipping fields.

- Listings must include at least one picture, and it needs to be an eBay-hosted photo, as shown in Figure 19.10.

- You must allow shoppers to pay by single, combined payment for their purchases. You can specify this by going to your Selling Preferences within My eBay. Look for the Shipping & Discount section (see Figure 19.11).

- You must use eBay checkout (as opposed to most third-party solutions) or the new checkout integration API for third-party order processing. If you are using a non-eBay checkout platform, contact the vendor to see whether Express is supported.

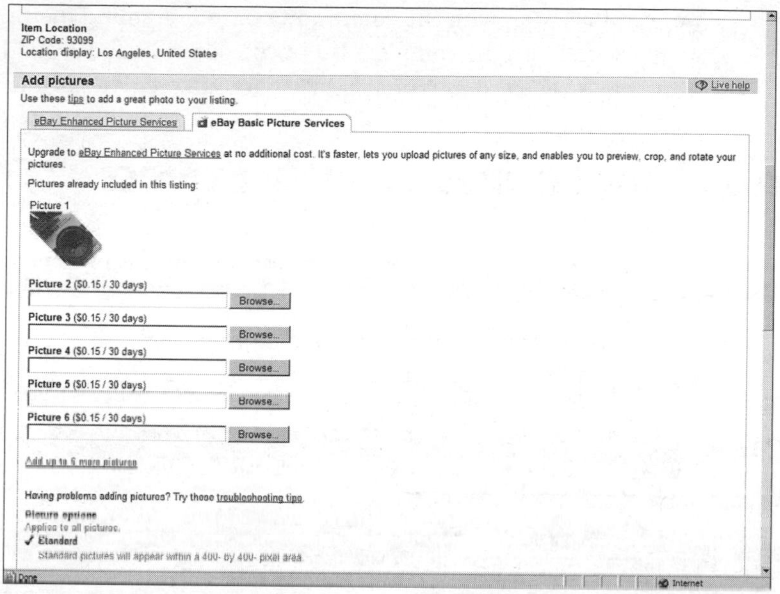

FIGURE 19.10

Be sure you use eBay's picture service for at least one photo if you want items to appear in Express.

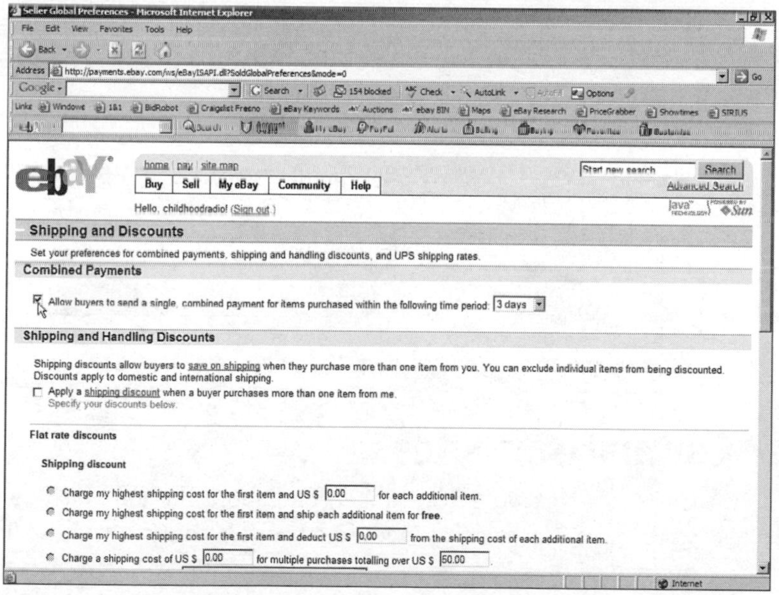

FIGURE 19.11

Be sure you enable Combined Payments if you use Express.

Meeting the Category Criteria

The majority of eBay.com categories are included in eBay Express. Categories not used in eBay Express at the time this book was written include those not covered by PayPal Buyer Protection and categories where Category Managers were still working with the community on representing their categories in eBay Express. See the complete list of categories included (and not included) at http://pages.ebay.com/express/service/about/categories.html.

Viewing Your Listings on eBay Express

You can check to see whether your items will appear in eBay Express by pasting the following link into your browser (obviously using your user ID instead of "youruserid"):

http://search.express.ebay.com/merchant/youruserid

Figure 19.12 shows an example.

FIGURE 19.12

Seeing your Express items.

Other Comparison Sites

Currently, NexTag, PriceGrabber, and Shopzilla don't display or compare eBay store items. However, as mentioned earlier, this is a volatile field these days, and you should keep your eye on it, particularly if you are selling popular items at attractive prices.

A good resource to help you watch all this moving and shaking is www.comparisonengines.com.

Really Simple Syndication (RSS)

Chances are you have at least heard the term *RSS*, perhaps while standing in the Starbuck's queue. Not exactly new technology (it's been around since about 1997). However, today RSS is pretty hot stuff. Now that so many RSS feeds are available, including some from eBay, if you are not RSS-savvy, you need to get started today. There are several ways to employ this technology as an eBay seller, with more uses on the horizon no doubt.

Really Simple Syndication, also known as *Real Simple Syndication* or *Rich Site Summary*, is a way for web content publishers (including eBay) to "push" information about updates into the hands of RSS subscribers.

Some examples of other RSS publishers include Yahoo! News, CNN, Forbes, and folks like that. The cool thing is that RSS feeds can provide you with a way to send rapidly updated information about your eBay listings to your customers. It's also a great way for you to check in on the progress of your auctions. Take a look.

What Do You Need?

To use eBay's RSS feeds, all you need is an RSS reader (also called an *aggregator*), and there are a bazillion of them, many free. Some browsers, including the Macintosh version of Safari, are also capable of reading RSS and bookmarking RSS feeds. Or you can use a standalone reader to download from sites such as the following:

- www.rssbandit.org
- www.sharpreader.com
- www.newsgator.com
- www.feeddemon.com

Alternatively, you can add RSS reading capabilities to many email programs. For example, Figure 20.1 shows my Thunderbird email program displaying the RSS feed for my eBay listings using the downloadable Live Bookmarks feature. There are similar add-ins for Outlook, of course, including some from the websites previously listed.

Using my email program, I can look at the latest information about by listings by simply clicking the links in the RSS "messages."

The subject lines of the email-like broadcasts contain the "headline" for each RSS "article," and the body contains the rest of the information.

I can also tell shoppers about my RSS feeds (I'll show you how in a moment), and then when I list new items, my customers will get feeds alerting them to the new items.

When new eBay listings launch, they appear in the RSS Feed folder of my email program. But my favorite way to get RSS feeds is via a little scrolling "ticker" that runs along the top of my screen. (Tickers can also be embedded in your web browser or placed at the bottom of your screen.)

Figure 20.2 shows an example. When I hover my mouse pointer over an item in the scrolling feed, it lets me check the progress and even click to go right to the listing.

You can read
RSS feeds from
many email
applications.

FIGURE 20.2

Scrolling news
readers let you
track listings
and jump to
them.

Creating RSS Feeds for Your eBay Listings

It's remarkably simple to start "broadcasting" information about your listings.
You visit the same page you did to enable search engine feeds back in Chapter
18, "Getting Noticed by Search Engines." Here are the steps involved:

1. Install and test an RSS reader if you don't already have one.

2. Log into My eBay.

3. Go to the Manage My Store page.

4. Choose the Listing Feeds link from the navigation area. You will see a
   screen like the one in Figure 20.3.

5. Click the "Distribute your listings via RSS" radio button.

6. Click the Apply button.

FIGURE 20.3

Turn on RSS feeds of your listings here.

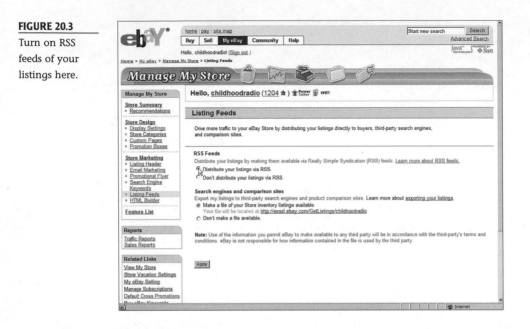

Seeing and Promoting Your RSS Feeds

Even promoting your eBay feeds is fairly simple, and eBay helps here, too. Once you have enabled feeds, eBay inserts a little RSS logo and link at the bottom of your store page, as shown in Figure 20.4.

When you (or your shoppers) click the RSS button, you will see the "raw" feed and be invited to copy and paste the URL into your browser or other reader. You need to copy and paste the URL from your browser's Address line, not the stuff in the main body of the page. The big arrow in Figure 20.5 shows what to copy and paste.

Where you paste the URL depends on what reader you use. In the case of Thunderbird or Firefox, for example, you place it in the Feed URL field, as shown in Figure 20.6.

FIGURE 20.4

The RSS logo appears on your store page when you enable feeds.

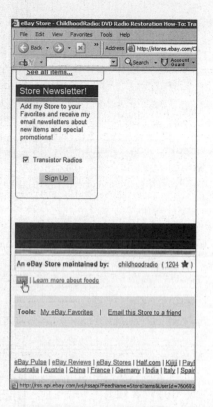

FIGURE 20.5

Subscribers need to copy and paste the long URL (above the arrow).

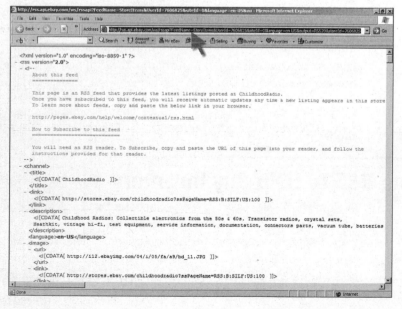

FIGURE 20.6

Paste the feed
URL into your
reader.

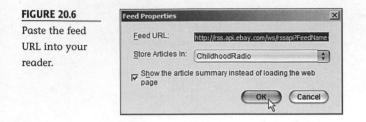

As RSS becomes more mainstream, people won't even blink when you tell
them they can watch your listings via RSS feeds. It's already time to start pub-
licizing your feed by including the URL (or maybe a prettied-up link to it) in
marketing emails.

For example, in my eBay newsletters I include the following phrase:

> *Oh, and have you discovered eBay's RSS feed feature yet? It's an even quicker
> way to get notified of new listings. You need an RSS reader, but it's all quite
> simple. Just Google "RSS How to."*
>
> *Here's my RSS feed link.*
>
> *Paste it into your reader and you will know almost instantly when I list new
> things.*

Getting News about eBay with RSS

Recently eBay started publishing news, policy changes, and system status via
RSS. You can expect this trend to continue. Two URLs for links worth subscribing to include http://www2.ebay.com/aw/announce.xml and http://www2.
ebay.com/aw/marketing.xml. Although these appear to be the same
announcements you can subscribe to via email, the system announcements
(http://www2.ebay.com/aw/announce.xml) might be worth adding to your
scrolling email reader because they could give you an early heads-up regarding technical issues.

Using RSS to Help Buy Inventory

A number of services are now available that will create custom RSS feeds for
you using criteria you define. For example, http://www.rssauction.com/ lets
you specify eBay searches including keywords, seller IDs, and much more.
These are similar to eBay's email-delivered search results, but are delivered via
RSS. Figure 20.7 shows a typical search setup page.

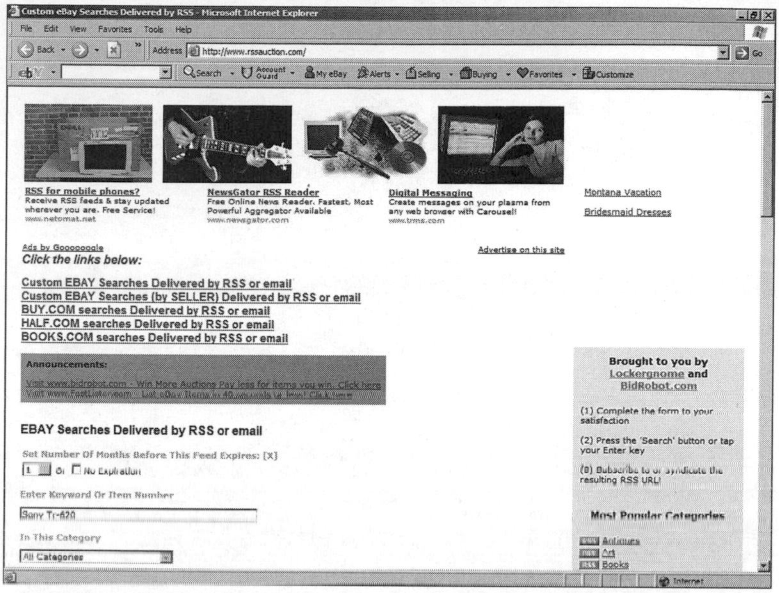

FIGURE 20.7

Some third parties will help you specify custom feeds.

By subscribing to RSS feeds from sources of merchandise that you buy to resell on eBay, you will know when your suppliers (manufacturers or eBay sellers, for example) have new items of interest to you. RSS feeds can often alert you to items before your competitors can see them and grab them. This strategy works particularly well for tracking down bargain Buy It Now and fixed-price items.

Part IV

Reports

Selling Manager Pro Summaries

Over the past year or two, eBay has beefed up the reporting features it provides to sellers. If you use Selling Manger Pro, you get some snapshots of your current activities and rough profit and loss calculations. Although these are no substitute for a "real" bookkeeping system, they can give you a running idea of how things are going. Let's take a look.

Selling Manager Pro Reports

Selling Manager Pro creates a series of simple profit and loss (P/L) reports that you can view online, print, or download. These reports should not be confused with the optional Store Sales Reports discussed in Chapter 22, "Using Store Sales Reports." Figure 22.1 shows a basic Selling Manager Pro report.

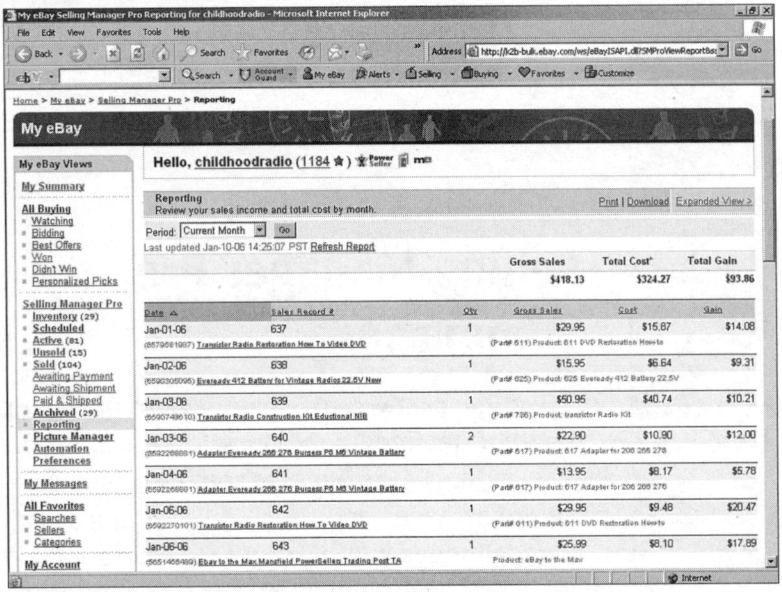

FIGURE 21.1

The unvarnished Selling Manager Pro report.

The unexpanded version of the report simply lists gross sales, total costs based on the cost data you've entered for each item, plus the associated selling fees, and it displays an approximate total gain or loss. The gross sales, costs, and loss or gain are shown next to each line item as well, representing the P/L of the sale.

These data are not automatically updated. The "Last updated" date and time information displayed under the Period area in the upper-left section of the report tells you when the data was last refreshed. Looking at Figure 21.2, you can see that eBay last updated the data used in the example on January 10 at about 2 p.m. You must click the Refresh Report link next to the updated date and time to make SMP fetch the current data for you.

When you click Refresh Report, the Reporting page will turn into something looking like Figure 21.3, telling you to wait for the update request to be processed. Clicking the Selling Manager Pro Summary link takes you back to the Summary screen.

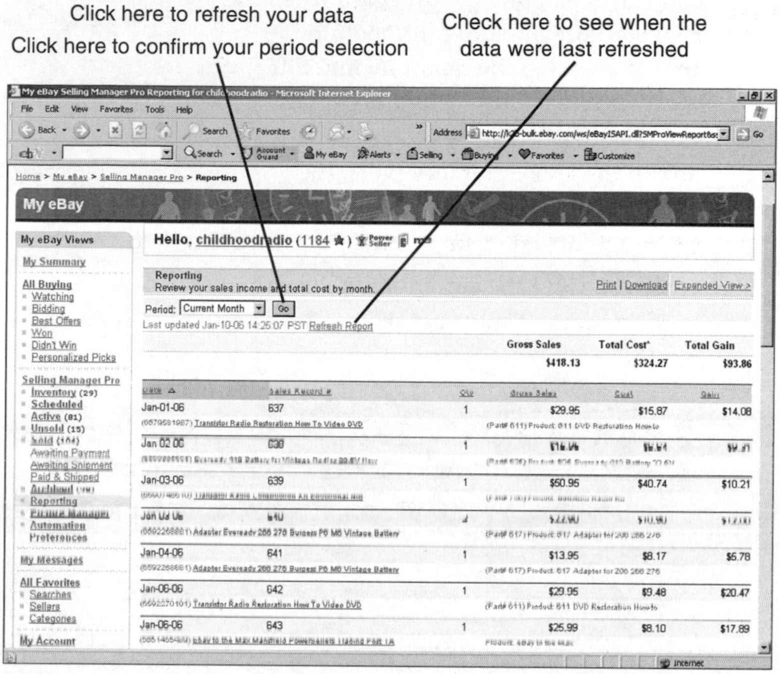

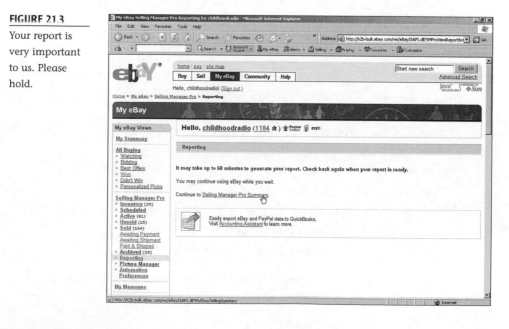

FIGURE 21.2
Remember to update reports before using them.

Click here to refresh your data
Click here to confirm your period selection
Check here to see when the data were last refreshed

The length of time it takes for updates to occur has to do with the size of your files, number of transactions, eBay's workload, and other factors.

FIGURE 21.3
Your report is very important to us. Please hold.

You will eventually get an email when the new data are in place (although the emails often lag the report availability considerably). Once the updating has completed, when you click the Reporting link in the SMP Summary page, the Reports page will reappear displaying the newly updated date and time and the current data.

> **note** You are only permitted to update reports once every 4 hours, so wait until you have finished any work you want reflected in your reports before refreshing.

Once you have the current data, it's useful to click the Expanded View button to get a more detailed breakdown by transaction. Figure 21.4 shows the results.

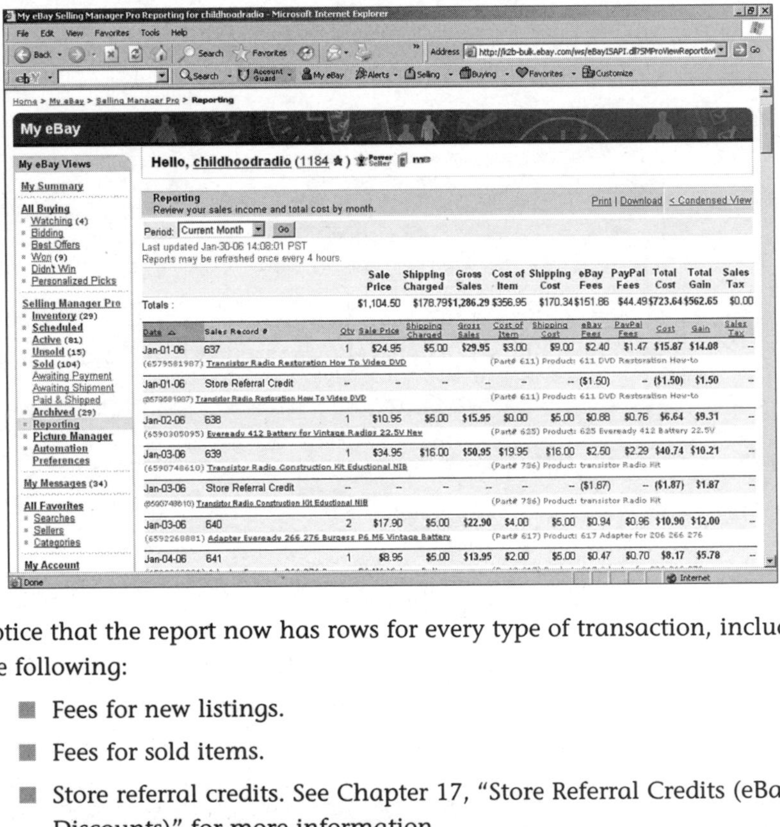

FIGURE 21.4
SMP's expanded report view shows line-by-line costs.

Notice that the report now has rows for every type of transaction, including the following:

- Fees for new listings.
- Fees for sold items.
- Store referral credits. See Chapter 17, "Store Referral Credits (eBay Fee Discounts)" for more information.
- Your notes and part numbers if you have entered them.

The top of the report in Figure 21.4 shows a row of subtotals, including these items:

- Sale Price

- Shipping Charged

- Gross Sales (final value + shipping income)

- Cost of Item (only accurate if you enter this information)

- Shipping Cost (only accurate if you enter/edit this information)

- eBay Fees

- PayPal Fees

- Total Cost (cost of item + shipping cost + fees)

- Total Gain (or loss)

- Sales Tax (if you have collected any)

note You can sort reports by clicking any of the column headings shown in Figure 21.4 (Qty, Sale Price, and so on). Alternate clicks switch between ascending and descending sort order.

If you sell multiple items to the same person, you will notice that these items are combined on a single row, as shown in Figure 21.5.

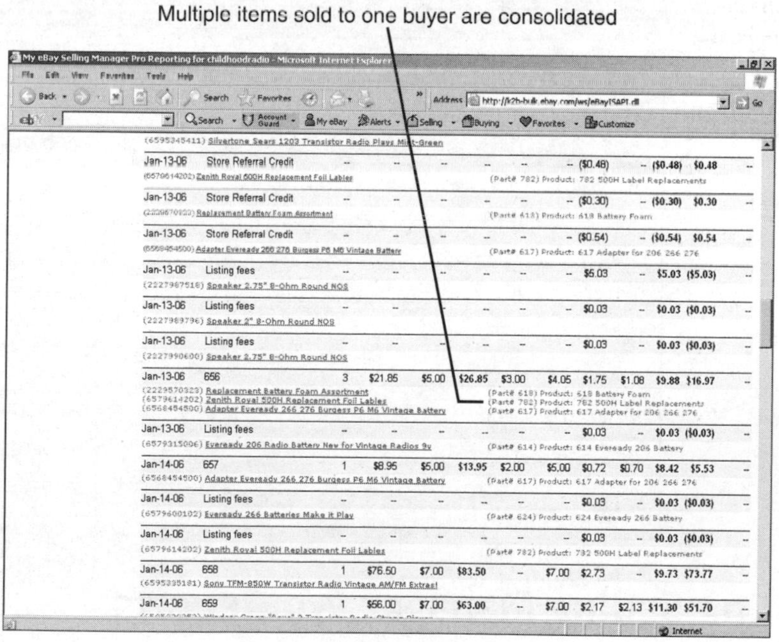

Multiple items sold to one buyer are consolidated

FIGURE 21.5

Combined shipping items are shown together.

Beneath the Totals line is a row of similar but not identical headings describing the columns in the report. Clicking these headings lets you sort the report by them. For example, in Figure 21.6 I've sorted by PayPal fees. By default, the report is sorted by date.

Although you probably won't use these reports for tax reporting and other "true" bookkeeping tasks, they can give you a good idea about how things are going, which items are popular and profitable, when and if eBay or PayPal fees are costing so much that you need to rethink your listing and pricing strategies, and so on.

You can also keep an eye on whether your store referral credit links (discussed in Chapter 17) are working right. Notice the three credits listed in Figure 21.5. This means that shoppers found these items via links from "off eBay," and as a result, the eBay final value fees were reduced. Seeing those credits here can be a quick way to see if your referral links are working properly.

The reports can show you how many people purchase multiple items from you at the same time as well. This is an indicator that your store is "sticky" and has multiple items of interest to shoppers. Figure 21.5 shows an example of one such sale on January 13.

FIGURE 21.6

Click the headings to sort your report (by PayPal fees in this example).

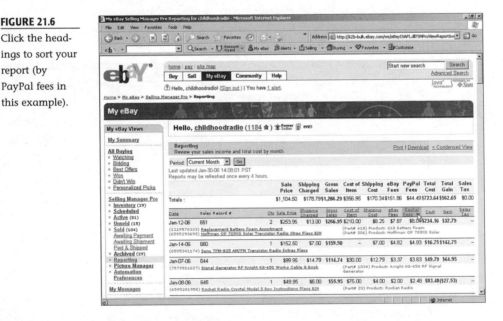

Printing Selling Manager Pro Reports

Clicking the Print link opens a new window containing only the report details, without the navigation bars and other screen clutter. Use your browser's Print command to print the resulting window. Figure 21.7 shows this.

FIGURE 21.7

Printing the
report is just a
click or two
away.

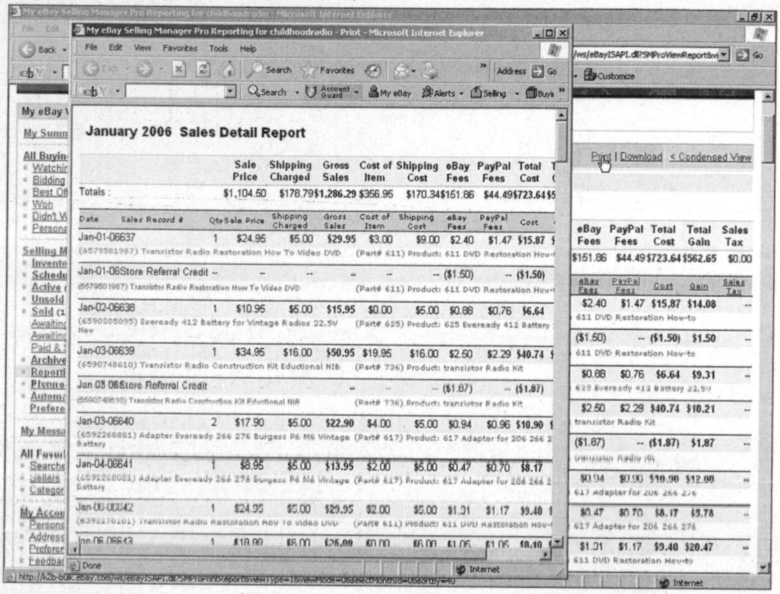

Downloading Reports

It is also possible to store the data from these reports to your hard disk. This is
great if you want to further massage the data in a spreadsheet or integrate the
data with a database you've created. Here are the steps:

1. Display the report you want to download, being sure the data are current, that you have selected the desired month, and, if the sequence is
important to you, that the onscreen report is sorted to your liking.

2. When you are ready, click the Download link. You will be presented
with a File Download dialog box like the one shown in Figure 21.8.
Click Save.

3. Specify the desired folder location (a separate eBay download folder
perhaps) for the resulting comma-separated value (.csv) file.

4. Click Save.

The data will be downloaded in this order:

- Date
- Sales Record #
- Item ID
- Item Title

- Part #
- Product Name
- Qty
- Sale Price
- Shipping Charged
- Gross Sales
- Cost of Item

- Shipping Cost
- eBay Fees
- PayPal Fees
- Cost
- Gain
- Sales Tax

FIGURE 21.8

Downloading
a report as a
.csv file.

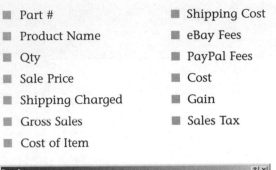

And if you have Microsoft Excel or a compatible spreadsheet program, you
can open the resulting .csv file. It should look something like Figure 21.9. You
can also import this stuff into a database if you prefer. Not all resulting cells
in a spreadsheet or fields in a database record will contain data.

As with all downloads it seems, some data massaging might need to be done.
For example, look at Figure 21.10. Do you remember those three combined
items back in Figure 21.5? They show up in the .csv file (and therefore in a
spreadsheet or database) as four rows with combined cost and income numbers and no dollar amounts in the individual items' cells. Stuff like this drives
accountants as well as spreadsheet and database folks to drink.

If you plan to automate your "real" bookkeeping tasks and import your data into
QuickBooks, you will want to use the tools
and techniques described in Chapter 12,
"Store Bookkeeping and QuickBooks,"
instead of, or perhaps in addition to, the
features in this chapter.

 note Mark your calendar.
Download all
PayPal and eBay data monthly.
Most of it is only available online
for 90 days or less.

FIGURE 21.9

Store data downloaded to a worksheet.

	A Date	B State Item Id	C Item Title	D Item #	E Part #	F Product Name	G Qty	H Sale Price	I Shipping C	J Gross Sal	K Cost of It	L Shipping C	M eBay Fee	N PayPal Fe	O Cost
2	Dec-01-05	668455419	Allied Knight 83Y/67	Trans-Midge	Transistor Radio Rare										$5.05
3	Dec-01-05	668561563	Global GR-711	Leather Case	amp; Box. Transistor Radio NR		$21.90	$10.00	$31.90	$0.00	$5.00	$4.20			$4.20
4	Dec-01-05	668456668	Continental TR-632	Power Pac.	Transistor Radio w/Extras		$19.99	$8.00	$28.99	$0.00	$5.00	$5.05			$5.05
5	Dec-01-05	668458659	Hitachi 666	Transistor	Radio Box. Instructions & Extras		$263.95	$13.00	$266.95	$210.00	$3.85	$5.05			$4.45
6	Dec-01-05	668461337	Zenith Royal 500H	Transistor	Radio Museum Quality NR						$13.16	$8.04			$4.45
7	Dec-01-05	583721313B	Craig TR-490	Tape	Recorder Vintage Cardige Format NR						$3.95				$24.40
8	Dec-01-05	583680123	Clarkstan Phono	Stylus	Pressure Gage Vintage Needle NIB		$27.77		$37.77	$7.00		$1.39	$79		$24.45
9	Dec-01-05	668480476	RCA 3RG21G	Transistor	Radio Vintage Extras Plays NR						$3.95			($0.46)	$0.70
10	Dec-01-05	668491693	Magnavox 2-AM-60	Pocket	Transistor Radio Vintage Plays						$7.95			($0.30)	$1.00
11	Dec-01-05	668497628	Philco T86-126	Pocket	Transistor Radio Vintage Plays NR						$3.85			($0.54)	$1.00
12	Dec-01-05	587931506	Eveready 2	614	614 Eveready 2	1	$10.95				$1.95			$5.03	$6.64
13	Dec-02-05	752798732	Amphenol 75-MC1M	Connector Vinta			$9.95			$2.00	$3.85			$0.03	$6.53
14	Dec-02-05	752799508	Amphenol 75-2 MINI	Connector Vinta			$9.95								$6.38
15	Dec-02-05	752798751	Amphenol 75-PC1M	Connector Vinta			$9.95								$7.26
16	Dec-02-05	766850213	Paco 6-30 RF	Signal	Pac G-30 Sign		$69.95			$13.16					$18.58
17	Dec-04-05	587981420	Zenith Roy	740	740 X2 Zenith Roy		$7.95			$3.85					$6.17
18	Dec-04-05	584351054	Eveready	1740	1740 X2 Eveready		$11.00			$5.00					$6.64
19	Dec-04-05	588724737	Allied Knight	Transist	Recap Kits		$9.95			$3.95					$6.10
20	Dec-04-05	587961420	Zenith Roy	762	762 500H Labe		$7.95			$0.60					$2.77
21	Dec-05-05	587961987	Transistor	611	611 DVD Resto		$24.95			$3.85					$8.57
22	Dec-05-05	584336729	Zenith Roy	782	782 500H Labe		$7.95			$0.64					$6.32
23	Dec-06-06	584020344	Regency TR1	Transis	Recap Kits		$9.95			$0.52					$10.25
24	Dec-06-06	598907050	Vintage Ra	1065	1065 Calendar 2006						$12.30				$12.30
25	Dec-07-05	648664760	Best of Discovery	Channel	DVD Volu		$16.50			$4.00					$5.88
26	Dec-07-05	598907050	Vintage Ra	1065	1065 Calendar 2006		$12.95			$3.85					$9.63
27	Dec-07-05	598907050	Vintage Ra	1065	1065 Calendar 2006		$12.95			$5.00					$11.50
28	Dec-07-05	648664600	Adapter E	617	617 Adapter for 206 266 276						$0.05				$0.05
29	Dec-10-00	210007441	Makku yu	Own	Tranistur Radiu Tee		$7.95			$8.00					$6.31
30	Dec-10-00	220	Nikku yu	Own	Stylus Pressure Ga		$11.60			$6.00					$8.47
31	Dec-11-05	589604533	Clarkstan Phono		Stylus Pressure Ga		$34.96				$0.66				$12.57
32	Dec-11-05	668455919	Allied Knight 83Y/67	Trans-Midge	Tr		$82.00			$0.40					$12.57
33	Dec-11-05	668456698	Continental TR-632	Power Pac.	Transis		$140.00			$4.50					$14.03
34	Dec-11-05								$4.53					

FIGURE 21.10

Multi-item sales export with combined dollar amounts.

Multiple items sold to one buyer are consolidated

	A	B	C State Item Id	D Item Title	E Item #	F Part #	G Product Name	H	I	J	K	L	M	N	O	P
28			668463423	EBay to the Max Mar			EBay to the Max				$0.00	$7.25	$13.30	$1.54	$13.30	$13.30
29		647	668036596	Eveready 2	625	625 Everei					$0.00	$6.00	$1.75	$1.05	$10.54	$21.36
30		648	668483423	Ebay to the Max Mar			eBay lo the Max eBay to th				$210.00	$8.25	$8.04	$1.05	$8.10	$17.89
31		651	220957023	Replacem	618	618 Battery Foam		$21.90	$10.00				$7.87		$234.16	$33.79
32		651	656035693	Hoffman O	306	306 Hoffman OP 709XS Solar		$19.99	$8.00							
33		652	669534411	Silvertone Sears	1203	1203 Transistor		$263.95	$13.00							
34			587814202	Zenith Roy	782	782 500H Label Replacements		$27.77				$7.00	$1.39	$1.40	$9.79	$27.98
35			220957023	Replacem	618	618 Battery Foam							($0.46)		($0.46)	$0.48
36			220957023	Replacem	618	618 Battery Foam							($0.30)		($0.30)	$0.30
37			668045000	Adapter E	617	617 Adapter for 206 266 276							($0.54)		($0.54)	$0.54
38			227289736	Speaker 2.75	8-Ohm	Round NOS*							$0.03		$0.03	($0.03)
39			227289736	Speaker 2.75	8-Ohm	Round NOS*							$0.03		$0.03	($0.03)
40			227289300	Speaker 2.75	8-Ohm	Round NOS*							$0.03		$0.03	($0.03)
41		656						$21.95			$3.00					
42		656	220957023	Replacem	618	618 Battery Foam	3	$21.95	$6.00	$26.95		$4.05	$1.75	$1.08	$9.88	$18.97
43		656	587814202	Zenith Roy	782	782 500H Label Replacements										
44		656	668045000	Adapter E	617	617 Adapter for 206 266 276										
45			587915006	Eveready 2	614	614 Eveready 206 Battery							$0.03		$0.03	($0.03)
46		657	587815006	Eveready 2	614	614 Eveready 206 Battery		$8.95			$5.00		$0.72	$0.70	$8.42	$5.53
47			668464600	Adapter E	617	617 Adapt							$0.05		$8.42	$5.53
48			587900102	Adapter E	624	624 Eveready 206 Battery							$2.73		$9.73	$73.77
49		658	587814202	Zenith Roy	782	782 500H Label Replacements		$8.95		$13.95			$2.17	$2.13	$11.30	$5.70
50		659	669533852	Windsor Green Boys* 2	Transist			$76.50		$83.50	$63.00	$7.00	$4.82	$4.93	$16.75	$14.75
51		660	669534174	Sony TFM-625	AM/FM	Transist		$56.00		$63.00	$63.00	$7.00	$2.00	$1.95	$10.95	$46.05
52		661	668534633	Hitachi 627R	Transistor	Radio S		$152.50		$159.50	$57.00	$7.00	$0.03		$0.03	($0.05)
53			218601267	Transistor Dial	String	Diagrams & String		$50.00		$57.00			$0.03		$0.03	($0.05)
54			668302507	DISASTER	AID 23	Crystal Radio Bomb Shelter Cold War							$3.05		$3.05	($3.05)
55			668020507	DISASTER	AID 23	Rocket Radio							$3.05		$3.05	($3.05)
56			589021866	Sony TFM		306	Hoffman OP 709XS Solar							$0.03		$0.03	($3.05)
57			595918382	Heatkit AJ	1092	Heathkit AJ-14 Tuner							$0.03		$0.03	($0.03)
58			668036596	Eveready	625	625 Eveready 412 Battery 22.5V							$0.03		$0.03	($0.03)
59			668036637	Eveready	782	782 Eveready 276 battery							$0.05		$0.05	($0.05)
60			669031382	Allied Knight	Transist	Recap Kits							$0.05		$0.05	($0.05)
61			669312000	GE P780	Transist	F Recap Kits							$0.05		$0.05	($0.05)
62			669312499	Regency TR1	Transis	Recap Kits							$0.05		$0.05	($0.05)

Using Store Sales Reports Plus

For many eBay sellers, their sales statistics are simple facts in such a small quantity that the numbers are easily carried around in their heads. If you are paying attention, it's not hard to mentally keep track of such things as last month's total sales, your sales to date this month, average selling prices, percentage of successful sales, and perhaps a notion of whether your auction items are selling better than your fixed-price or store items. But eventually things will get out of hand. You will have too many products, too many months, and too many numbers to remember even in a slow month. You will need reports. In this chapter, I tell you how to use all that information available to you.

Sales Reports Plus

As an eBay seller, you can obtain plenty of reports, perhaps even too many. In addition to the basic reports discussed in the previous chapter, store owners should subscribe to optional sales reports that come in two flavors—Sales Reports and Sales Reports *Plus*. If you have a Featured store (and I think that you should), you will get the Plus reports at no extra cost as part of your store fees, so that's the version of reports we will examine here and in the next chapter as well.

Important Concepts

As you rattle around in eBay's reporting, you need to keep several concepts in mind. Let's take a moment to think about the terms *metrics*, *items*, and *listings*, and also ponder the limitations of this type of reporting in general:

- **Metrics**—You will see the term *metrics* used in some of eBay's screens. This refers to your operational statistics. Average selling price, percent of successful sales, and number of items sold are all metrics.

- **Items vs. listings**—Many of us have fallen into the bad habit of using the terms *items* and *listings* interchangeably, especially those of us who have sold long enough on eBay to remember when the terms actually were synonymous. But now that we can launch one listing to sell multiple items, the difference is an important one, particularly where reporting is concerned. Think of listings as unique "ad pages." One listing might contain a single doll you want to auction. Another listing might offer a hundred iPods you want to sell, one at a time, to multiple buyers at a fixed price over a specified period of time--over the next 7 days, for example.

To muddy things just a bit more, remember that with eBay's new Good 'Til Sold auctions, "over time" can mean over a really long, unpredictable period of time.

As you will see when we get to the reports, eBay handles these situations very differently for reporting purposes.

Let's say you launched three listings that ended in the same month with the following results:

- Listing 1: One item, which sold
- Listing 2: One item that did not sell
- Listing 3: Three items, one of which sold and two that did not

In eBay's way of thinking, that's a total of three ended *listings*. Two of the listings ended successfully, even though not all of Listing 3's items sold. However, because one item sold in Listing 3, eBay counts the listing as successful.

In this scenario, eBay counts five ended *items* and will report two successful items sales.

Your successful *listings* report would show 67% (two of three listings had at least one item sold), but your sold items percentage would be displayed as 40% because only two out of five items sold. Got it?

So, if you are doing a lot of multiple item listings, the Items reports will probably be more accurate, or at least more informative than the Listings reports.

Other Reporting Limitations

The old adage about having one foot in hot water and the other in cold making you comfortable "on average" certainly applies to many of the statistics you will see in eBay's (and most other) sales reports.

For example, if you look at a report showing the average selling price on eBay for items in the cell phones category, you would be looking at such a wide variation of products that the numbers would be nearly meaningless.

The report would include the results of adding up the selling price of such disparate things as new and used phones, plain and absurdly overfeatured phones, case shipments of 24 phones, $10 phones requiring an annual subscription not billed through eBay, and even accessories that have been miscategorized intentionally or accidentally.

If you are really interested in how much a particular model of a new cell phone is fetching on eBay, you need to do some serious "drilling down" to find the truth.

These same anomalies will creep into data about your own eBay sales. So, although it's interesting and even useful to comb through reports to spot trends and identify things you can fine-tune, realize that simple answers are often wrong answers, even when using your own data.

What the reports described in this chapter do best is help you spot, and perhaps even understand, historical trends regarding things you have sold. At a minimum they will get you thinking about how to better your business.

Paralysis by Analysis

One last thought: It is easy to get so caught up in looking at reports and trying to figure out how the numbers got there and what they mean that you get distracted from actually running the business. Don't get distracted.

Put aside a specific period of time each week or month to look at the reports and then get back to work. The true measure of success will be your ending checkbook balance, and only some of the things that you can do to improve your bank balance show up in these sales reports, not everything.

Subscribing to Reports Plus

If you have never used Sales Reports Plus before, you will need to subscribe. Then eBay will generate the first batch of reports, and keep generating them thereafter, as long as you continue to view your reports occasionally.

note After the first report generation, which can take up to 72 hours (but probably won't), new weekly reports will be available by each Thursday of the following week.

Begin by visiting your My eBay page and scrolling until you see the My Subscriptions link on the left side of the screen, as shown in Figure 22.1. If you don't see any report links, you have not yet subscribed and should click Manage My Store to start the process.

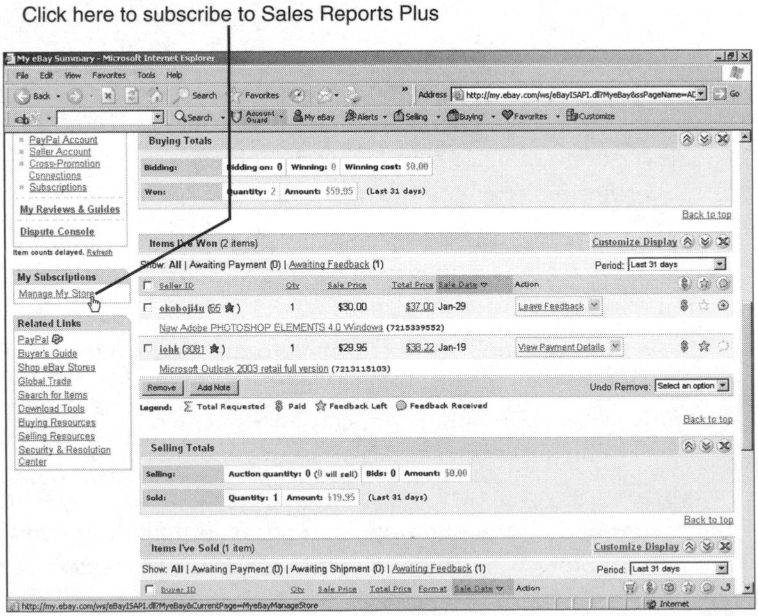

Click here to subscribe to Sales Reports Plus

FIGURE 22.1

Beyond here lies reporting....

The Manage My Store page contains a Reports section in the left navigation area. Click the Sales Reports link there. You will be told that you have not yet subscribed. (You knew that already, huh?) Click the Sales Reports link on this Sales Reports screen, as shown in Figure 22.2.

FIGURE 22.2

I know, I know, I want them!

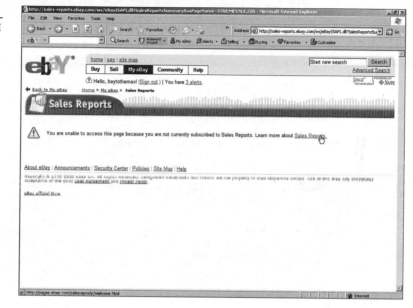

You will be taken to the Sales Report overview page and see two Sign Up Now buttons—one for Sales Reports, the other for Sales Reports Plus.

The basic reports are free for all store owners. The Plus reports are free for Featured and Anchored stores. Otherwise, you will be charged $4.99 per month. A 30-day free trial is available, so you should probably try the Plus version, even if you are not running a Featured store and are skeptical of reporting in general. Click the desired Sign Up Now button.

You will be asked to sign into your eBay account (again) and then to read and agree to the terms by clicking the Agree box. Click it and then click the Start My Subscription button.

You should see a Congratulations screen with a tantalizing View Your Report button; however, clicking that button will probably result in a screen telling you that the first report might take up to 72 hours to appear (although it will probably be ready sooner than that). You will also get a welcoming email almost instantly, again asking you to be patient.

Even before the reports are ready, if you go back to your My eBay page and scroll down, you should see Sales Reports listed as an option in the My Subscriptions section of the left navigation area (see Figure 22.3).

FIGURE 22.3

After subscribing to Sales Reports Plus, a new link appears here.

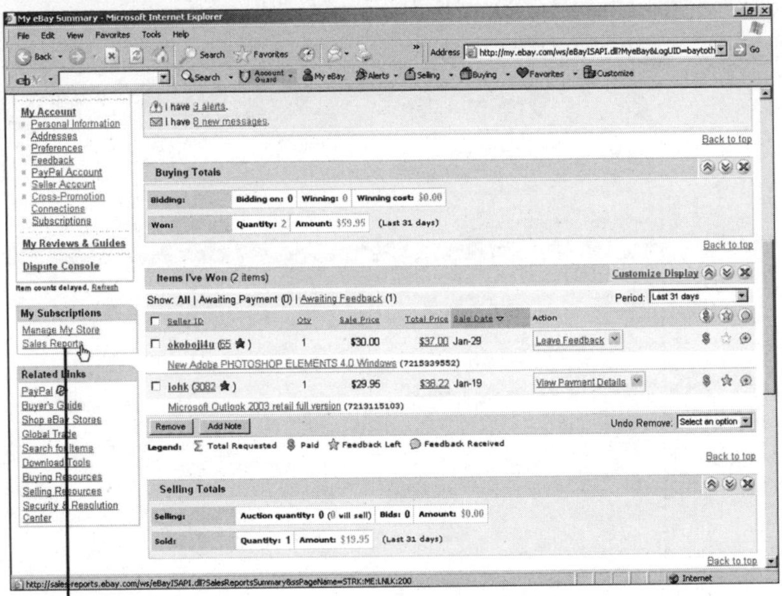

Link appears when you subscribe to Sales Reports Plus

Eventually, when the reports are ready, you will be able to see them by clicking that new link. For now, let's look at some sample reports from one of my selling accounts in the next section.

Categories of Reports

Reports fall into the following three broad categories:

- Sales Summary (Sales, Fees, and Unpaid)
- Sales by Format (Type, Ending Day, Time, and Duration)
- Sales by Category
- Marketplace Comparisons (All Sellers in Specific Categories)

Sales Summary

Let's start by looking at the default opening screen, a Sales Summary containing the most recent full month, and the prior 2 months if you have data going back that far. Figure 22.4 shows an example.

FIGURE 22.4

The Sales Summary compares up to 3 months' worth of history.

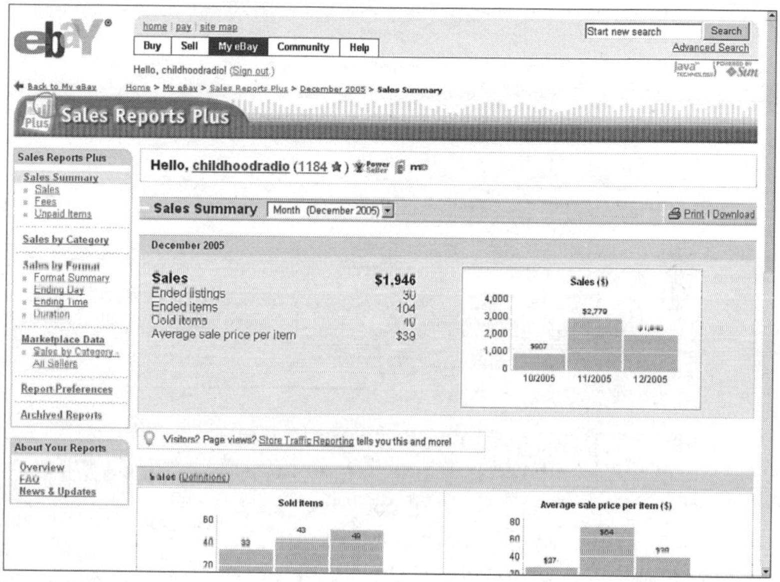

In Figure 22.4, you can see the top of the Sales Summary for December 2005, with sales of $1,946 coming from 30 listings, 104 ended items, and 49 sold items.

To the right you see a graph comparing December's Sales with two prior months'. October's total was $907 and November's was $2,779. Scroll down this page a bit until you see something resembling Figure 22.5.

Now you can see a chart with the number of sold items for each of the three months, and the average selling prices for the same time periods.

Beneath the charts you see detailed breakouts. These are mostly the data used to create the charts, but look carefully. For example, there's a Repeat buyers line in the chart that can tell you about customer loyalty trends.

By watching these statistics over time, you can learn what's working and what's not. For example, in October, 95.2% of the items sold. In December, only 24.2% of the items sold. What the heck is going on here? What I would really like is more months like November, with relatively high selling prices, sell-thru rates, sold item %, and positive sales growth. Or do I? Perhaps the answer lies in the rest of the reports.

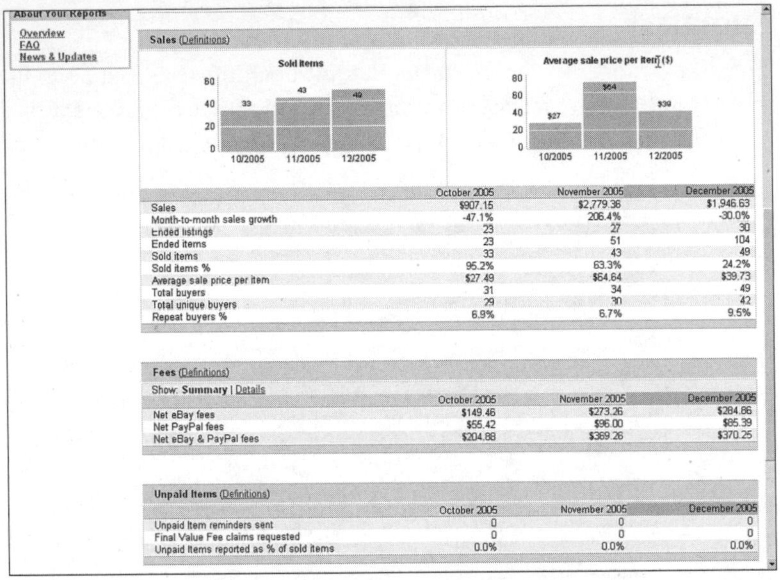

FIGURE 22.5

FIGURE 22.5

The Sales Summary shows you a high-level view of how your store has performed.

About Your Reports
Overview
FAQ
News & Updates

Sales (Definitions)

	October 2005	November 2005	December 2005
Sales	$907.15	$2,779.36	$1,946.63
Month-to-month sales growth	-47.1%	206.4%	-30.0%
Ended listings	23	27	30
Ended items	23	51	104
Sold items	33	43	49
Sold items %	95.2%	63.3%	24.2%
Average sale price per item	$27.49	$64.64	$39.73
Total buyers	31	34	49
Total unique buyers	29	30	42
Repeat buyers %	6.9%	6.7%	9.5%

Fees (Definitions)
Show: Summary | Details

	October 2005	November 2005	December 2005
Net eBay fees	$149.46	$273.26	$284.86
Net PayPal fees	$55.42	$96.00	$85.39
Net eBay & PayPal fees	$204.88	$369.26	$370.25

Unpaid Items (Definitions)

	October 2005	November 2005	December 2005
Unpaid Item reminders sent	0	0	0
Final Value Fee claims requested	0	0	0
Unpaid Items reported as % of sold items	0.0%	0.0%	0.0%

Before moving on, though, I want to mention that the bottom of this first report will show you a breakdown of eBay fees. Below that will be information about unpaid items, if any, and the starting date of your report subscription is displayed.

note You can pick different time periods by using the drop-down list of available reports positioned next to the Sales Summary title near the top of the report.

Sales by Category

Following the order of report links on the navigation bar, we get to a series of reports called Sales by Category. Figure 22.6 shows the default opening report, with breakdowns for only the categories you have sold in over the time period you are examining.

In this example, five eBay categories are listed—Transistor Radios, Signal, and so on. Actually these labels are abbreviations of the last level of the associated eBay category. For example, Signal is actually the category "Business & Industrial > Industrial Electrical & Test > Test Equipment > Signal Sources, Generators >, (97198)."

In Figure 22.6, you can see that most of the dollars ($1,740) came from transistor radio sales, and most of the items sold (39) were those same radios.

By default, you get to see numbers displayed for all types of sales (Online Auction, Fixed Price, and Store Inventory), but you can look at a particular venue and format separately by clicking an associated Show link, which you can see at the top of Figure 22.6. Clicking the Store Inventory report shows only items sold from the store, excluding auctions and fixed-priced listings, as illustrated in Figure 22.7.

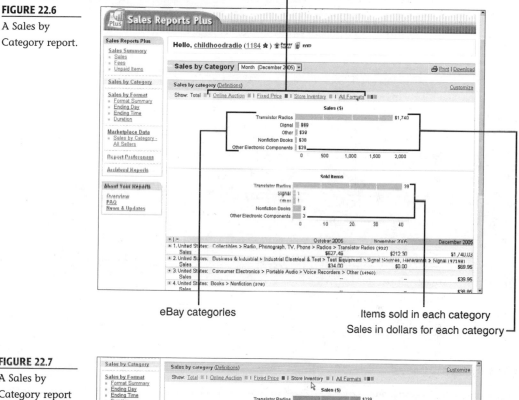

Click these links to choose the type of auction data shown

FIGURE 22.6

A Sales by Category report.

eBay categories

Items sold in each category

Sales in dollars for each category

FIGURE 22.7

A Sales by Category report filtered to display just store items and exclude items such as auction sales and fixed-price listings.

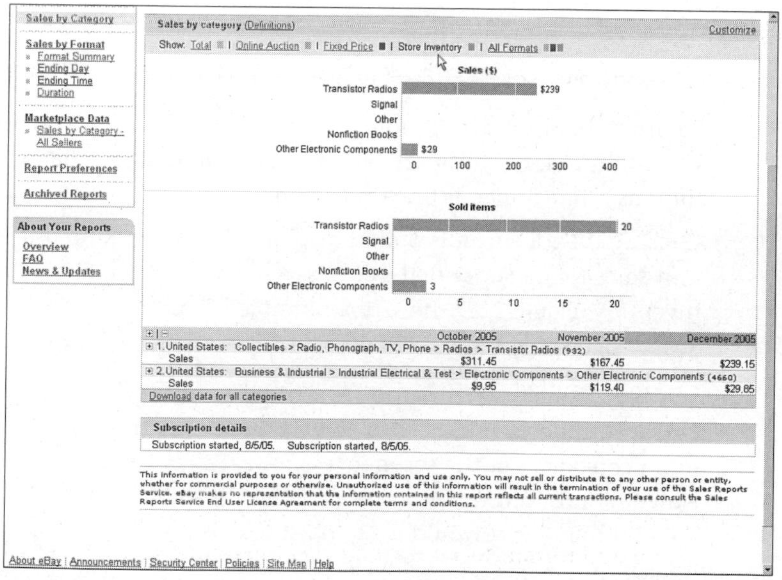

Exploring Category Sales Details

As with other reports, you can see "behind the scenes" data, this time for each category in which you have sold. Clicking the + buttons in the category lists shows the underlying numbers (see Figure 22.8).

> **note** Even though this is a book about stores, and stores have "store categories," the reports you generate using the techniques in this chapter sort things by eBay's *selling* categories, not your store categories.

Click the + and – buttons to show and hide the details associated with each piece of data

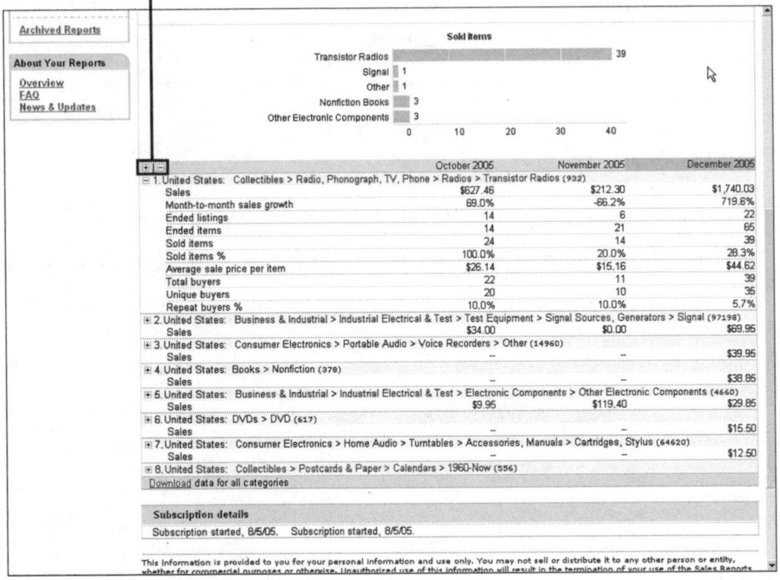

FIGURE 22.8

Click to see underlying category details.

So, using these data, you not only can see which categories do best for you, you can also learn if a particular category of item sells better in your store than as a fixed-price listing and so on.

Clicking the All Formats option displays charts breaking out sales dollars and unit sales for all supported formats—Online Auction, Fixed Price, and Store Inventory. Figure 22.9 shows an example of this.

Again, you are offered the opportunity to explore the underlying details by clicking + buttons in the lists following the charts, as shown in Figure 22.10.

One last thing: If you use two eBay categories to sell the same item, only the main category, not the secondary, shows. So if you have two Elvis Presley watches and want to test to see which is the better category—Watches or Elvis Memorabilia—you would need to list one using Watches as the primary (and only) category, and list the second watch with Elvis Memorabilia as the primary (and only) category. If you use two categories, there's no easy way (that I know of) to tell whether the second category worked.

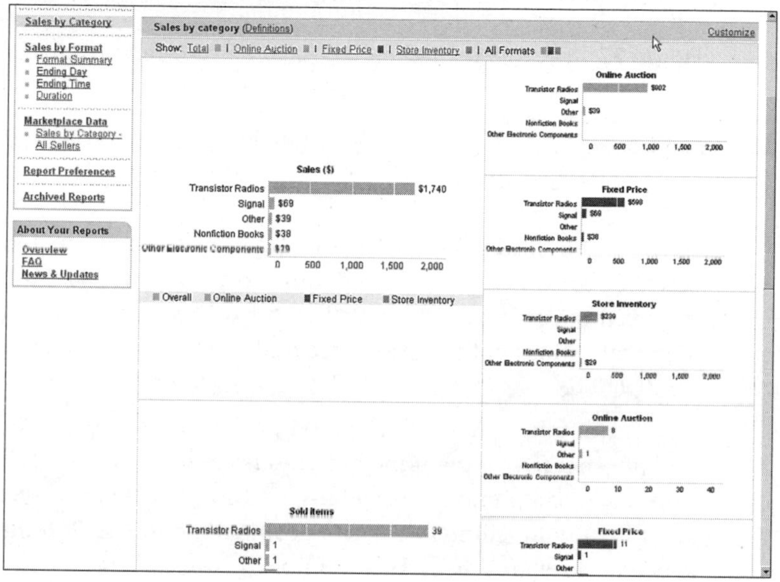

FIGURE 22.9

The All Formats category display.

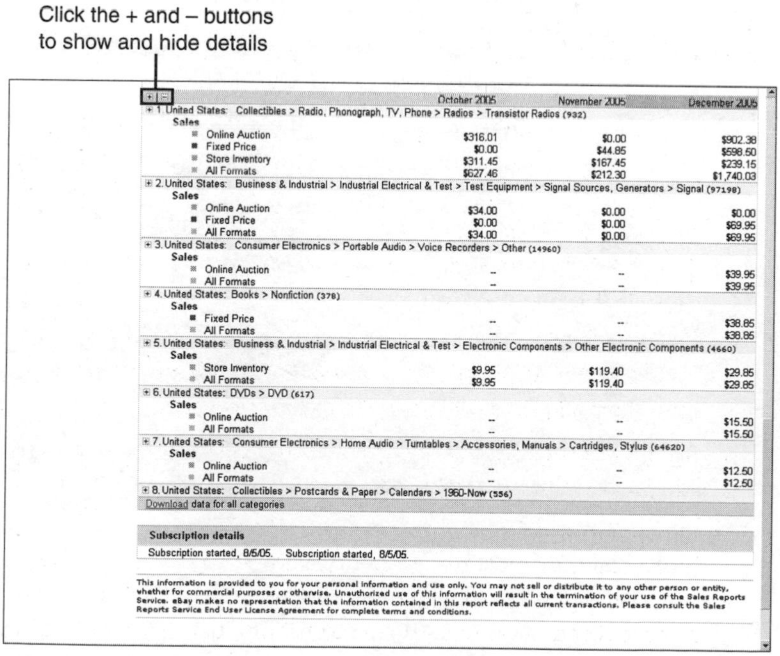

Click the + and – buttons
to show and hide details

FIGURE 22.10

Detailed breakdowns are available in this Category view as well.

Sales by Format

The next major report category is Sales by Format. Here, you can explore the potentially best format choice (Online Auction, Fixed Price, Store Inventory), ending strategies, and listing duration options.

Figure 22.11 shows the default Sales by Format report, which begins with two bar charts depicting dollar sales by selling format and average selling price per item in each selling format.

As you scroll down, you will once again see the underlying detail, as depicted in Figure 22.12.

However, for this kind of pondering to produce useful conclusions, you need to have the same item for sale under the various scenarios that interest you. For instance, to compare store and "Buy It Now" approaches, you need to have identical listings both in your store and as Buy It Now offerings over the same time period.

As an example, you would need to have five batteries in your store inventory and another five of the same batteries listed as 7-day Buy It Now listings, both using identical photos, descriptions, and so on. Otherwise, you will just be looking at data telling you where people were able to find things of yours they needed. See what I mean by no simple answers?

FIGURE 22.11

The default Sales by Format report.

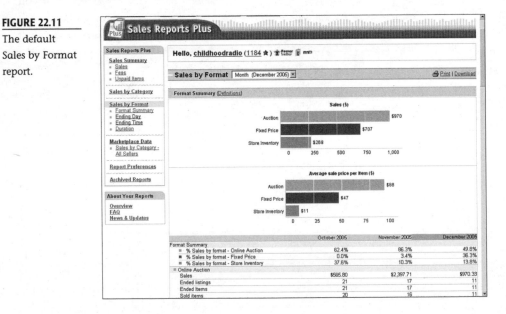

FIGURE 22.12

The Sales by
Format details.

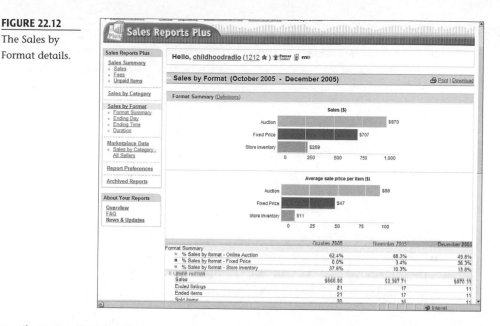

Ending-Day Reports

Scrolling further reveals Sales by Ending Day. Here, too, the charts will only reflect what actually happened to you during the timeframe selected. If you run only auctions and you never end them on Wednesday, for you, Wednesday is going to be a rotten ending day. So again, the reports are just showing you what happened to you on eBay given what you did, which is no small thing, by the way.

In Figure 22.13, I have chosen the fancier All Formats option to show you an overview of the Selling Day charts.

Looks like I had better think about ending things on Wednesday once in awhile, huh? This is especially true because good auctions drive shoppers to sellers' stores and fixed-price items, so by not having auctions end on Wednesday, I am probably cheating myself out of incremental store and fixed-price sales, too.

As with the other reports visited so far, if you scroll down you will see and be able to expand the underlying details.

Ending-Time Reports

Here again, the reports can only compare the ending times you use for auctions, but fixed-priced and store items can end at any time of the day or night, particularly if you sell internationally.

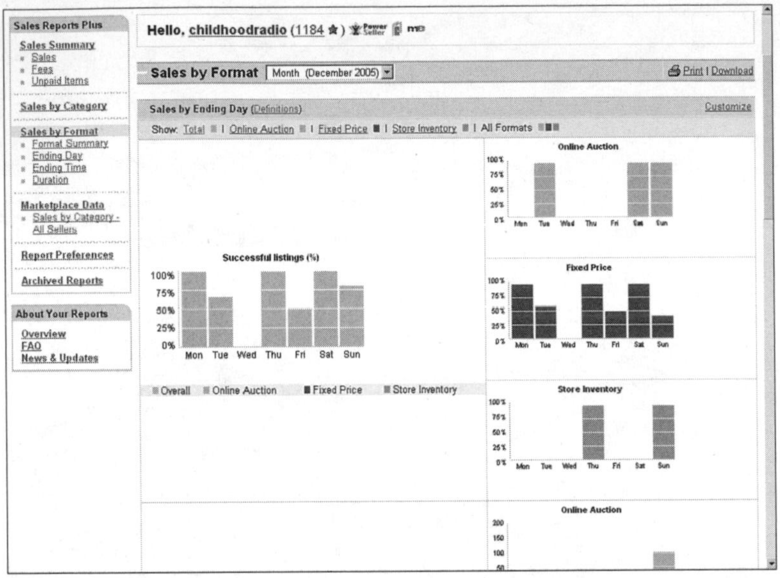

FIGURE 22.13

Ending Day reports show what happened, not what might have happened.

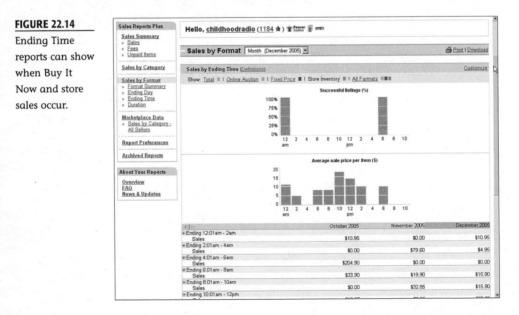

Figure 22.14 shows part of a typical Ending Time report, this time filtered to show only store sales. What are all those people doing in my store in the middle of the night and early morning? Well, they are buying things, of course. Maybe I should have an auction or two ending then also to attract more of this late night (mostly international) crowd.

FIGURE 22.14

Ending Time reports can show when Buy It Now and store sales occur.

Duration Reports

Everybody has an opinion about how long auctions should run. I think it depends on, among other things, the category and whether the item is a commodity item in ample supply or rare—even a weird collectible with a very small following.

If you are selling common items to the masses, you will probably do well to have a mix of quick auctions or Buy It Now listings beginning and therefore ending each day of the week—along with a few, if any, 7- and 10-day auctions.

note Starting 10-day auctions on Thursdays gets you two weekends of exposure, great for "oddball" items with potentially small but eager crowds, especially individual collectors.

If, on the other hand, you want to sell a left rear fender for a yellow Nash Rambler from the '50s, you might want to keep the auction running as long as possible so that the, um, "crowd" can gather. Ten-day auctions are best for this unless you know the value of the item and have a firm price in mind. Then a Good 'Til Sold strategy might work best.

And so we turn to the report to see how those strategies are working for you. The problem, of course, is if you don't run any 5-day listings, there won't be any to display, as you can see in Figure 22.15.

FIGURE 22.15

Duration reports only show what you have tried.

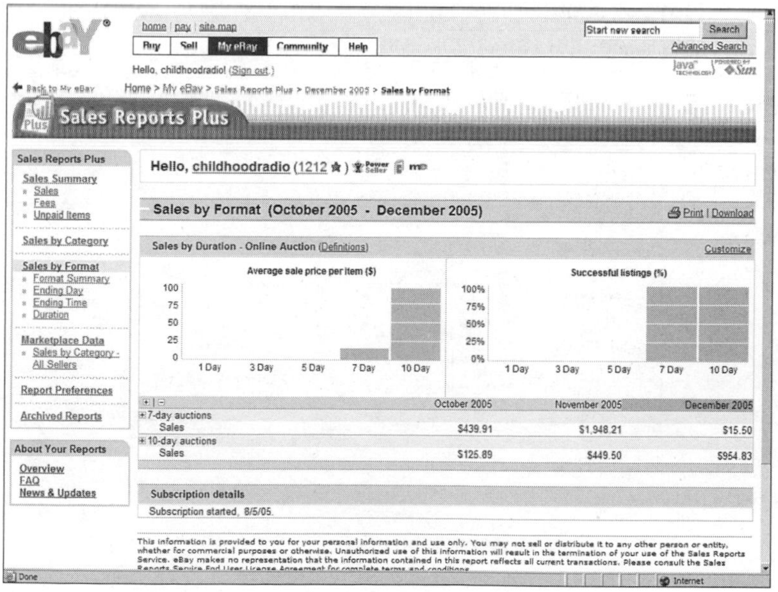

Being a guy who sells the electronic equivalent of Nash Rambler fenders under this seller ID, I have not tried any short auctions, but probably should. For me, though, it looks like 10-day auctions work better than 7-day auctions, at least in December 2005. And because I have also looked back at a number of my earlier months, I can tell you that, for my category and crowd, the extra cost of 10-day auctions pays off. And that's the whole reason to look at these reports—to get perspective, to see what needs attention, and to see what should be left alone.

So again, you need to look at this stuff over time, and with a skeptical eye, especially if you are dealing with a small volume of expensive items because there won't be many data points from which to draw sensible conclusions.

Marketplace Data

The link titled "Sales by Category—All Sellers" lets you compare your results with all other sellers by category. See Figure 22.16 for an example of this.

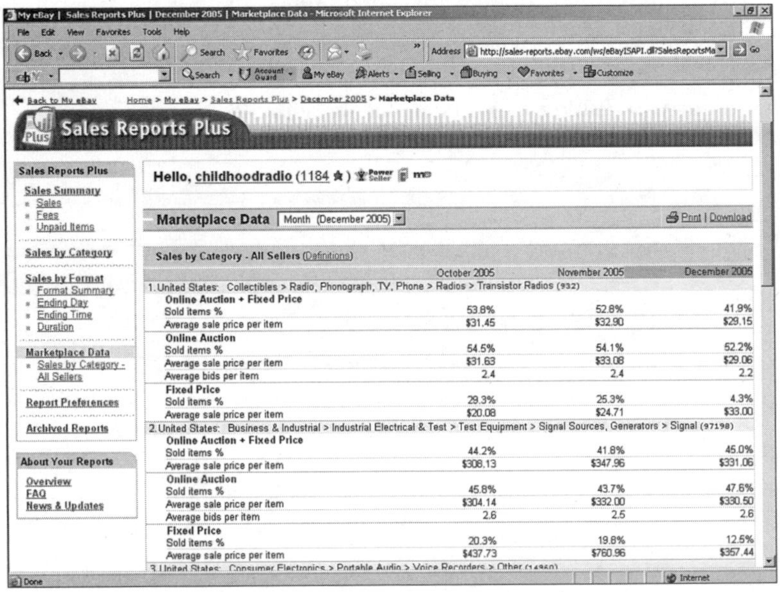

FIGURE 22.16

The Sales by Category – All Sellers report.

Viewing Prior (Archived) Reports

To go back in time, simply choose the Archived Reports link near the bottom of the left navigation area. After you have been creating reports for a while, you will see a list of them, similar to the one shown in Figure 22.17.

FIGURE 22.17

Picking historical reports.

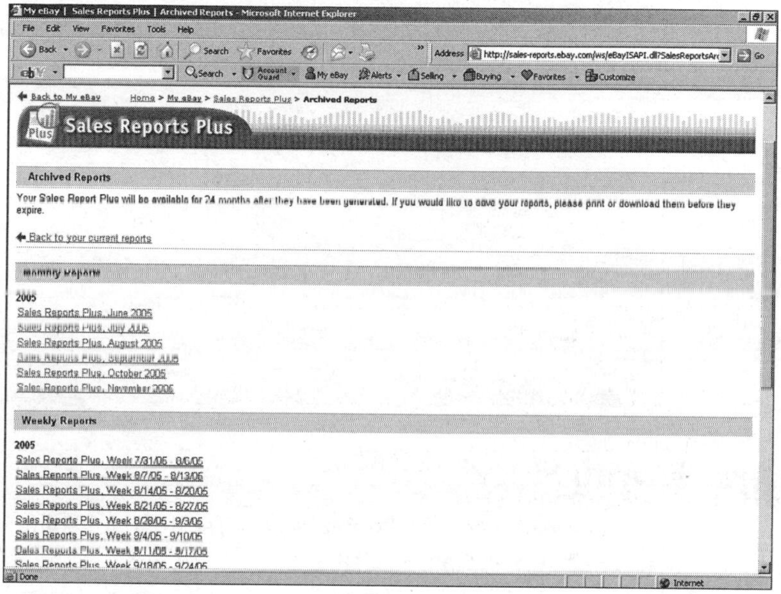

As you can see, it's possible to pick prior months or even weeks for review. The date range you have chosen is displayed at the top of the reports, as shown in Figure 22.18.

If you use this feature, be certain to get in the habit of looking closely at the period covered when viewing reports. Otherwise, you might think you are looking at September, October, and November when you are really looking at June through August. The date ranges "stick," so if you look back to last year for one report and then switch to a different report, you will see the historical data for the second report as well, unless you switch back to the current month.

To go back to current reports, return to the Archived Reports screen, shown in Figure 22.17, and click the "Back to your current reports" link.

Archived reports will disappear after 24 months, so if you are fond of history, remember to print (or download and save) them before they disappear.

FIGURE 22.18

Make sure you
are looking at
the right
months.

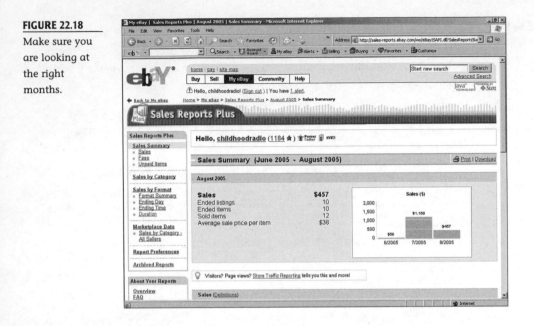

Printing Reports

To print a report, click the Printer icon or use the Print command from the File
menu, as shown in Figure 22.19.

In order for charts to print properly, you might need to fiddle with your
browser settings, which will, of course, affect any other browser printing you
do thereafter unless you restore the old settings after printing eBay reports.
What you want to do is to enable background color printing, even if you have
a black-and-white printer. Otherwise, the bars won't print.

Printing from Internet Explorer

Here are the steps for printing from Internet Explorer (see Figure 22.20):

1. Select Internet Options from the Tools menu.
2. Click the Advanced tab.
3. Scroll down to Printing options.
4. Check the "Print background colors and images" box if it's unchecked.
5. Click OK to save your changes.

FIGURE 22.19

Report printing.

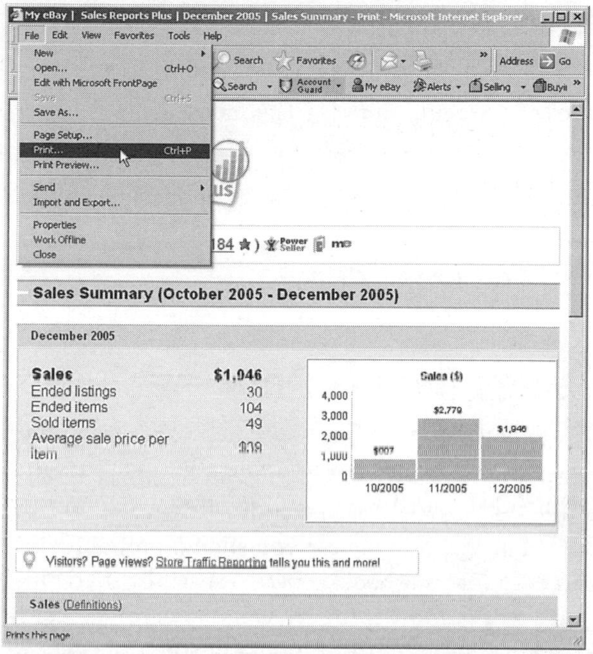

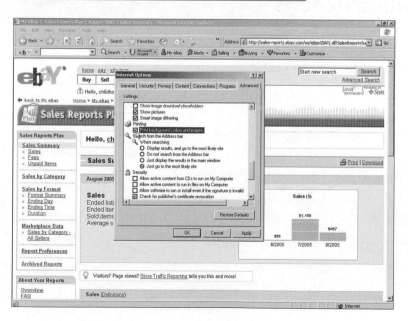

FIGURE 22.20

Configure your
IE browser to
print colored
backgrounds for
chart printing.

Printing from Netscape Navigator

To print reports from Netscape Navigator, follow these steps:

1. Choose Page Setup from the File menu.

2. Click the Format & Options tab to see the printing options.

3. Enable Print Background (colors & images) by checking the appropriate box.

4. Click OK to save your changes.

Downloading Sales Report Data

It is possible to download comma-separated value (CSV) files of most reports. Microsoft Excel, Access, and similar applications can use these reports. Charts are not downloaded, just the supporting data in tabular form.

As I mentioned in the last chapter, you should probably not rely on this downloaded data for your bookkeeping, especially if you like to "tie out" to the penny. It's real purpose is to give you a general feel for how things are going. If you have an in-house database or spreadsheet guru (or are one yourself), you might be able to combine months or create other new ways to use the downloaded data.

For most of us, however, viewing and perhaps printing the reports should accomplish the intended purpose—providing an overview of what's going on.

Clicking the Download Report button should start the download automatically, but you might need to intercede if your computer's security features object, as shown in Figure 22.21.

It takes a while for the data to come down, after which you will be asked to save it as a file on your hard disk. If the download fails, try again. Eventually you should see a screen similar to Figure 22.22.

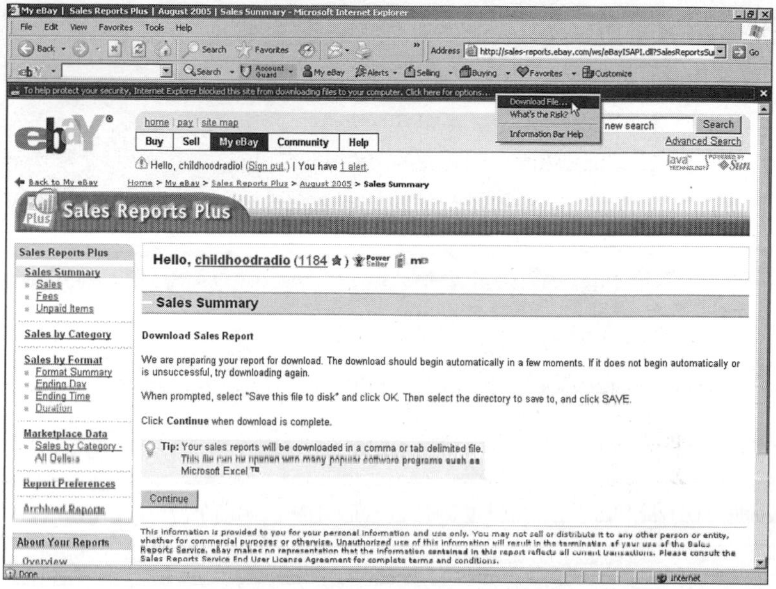

FIGURE 22.21

You might need to override browser security features to download the file.

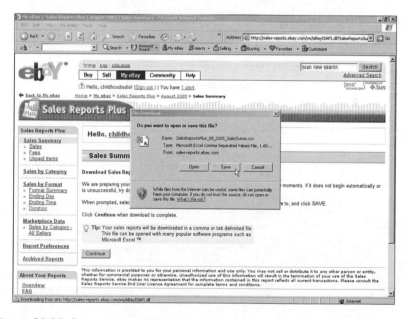

FIGURE 22.22

Click Save to specify a file-name and desti-nation. Once the file has been saved, you can open it in Excel or any other program com-patible with CSV files.

Figure 22.23 shows a typical Excel worksheet created from the sales report. You might need to fiddle with column widths to make the worksheets look right.

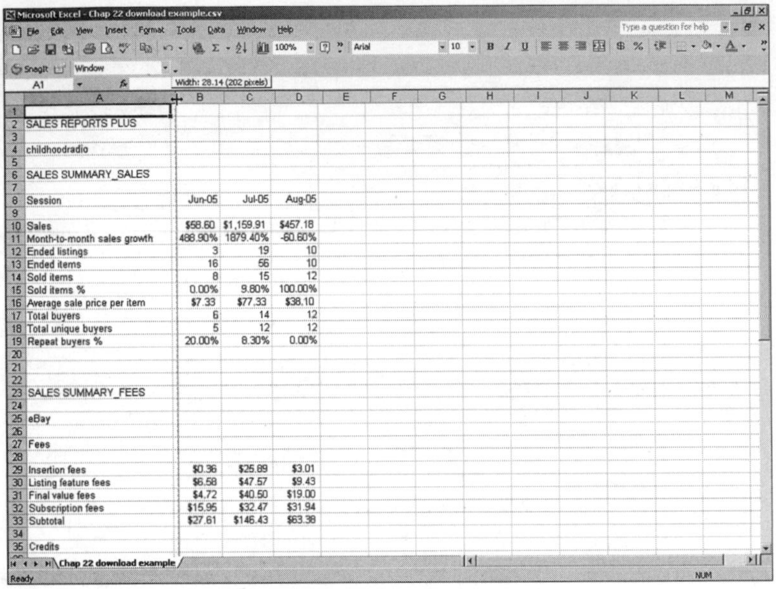

FIGURE 22.23

An Excel
worksheet from
a report
download.

Report Preference Settings

Nearing the end of our Sales Reports Plus tour, take a quick peek at Figure
22.24, the Report Preferences screen. It's reached by clicking the Reports
Preference link in the left navigation area.

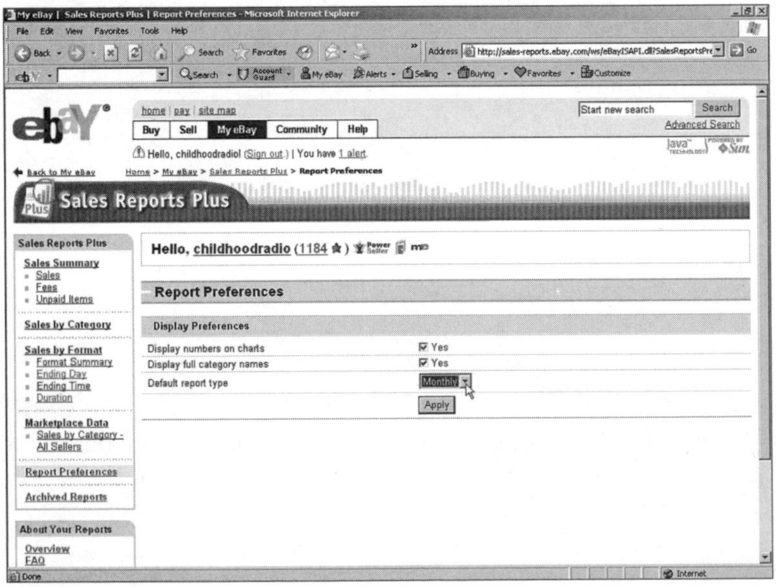

FIGURE 22.24

The Report
Preferences
screen.

There aren't many choices, and they are pretty self-explanatory. We can probably expect to see this screen evolve over time, so yours might not look exactly like this one.

Unsubscribing

If for some reason you do not have a Featured or Anchor store, and don't want to pay for Sales Reports Plus, you can cancel your subscription by going to your My eBay screen and visiting the Subscriptions link under the My Account heading in the left navigation area (see Figure 22.25). You will obviously want to keep an eye on your eBay bill to make sure the fee has stopped.

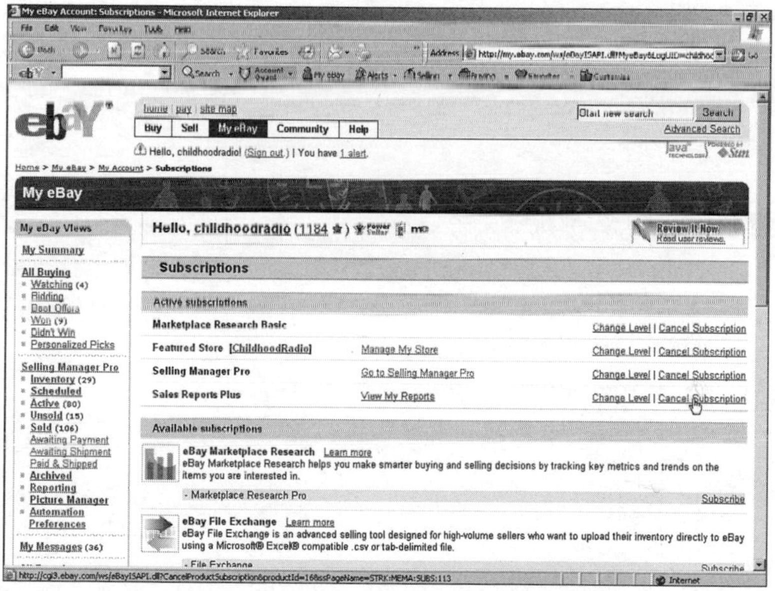

FIGURE 22.25

Unsubscribing to Sales Reports Plus.

Using eBay Store Traffic Reports

How do people find your store? What do they look at when they enter? How long do they stay? Are your off-eBay promotional efforts working? What's getting ignored? You can answer these and many other interesting questions by studying eBay's traffic reports.

Enabling and Viewing Traffic Reports

Traffic reports are *not* reached by visiting the Sales Reports link. Instead, you get to them via the Manage My Store link, also found near the bottom of the left navigation area in the My Subscriptions subgroup, as illustrated in Figure 23.1.

FIGURE 23.1

Use the Manage My Store link to reach traffic reports.

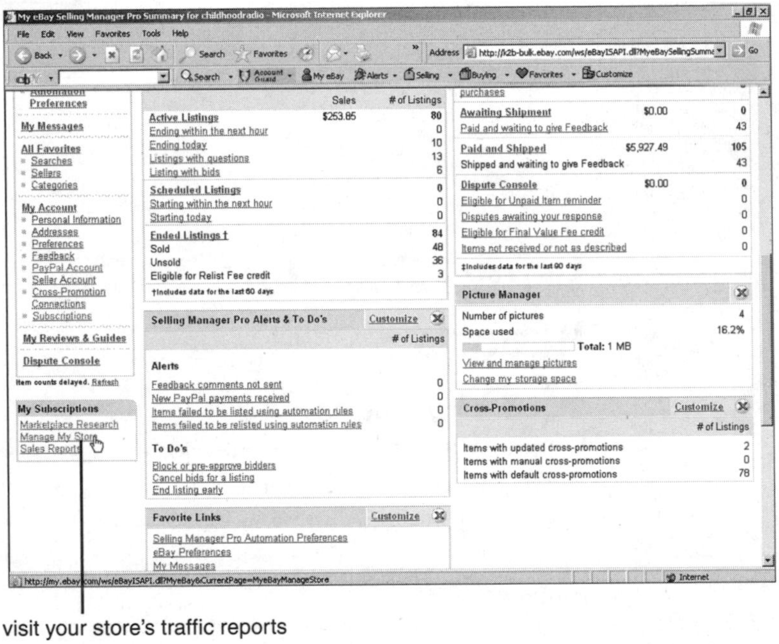

Click here to visit your store's traffic reports

Visit the Manage My Store main screen. In the Reports area of the left navigation bar you will see a Traffic Reports link, like the one in Figure 23.2. Click it.

You will be asked to log in again. If you are accessing traffic reports for the first time, you will need to give eBay permission to transfer traffic information to Omniture, a third-party website that partners with eBay to provide the reporting services. Do this by reading the agreement and clicking the "I agree" box; then click the Agree and Continue button to continue.

There's yet another agreement to make—this one with Omniture. Read it, check the box, and click the Continue button. This

> **note** You must view traffic reports at least once every 90 days to maintain an active, uninterrupted subscription. If you go longer than 90 days without visiting your traffic reports, you will need to resubscribe to them.

will take you to a Traffic Reports "My Summary" page, similar to the one in Figure 23.3.

FIGURE 23.2

Click Traffic Reports in the Manage My Store main screen to get started.

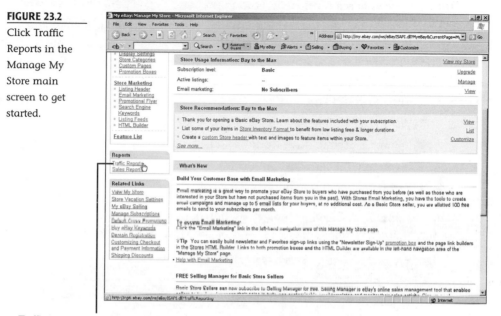

Traffic reports are accessed here

FIGURE 23.3

The top half of the main Traffic Reports "My Summary" screen.

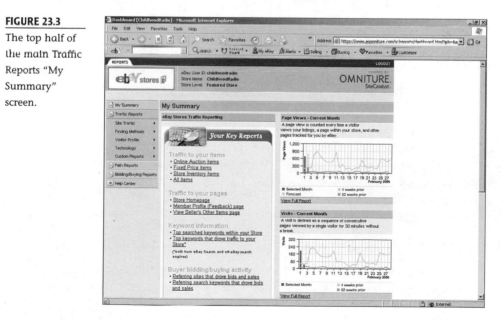

Fortunately, you only need to go through the signup process once, although you will need to log into Omniture using your eBay ID and password each time you want to see traffic reports.

As you saw in glimpses earlier in this book, this summary page is the literal tip of an iceberg. It is possible to drill way, way, way down into the data related to activity in and around your store. You can explore and better understand the following:

- Visits to your items
- Visits to your pages (store landing page, profile page, and so on)
- Keywords used to drive traffic, and keywords used to search in the store
- Buyer and bidder activities
- Technology and languages used by visitors

The My Summary screen is another of those long ones, so be sure to scroll down. Figure 23.4 shows the other half of the My Summary page.

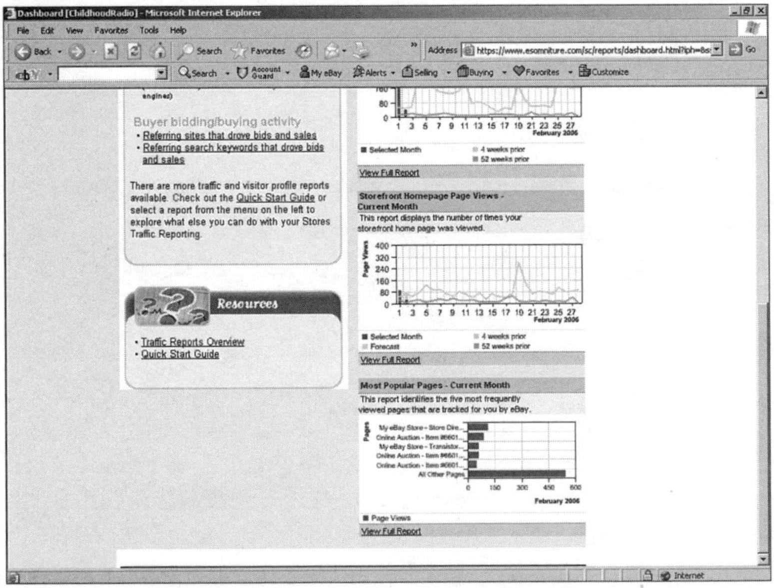

FIGURE 23.4

The second half of the main Traffic Reports "My Summary" screen.

Page Views and Visits Graphs

The top half of the My Summary page includes two charts that show you graphically how many pages have been viewed and how many folks have visited so far this month, over the same days over the prior four weeks, and over the prior year. This month's data are displayed as bars. The prior data appear as lines. Look at Figure 23.5.

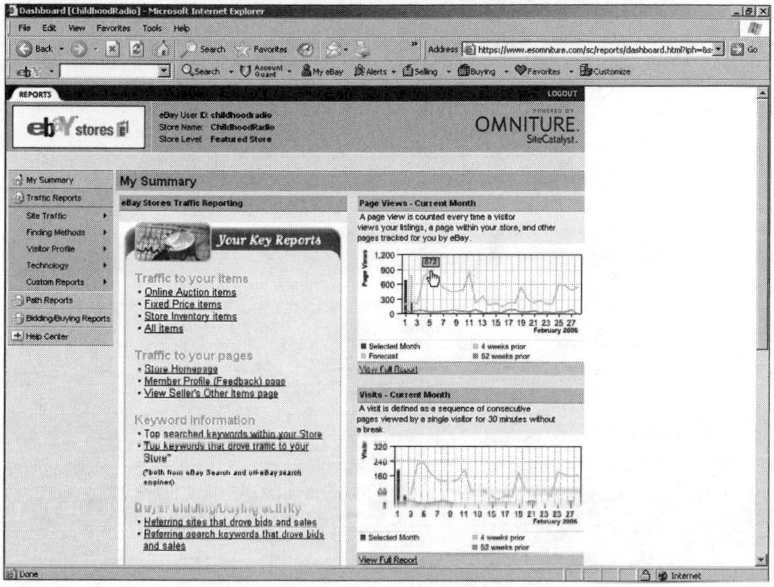

FIGURE 23.5

The Page Views and Visits graphs show the current month and history.

Hovering your mouse over points on the graph displays the actual numbers associated with the plot point. You see an example of this in Figure 23.5.

Clicking the View Full Report link under one of these charts reveals a larger version of the chart and the underlying data. Notice in Figure 23.6 that because this report was run on the morning of February 2, there are no data for later days in February yet. You can go back to look at last month, last year, or a particular date range if you like.

Specifying Date Ranges

This is a great place to point out how to review historical data in detail by specifying date and time ranges. Notice the little calendar in the upper-left corner of Figure 23.6. Clicking the month arrows moves you forward and backward a month at a time, and if you have multiple years' worth of data, the year arrows will move you a year at a time.

You can also specify specific date ranges (a quarter, for example, or the dates you consider to be your holiday selling season perhaps). Do this by clicking the Range link up near the calendar. As you can see in Figure 23.7, you have a variety of ways to configure these custom date range reports.

Some of the preset choices include Today, Yesterday, Last 60 days, Last year, and so on. Or you can specify specific "to and from" dates.

FIGURE 23.6

The Full Report version of the Page Views report for a new month.

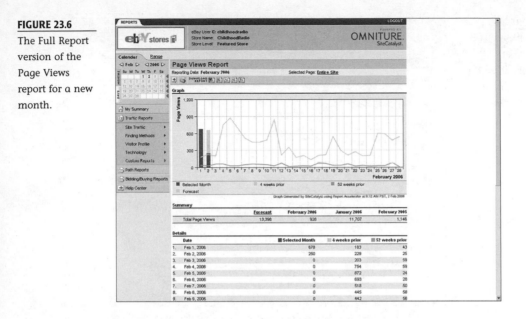

In addition, you can define how much detail you want and how it will be displayed by using the "Show by" drop-down. These are called "granularity" ranges, and they must be compatible with the date ranges you pick. For example, you can specify a granularity (Shown by) option of Days to view a month's worth of data, but not a granularity option of Year to display a month's worth of data. You will be prompted to correct any mismatched granularity and date range choices.

As an example, Figure 23.7 shows a month's worth of visits displayed by day.

We can cut this data more thinly, within reason. For example, Figure 23.8 shows 14 days of page views by hour. Hovering will display the hit counts, or you can scroll down to look at the underlying numbers themselves.

note Currently you can only display 14 days' worth of data in hourly slices.

FIGURE 23.7
How to specify a month's worth of visits displayed by day.

FIGURE 23.8
The Page Views by hour can give insight into the best ending times.

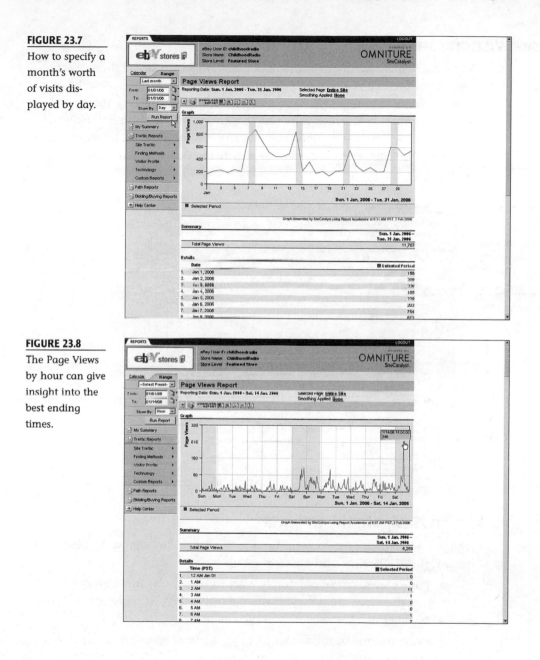

Visits, Visitors, and Views

Visits are defined as any sequence of pages viewed by a single shopper who moves from one of your pages to another without a break. Visits can be analyzed in summary on your My Summary page, or you can click the related View Full Report link, which will bring you charts and details reminiscent of the Page View reports—but this time tracking visitors. Figure 23.9 shows an example. You can do the same slicing and dicing here—by day, hour, and so on.

FIGURE 23.9

The Visits reports are similar to Page reports, but track unique shopping visits.

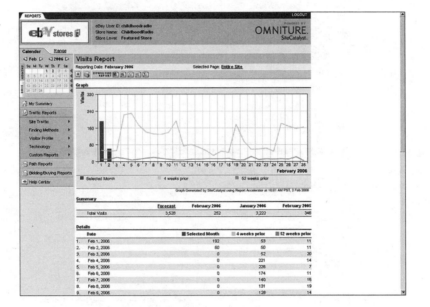

Another Way to Navigate the Reports

The left navigation area contains links to the site and visitor traffic reports as well. Figure 23.10 shows the choices:

- **Page views**—Views are simply a count how many times every page gets displayed regardless of who did the visiting. If you visit your pages 10 times, the Views count will increment by 10.

- **Daily unique visitors**—Daily Unique Visitor counts are incremented during a visitor's first trip to your store, listing, Seller's Other Items page, Member Profile (feedback) page, and several other pages *on a given day*. Therefore, if the same person visits your store and views your store home page three times, your feedback page twice, and several other pages once each, the Daily Unique Visitors report records that person as one "unique visitor"—unless, of course, the shopper uses different computers (IP addresses, actually). In this case, he or she will show up as multiple visitors.

- **Monthly unique visitors**—The sum of unique visitors over one month.

- **Visits**—Any sequence of pages viewed by a single shopper who moves from one of your pages to another without a break.

FIGURE 23.10

You can choose reports from the left navigation area as well.

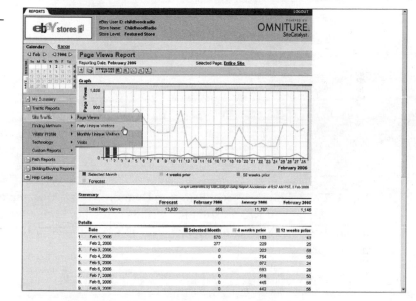

Finding Methods

Understanding how people find your store is key to building an effective mix of on- and off-eBay promotional activities. The Finding Methods reports help you understand the present and watch your progress as you tweak.

Let's start with the Referring Domains report, which can help you learn where visitors were before visiting your store or listings. Use the information to review the effectiveness of your search engine placements, banner ad buys, links from other sites, and so on.

See a Referring Domains report by choosing the Referring Domains sub-choice from the Finding Methods menu in the left navigation area (see Figure 23.11). Notice that you can also narrow things down from this submenu by choosing Search Engines, Search Keywords, or Return Frequency.

See how each visitor reached your store

FIGURE 23.11
Click on Finding
Methods and
then Referring
Domains.

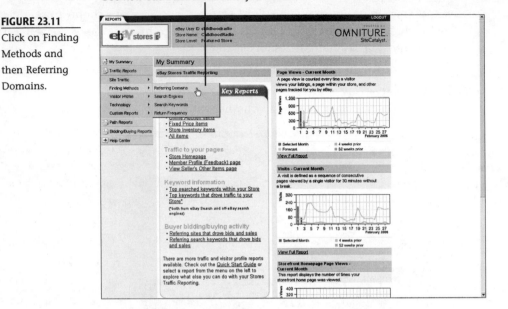

Figure 23.12 shows a typical Referring Domains report, this one covering only
2 days. More than two-thirds of the visitors came from other websites, 22.5%
found the store via a search engine, and 11.6% of the visitors had book-
marked my store.

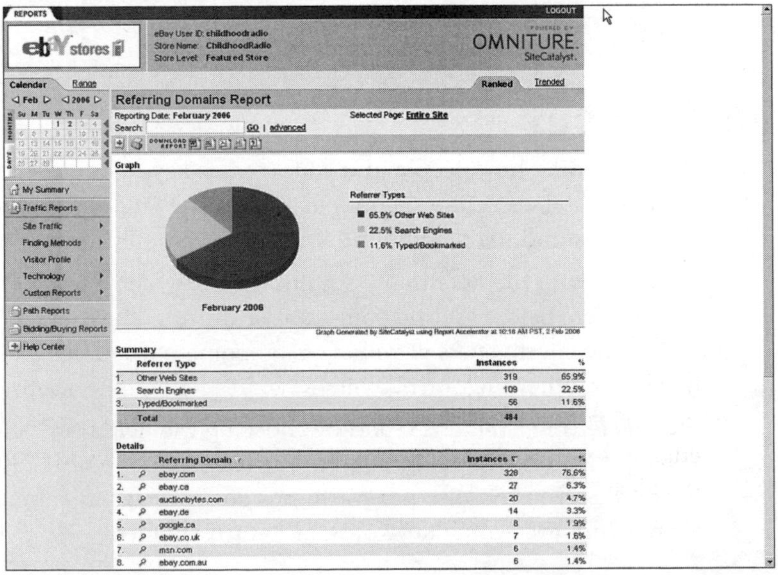

FIGURE 23.12
The Referring
Domains report.

Below the graph you will see the underlying details. The majority of visitors came from eBay, of course, but nearly 5% came from a link in an article I wrote for Auctionbytes.com, which tells me that this was an extremely helpful public relations move.

Search Engines Reports

Search Engines reports not only can tell you how easy it is to find you, they can also tell you who is interested in the things you sell. For example, look at Figure 23.13. Running the Search Engines report for last year turns up a lot of Google searches from outside of the United States, which tells me I should (continue to) sell internationally, and perhaps even put some more effort into picking ending times and products that appeal to this audience.

This report also makes me want to refocus on search engine visibility in general because I would like to see a higher percentage of visits coming from "off-eBay" sites.

FIGURE 23.13

You can see which search engines bring you traffic, and which need work.

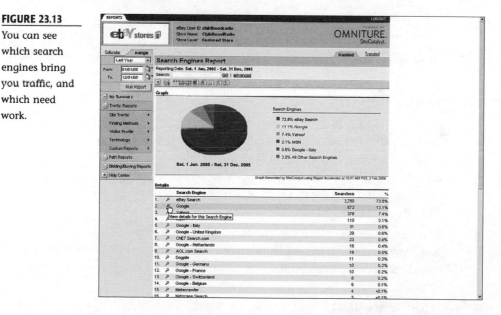

Notice the little magnifying glasses next to the various search sites in the listings beneath the graph. Clicking them brings up the details for each search engine, as illustrated in Figure 23.14. You can actually see the queries themselves.

Text from the search engine query

FIGURE 23.14

See the details
by clicking the
magnifying
glass icon.

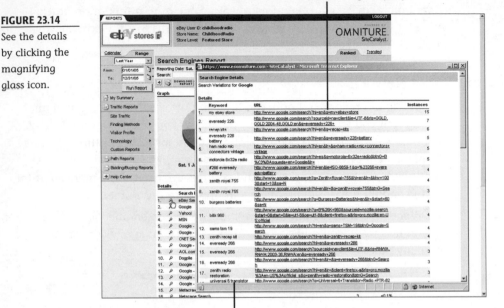

Keywords visitors used that led them to my eBay store

Search Keywords Reports

Search Keywords reports (the next submenu choice on the Finding Methods
menu in the navigation area) might be the most illuminating. It shows what
people were searching for when they found you. As with the other reports, you
can slice this down to a month, a week, or whatever, but you might want to
start by looking at a year's worth of data just to see how diverse peoples'
searches can be.

Figure 23.15 shows a year's worth of search data from my ChildhoodRadio
store. Again, clicking the magnifying glass icon will provide more details, this
time showing variations on the search terms, such as category restrictions.

Return Frequency Reports

Here's another interesting way to look at things. How many return visits do
you get from the same folks, and how long do they wait before returning? In
other words, do you have a loyal following? Figure 23.16 shows an example
with a fairly nice number of regular, frequent repeaters. This means visitors
probably like the store, and maybe wish it had more new things in it. By
watching this report (and others) over time, you can see whether the changes
you make are working.

FIGURE 23.15
Search Keyword reports show what people typed when searching.

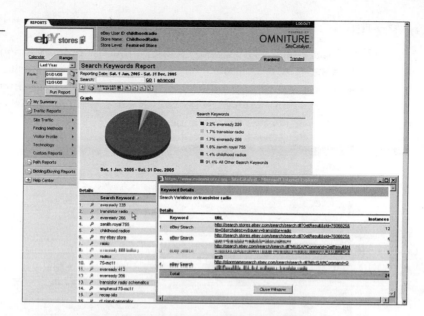

FIGURE 23.16
The Return Frequency reports help you understand loyalty and appeal.

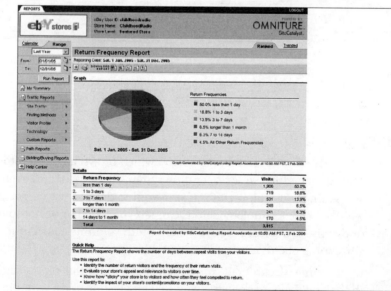

Visitor Profile

The Visitor Profile screen gives you insight into the primary language declared by visitors, or more accurately tells you which country's eBay site they used. It can give you some insight into which countries are interested in your items. As you can see in Figure 23.17, nearly 18% of my visitors come to this store from somewhere other than America.

Technology Used

The Technology Used reports tell you which browsers your visitors employed during their visits, which operating systems they used, and even the screen size settings—useful, perhaps if you want to design custom pages with fixed widths. These technology details can tell you whether or not to add fancy bells and whistles to listings such as fixed-width columns, Flash animation, video clips, large photos, and so on.

It's a shame we can't tell connection speeds from this report series because that could really change the way we embellish listings, with big photos, video, and so on. Figure 23.18 shows the Monitor Resolutions report.

FIGURE 23.18

FIGURE 23.18

Not everyone
has a high-
resolution moni-
tor, so you need
to use some care
when designing
custom pages
with fixed
widths.

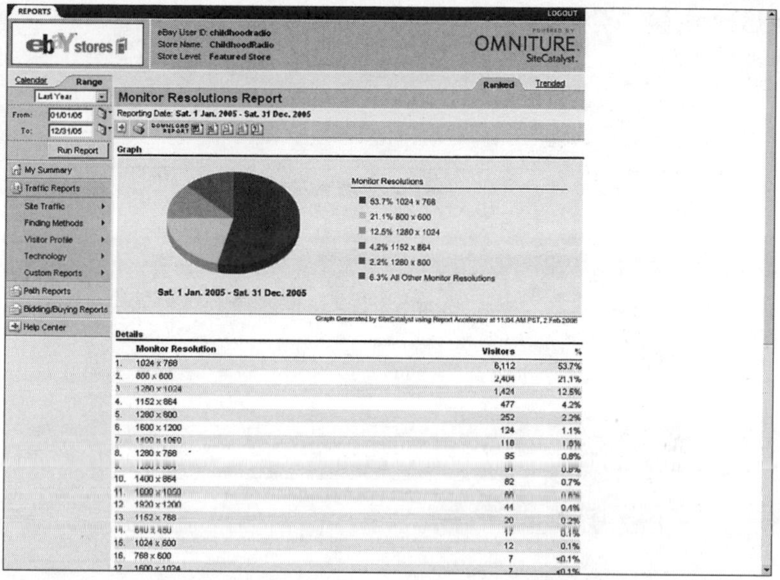

Custom Traffic Reports

Custom Traffic reports let you quickly spot your most popular store pages, listings, search terms, and more. As with the other reports, you can refine these
by defining date ranges and other options. Also, a built-in search tool can you
help further narrow the views. Figure 23.19 shows a snapshot of a week's most
popular listings, for example. Notice that among the top five, one is a fixed-
priced listing and the rest are auctions.

To use the search feature of these customizable reports, select the desired date
range (for example, I've used "Last Year" in Figure 23.20) and then type key-
word(s) in the Search box.

In this example, I've used the word *battery*, and the search returned a list of
the most popular items with this word in their titles.

Storefront Homepage Views Report

The Storefront Homepage Views report
can show you the number of visits to the
"entrance" of your store over a period of
time you specify. It will track the default
eBay store homepage or a custom landing
page if you have created one (see Chapter 8, "Custom Store Pages").

note When using the
Search feature, click
the little Go button to the right of
the box, not the bigger Run Report
button.

FIGURE 23.19

A custom Most Popular Listings report.

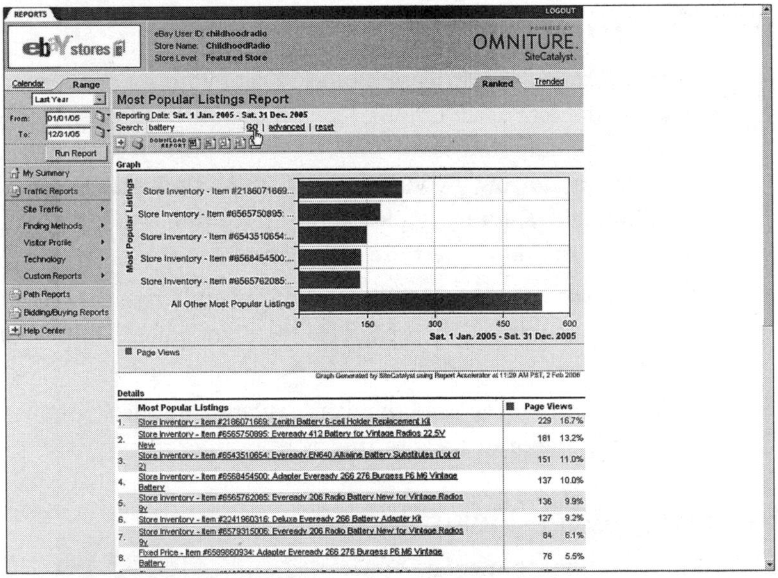

FIGURE 23.20

Use the Search feature to narrow custom reports.

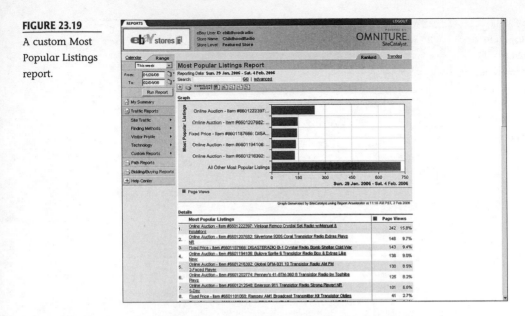

Figure 23.21 shows a year's worth of store homepage visits. It looks like my efforts to drive folks to the store are starting to work.

FIGURE 23.21
Tracking store homepage visits over a year's time.

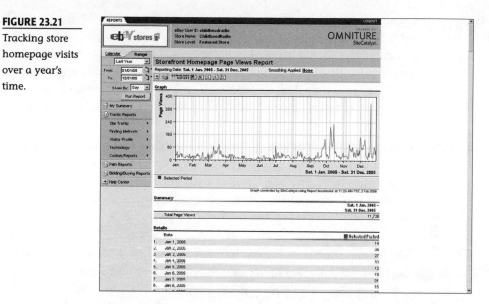

Store Search Terms Report

The last custom report we will look at is the Store Search Terms report, which might give you wildly different results if you search over long periods of time (a year, let's say, as opposed to a week or two). Figure 23.22 shows a 2-week report. Scrolling down to view the details of these reports can show you keywords people use in your store for items you might not have, but should consider adding. It's also a way to learn how to fine-tune listing titles.

FIGURE 23.22
Store search terms can tell you what to add to your inventory.

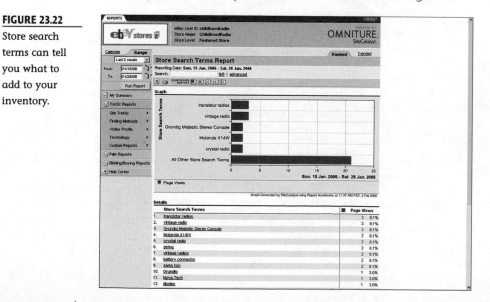

Path Reports

Path reports can be hypnotizing. Many of them are simply rehashes of other reports we've already discussed. But two in particular—Full Paths and Time Spent—are intriguing, no doubt. It's possible to spend way more time here than is prudent, but come along for a quick peek at the Full Paths report first. Figure 23.23 shows an example.

The Full Paths report shows you the most popular complete paths visitors took through your pages on eBay. Paths are displayed on alternating horizontal rows of gray and white. The beginning of each path is shown with a green arrow and the text "Entered Site." The end of each path is shown with a red arrow and the text "Exited Site." In between, all pages visited are shown with a page icon next to each.

For example, in Figure 23.23, Visitor number 24 found me by looking at one of my auctions (for a Bulova radio) and then looked at and bid on a number of other auction items. This person never visited the store, though.

See how each visitor found you

FIGURE 23.23

The path of an avid radio bidder.

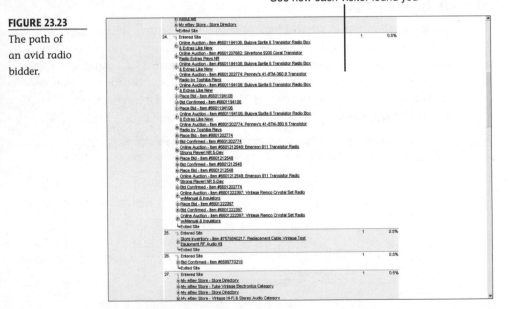

Figure 23.24 shows a visitor who came to the store, looked around, bought a store inventory item (the Zenith Royal 500h labels, about a third of the way down), used the store category "Transistor Radios" to find a live auction of

mine, placed a bid, went back to the store and looked around quite a while before leaving. This shows how important it is to have both store and inventory items cross-promoted. They can work together to keep shoppers interested in you.

FIGURE 23.24

Stores can build auction traffic, too.

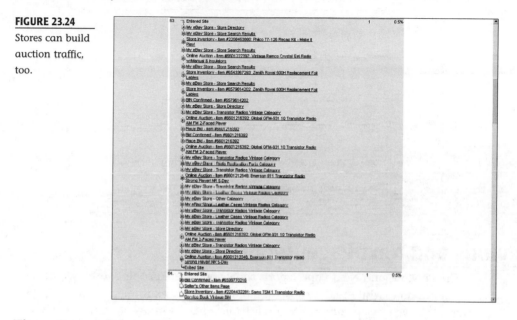

Time Spent Reports

The Time Spent reports can show you how "sticky" your listings are. Figure 23.25 shows an example. Generally, the longer shoppers hang around, the better. Over time you can see how your efforts to make the store more interesting have succeeded or failed.

Of course, people can sometimes spend a long time trying but not finding what they want, and this will result in long stays, but miserable success and revisit rates.

Again, simple answers aren't always the right ones. Dig a little, especially if your checkbook balance (my favorite report) is stagnant or going down rather than up.

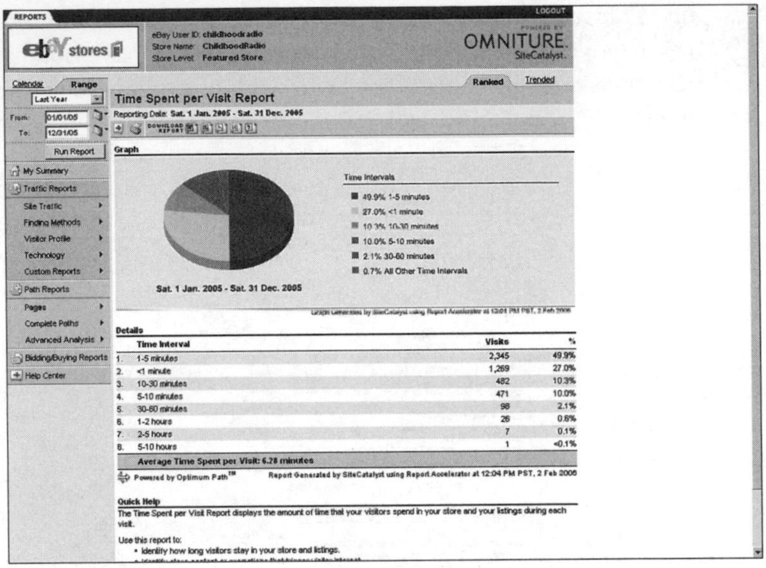

FIGURE 23.25

Time spent can be evidence of a great store or a frustrating one.

Previous and Next Page Reports

The Previous and Next Page reports show you where people most often come from or go to while visiting specific store pages. For example, in Figure 23.26, the top five ways people got to a particular auction in my store was to enter eBay directly, look at my store listings, look at another of my listings, or find the auction from my "Other items" page.

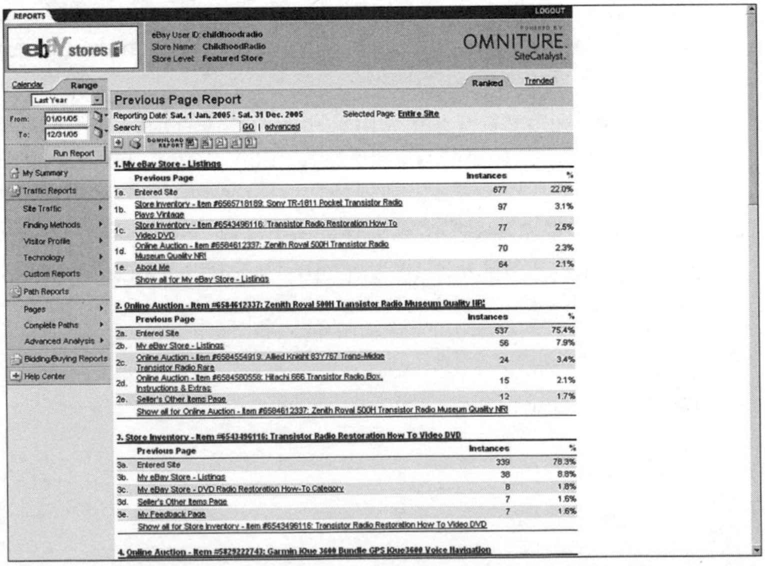

FIGURE 23.26

Tracking previous page visits.

Bidding/Buying Reports

This series of reports can show you when bids and "Buy It Now" purchases occur, and even where the buyers came from. Remember, though, you can only have bids when you are running auctions, and your Buy It Now sales require items to be in the store. For example, when I am working on a book or other project, I often don't list auction items because I like to give them the attention they deserve, and I can't do this when writing. Figure 23.27 graphically illustrates this phenomenon. It's a report of bid activity on my auctions over the past 3 months.

FIGURE 23.27

Tracking bids over time.

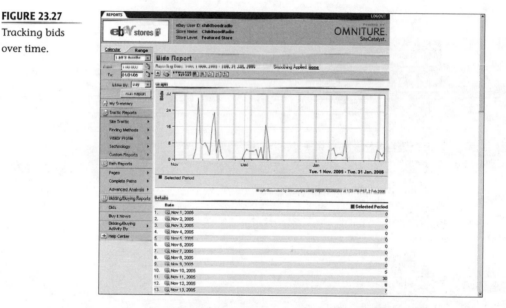

You can see reports like this and the behind-the-scenes details for auctions and Buy It Now purchases. It's also possible to examine bidding and buying activity by listings, referring domains, search engines, keyword entry pages, and original entry pages by picking the desired subreport from the Bidding/Buying Activity By choice in the navigation area (see Figure 23.28).

These reports will remind you of others you have seen, but they pertain only to cases where someone actually bid on an item or bought a fixed-price item you offered. You can tell, for example, which auction pages resulted in the most bids, as depicted in Figure 23.29.

FIGURE 23.28

Choosing
Bidding/Buying
reports.

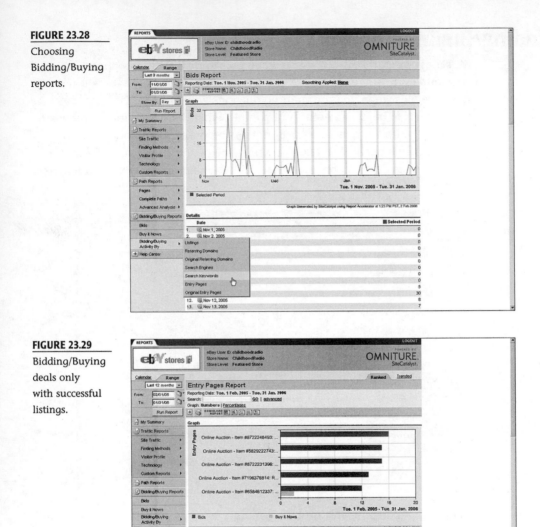

FIGURE 23.29

Bidding/Buying
deals only
with successful
listings.

Downloading Reports

You can download report data in five formats:

- Word (.rtf)
- Excel (.xls)

- PDF/Acrobat (.pdf)
- HTML (delivered as HTML emails)
- Comma Separated Values (.csv)

note The "Download this report immediately" option is not available for HTML reports. They are always emailed.

What gets saved depends on what format you choose. Further, you can choose to save the report to disk or email it to yourself or elsewhere. You can also compress it (get it as a zip file if you like).

Figure 23.30 shows the jumping-off point. Clicking any of the download buttons brings up the Download Report dialog box, where you can choose the desired report format, number of entries (limited to 500), destination, and your decision about compressing. You must always enter a "To" and "From" email address in case the report can't be generated immediately. You can use the same email address for both (your own address, probably) or mail reports to someone else.

FIGURE 23.30

Specifying download options.

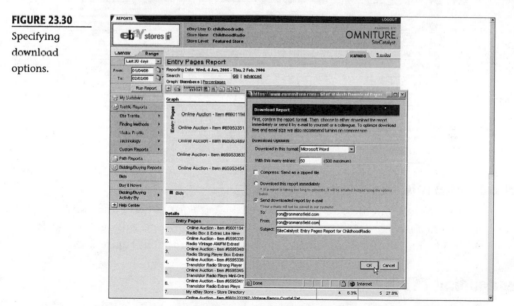

Either your report will be generated immediately and you will be prompted for a destination location on the disk, or you will be informed that the report will be emailed. In either case, you need to close the Download Report dialog box after receiving the file or the email promise.

Downloading PDF Reports

As I mentioned earlier, the information you download and its final appearance varies with the format chosen. PDF files look pretty much like screen captures without the navigation area. You will need a PDF reader (Adobe Reader or whatever) to open them. Figure 23.31 shows an example of this. They are searchable, by the way. Cool.

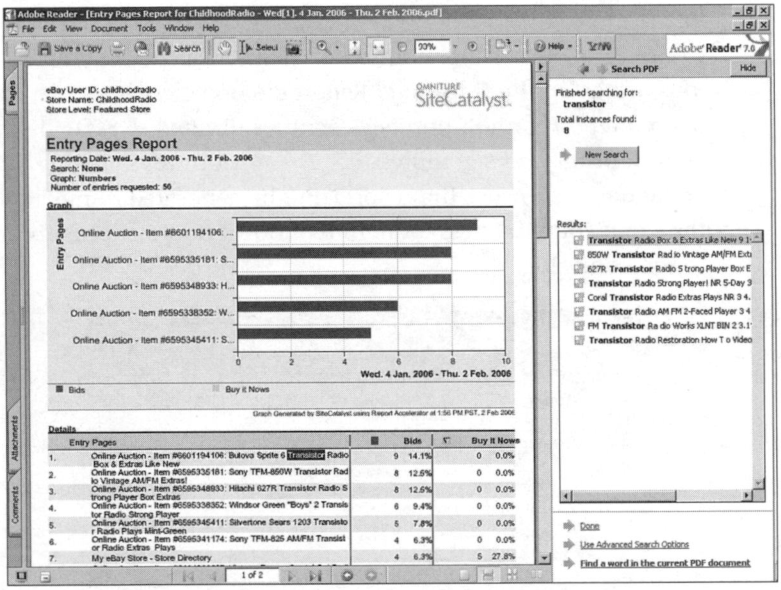

FIGURE 23.31

A report downloaded in PDF format.

Downloading Microsoft Word Reports

Microsoft Word files are delivered in Rich Text Format (RTF) and can be opened by a compatible application, not just Word. You will get the charts and editable tables containing the data, as illustrated in Figure 23.32.

Downloading CSV Reports

Comma Separated Value downloads don't contain charts, of course, but can be opened in any program that can import CSV files—Microsoft Excel, Word, a database program, and so on (see Figure 23.33).

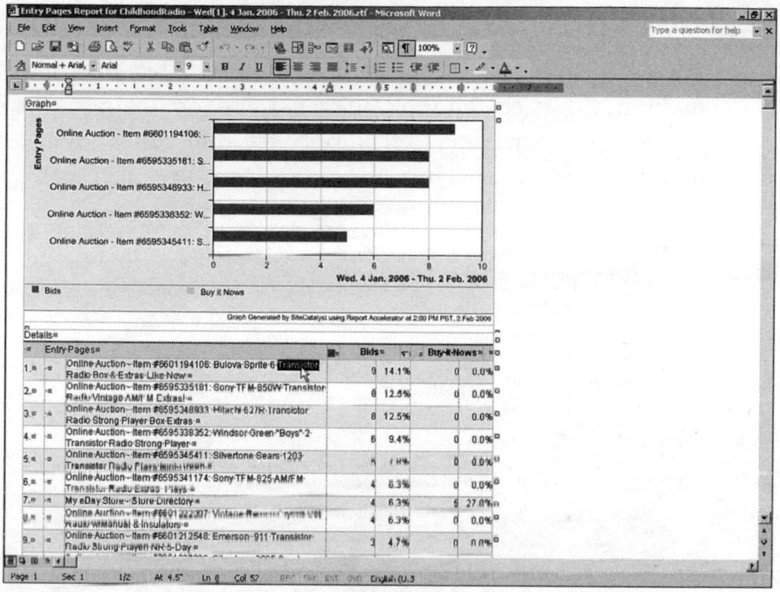

FIGURE 23.32

Word downloads can be edited.

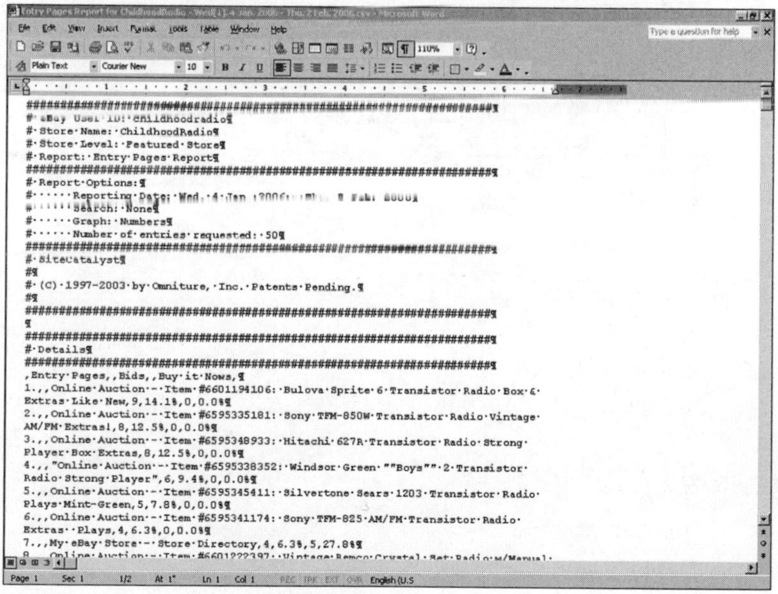

FIGURE 23.33

A typical Comma Separated Value download (opened in Microsoft Word).

Downloading Microsoft Excel Reports

Microsoft Excel reports contain charts, are editable, and might need some fiddling with to get data to display properly. For example, in Figure 23.34, a column needs widening to replace ##### with values. By the way, the charts aren't actually Excel charts; they are just pictures of charts.

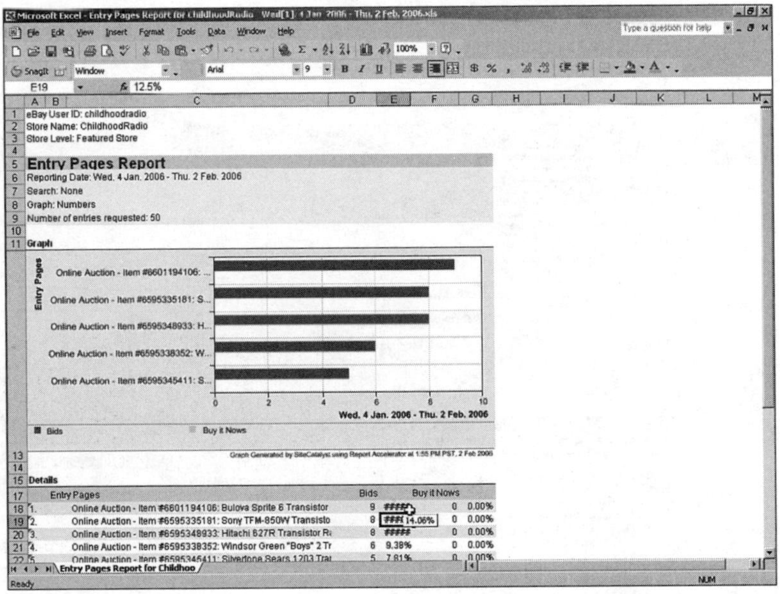

FIGURE 23.34

Microsoft Excel files contain charts and might need minor formatting.

Downloading HTML Reports

Because HTML reports always arrive as emails, you will need to be a little resourceful if it's the HTML *code* you are really wanting. Figure 23.35 shows one approach, which is using the View Source feature in my mail application (Thunderbird) to reveal, copy, and repurpose the HTML itself.

Index

N

eBay
Auction Templates
Starter Kit
0-7897-3563-6

This combination book/CD is designed to help all levels of eBay sellers create better-looking eBay auction listings.

* * * * * * * * * *

Launching a
Successful eBay
Store
0-7897-3575-X

Find out how to set up a new store, perform bookkeeping, manage inventory, promote the store on and off eBay, purchase eBay keywords and more.

* * * * * * * * *

Tricks of the eBay
Masters, 2nd Editon
0-7897-3543-1

Are you slowly buying and selling your way to PowerSeller status? Get there faster with the help of *Tricks of the eBay Masters*!

* * * * * * * * *

eBay to the Max
0-7897-3468-0

This one-of-a kind book shows how to become a PowerSeller, Trading Assistant, and open and run a retail Trading Post.

* * * * * * * * * * * *

I Married
an eBay Maniac
0-7897-3562-8

I Married an eBay Maniac offers a unique and interesting glimpse into the world of eBay, from an eBay Maniac and his wife.

eBay In a Snap
0-6723-2837-2

eBay In a Snap's unique, random-access approach lets you zero right in on the thing you want to learn about and get back to winning a bid or selling a product at the highest price.

Making a Living
from Your eBay
Business
0-7897-3366-8

This guide shows you how to set up and run different types of eBay businesses, including official retailer, second hand seller and trading assistant.

eBay Strategies
0-3212-5616-6

Whether you are just getting started selling on eBay or have been at it for years, the proven methods presented in *eBay Strategies* take you beyond the basics, helping you maximize your business while avoiding common mistakes.

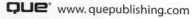

HOW IT WORKS

The How It Works series offers a unique, visual, four-color approach designed to educate curious readers. From machine code to hard-drive design to wireless communication, the How It Works series offers a clear and concise approach to understanding technology—a perfect source for those who prefer to learn visually. Check out other books in this best-selling series by Que:

How Computers Work, Eighth Edition
ISBN: 0-7897-3424-9

How Computers Work, Eighth Edition offers a unique and detailed look at the inner workings of your computer. From keyboards to virtual reality helmets, this book covers it all.

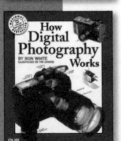

How Personal & Internet Security Work
ISBN: 0-7897-3553-9

How Personal & Internet Security Work clearly explains every aspect of security concerns that have become so important in an increasingly insecure world—everything from spyware, viruses to anti-terrorist screening systems in airports.

How Wireless Works, Seventh Edition
ISBN: 0-7897-3344-7

How Wireless Works gives you an insider's view on how all things wireless work, from WiFi networking, to hot spots, to wireless web surfing, to cell phones and more.

How Digital Photography Works
ISBN: 0-7897-3309-9

How Digital Photography Works offers a behind the scenes look at digital photography. You'll understand how your digital camera captures images and how your software fixes your mistakes.